Urban Problems
and Prospects

Urban Problems and Prospects

Second Edition

Anthony Downs

Chairman of the Board
Real Estate Research Corporation

Rand McNally College Publishing Company/Chicago

Current printing (last digit)
15 14 13 12 11 10 9 8 7 6 5 4 3 2 1

Contents

Introduction

Nearly all aspects of urban life in America are changing faster than ever before, but not with equal speed. Technical and economic factors, plus cultural and spiritual ones, are shifting much more rapidly than our legal and social institutions. The result is an escalation of general tensions and conflicts, and great pressure for major alterations in even the most basic institutions.

This book is about how our society might cope with such pressures by altering some of its existing urban policies and programs. It contains thirteen articles concerning urban growth in general, race relations, how public opinion affects urban problems, housing, new communities, transportation, government administration, urban research, and education. Six of these essays appeared in the first edition of this book, though they have been revised somewhat for this edition. The other seven are new to this collection and are drawn from various articles, reports, and speeches I have made in the past few years. Nearly all these articles focus upon how to change the key institutions in the fields concerned. By *institutions,* I mean established laws and organizational structures, their rules, their interrelations, and the entrenched patterns of behavior built around them.

This emphasis results from my belief that significant progress towards curing our most serious urban ills—including pollution, high crime rates, hunger, poverty, racism, poor housing, and poor education —cannot be made without major changes in existing institutions. True, marginal alterations in present institutional policies can help alleviate a few symptoms. Moreover, attacking symptoms is frequently both effective and worthwhile. But it is not enough to accommodate the pressures for change generated by our media-saturated culture. President Nixon recognized this in his State of the Union Message in January 1970, when he said, "As we enter the seventies, we should enter also a great age of reform of the institutions of American government."

Unfortunately, in recent decades, social scientists have not devoted much of their attention to urban institutions. A few excellent studies have been made. But there is a serious dearth of knowledge about the way new concepts and ideas get translated—or fail to get translated—into working policies and programs through institutional change. Institutions have not been studied enough partly because it is so easy to take them for granted. They appear so well-established, so much a part of the landscape, that they become almost invisible even to professional analysts. Yet I believe it is vital for social scientists in general, and social policy designers in particular, to start reexamining this institutional background. In working on a particular problem, they should challenge the "conventional wisdom," and take very little of the relevant institutional structure as "given" or unchangeable. The traumatic history of the twentieth century proves beyond doubt that even the most fundamental assumptions about society do not always hold true. The average citizen usually assumes—and should assume—that the basic fabric of society is stable and can be relied upon from day to day. But policy analysts should not.

Yet this conclusion does not imply that every analyst must consider the entire universe in every policy study. True, the complex interdependencies inherent in our society mean that "everything depends upon everything else" to an important degree. This "wholeness" has been emphasized recently by ecologists in their attacks upon pollution. But it is both naive and false to leap from this true insight to the false assertion that no specialized or particular analyses can be valid or meaningful. On the contrary, thorough, highly specialized knowledge, analysis, and action are among the keystones of western civilization, and will remain so. Our world is vastly too complicated to allow everyone grappling with a particular issue or problem to reexamine every facet of life, or to eschew specialized concentration upon a relatively narrow subject. Thus, in the jargon of economics, suboptimization is inescapable.

Yet my initial emphasis upon not taking institutions for granted is perfectly consistent with focusing upon particular problems or areas of activity in policy studies. I hope this is demonstrated by the articles in this book. All of them are specialized in subject matter, but some propose rather sweeping changes in existing institutions.

However, I have deliberately avoided presenting any single all-encompassing or overarching theme or theory of urban development, urban problems, or urban growth. The main reason is simple: I do not have one. Other analysts have developed excellent fragments of such a theme or theory—even large-sized fragments. And every competent urban analyst has some unconscious or partly formed "images" or "models" of how the larger context of urban society works. An example is my use of the "trickle-down" process as a central image of how urban housing markets work. This model plays a key role in several of the essays in this book.

But formulating such fragments into a unified, coherent theory that might be useful (comparable in scope to my theories of democracy and bureaucracy in earlier works) is beyond my own present capabilities for three reasons. First, the urban world is too complex. Even the most highly sophisticated, computerized models cannot yet encompass most of its significant subtleties, in my opinion. Second, the pace of change is too swift. Today's brilliant global generalization about urban affairs is tomorrow's laughable blunder, outmoded by some unpredictable change in behavior, or new empirical finding. Third, I am paid to think about specific problems, though in a broad context; so that is what I have concentrated my energies upon.

In doing so, I have employed certain specific techniques embodied in these studies. None are original with me, but I believe all are worth using in analyzing urban affairs. They are:

1.   Clearly defining, in operational terms, basic concepts that are widely used but normally considered so "obvious" their meanings are rarely spelled out. Consequently, different people use them to denote very different ideas, conditions, or policies. The resulting ambiguities often generate confusion and needless controversies. Examples treated in this book are *new cities* and *racism*.

2.   Using simple and straightforward language instead of technical or professional jargon. Policy ideas are useless unless they can be easily understood by those who can translate them into action.

3.   Carefully evaluating all widely quoted bits of "conventional wisdom" that derive their authority from repetition, familiarity, or association with high officialdom. Such wisdom often consists of sheer myths based upon erroneous analysis or data. Examples discussed herein include the Census Bureau's population projections, and the belief that a great deal of future urban growth will—or should—occur in "new cities."

4.   Formulating several alternative courses of future action, rather than just one preferred course. One of the alternatives should usually describe what will happen if present policies are continued unchanged. This "alternative futures" technique forces people to confront the consequences of their own actions—or inactions—by comparing them with the consequences of those policies the analyst really prefers. Thus, it denies potential critics the intellectual luxury of attacking the analyst's preferred course without offering any alternatives of their own. It also

provides them with the basis for selecting different policies in case their preferences are not the same as the analyst's. This method is best illustrated in my study of possible housing policy strategies, which is a chapter excerpted from a book on federal housing subsidies (*Federal Housing Subsidies: How Are They Working?*, Lexington Books, 1973).

5. Using an "all feasible combinations" approach in designing multiple future alternatives. This consists of the following steps: (a) Selecting those specific traits or variables which are most significant in regard to a given problem; (b) Estimating a few alternative possible future values for each variable; (c) Calculating the total number of possible combinations of these values, taking all the key variables into account (this may be in the millions); (d) Designing criteria for eliminating most of these combinations; and (e) Narrowing down the number to a manageable few for more detailed analysis. This technique is employed in considering alternative forms of future urban growth and alternative housing strategies.

6. Using arbitrary, but bold and imaginative, judgments and assumptions in analyzing behavior patterns and formulating policies. I believe that extremely arbitrary—even ridiculous—simplified judgments are often useful in advancing perception, analysis, or prescription. For example, I divide all expressway commuters into two categories: explorers and sheep. Similarly, the complex formation of overall national housing strategies encompasses hundreds of issues, but important insights can be gained by reducing them to just seven key questions. Another application of this approach is assuming that seemingly permanent conditions can be changed by deliberate policies. Examples are achieving greater suburban dispersal of the U.S. black population, and lowering quality standards for new housing.

7. Making very rough calculations in order to gain some quantitative insights into various policy alternatives. In countless policy decisions, the *magnitude* of a proposed change, rather than its *direction,* is the critical factor. Whenever this is true, even crude calculations are vastly superior to none. An example herein is the estimation of housing subsidy cost per low-income household aided by different specific forms of subsidy.

8. Taking explicit account of redistribution effects in evaluating policy alternatives. I reject the common assumption that all the costs and benefits of any policy are borne by the same people; so redistribution effects can be ignored. Economists in particular are fond of isolating the so-called "efficiency implications" of a policy from its "income redistribution implications." They often make policy recommendations based solely upon the former, while assuming the latter can be handled through a set of taxes and payments treated somewhere else in society. In my opinion, this procedure is both totally unrealistic

and harmful. True, efficiency and redistribution effects should often be separated analytically. But they must both be considered in designing policy recommendations, because congressmen and other real actors do not separate them when adopting policies. Moreover, in most cases, the redistribution impacts of a policy are vitally important in determining its desirability. This means most public policy decisions are strongly political in nature, and cannot be treated as purely economic or scientific. But I believe we should face this fact squarely, rather than ignore it so as to arrive at less ambiguous policy recommendations.

The thirteen essays in this book were written over fourteen years under many different circumstances. Some were purely academic in origin; others were prepared as parts of assignments for various clients; a few originated as speeches; and some combine these elements. This diversity makes it impossible for me to acknowledge all the many others who contributed ideas to these essays or otherwise aided in their creation. I wish I could claim that any errors are due to those others, while I am solely responsible for everything either original or valuable. However, honesty forbids such immodesty. It also requires me to single out three people who made major contributions for which I am especially grateful. They are John McKnight, whose ideas comprise much of the essay on racism; Leanne Lachman, my invaluable assistant and colleague whose wisdom helps me separate good ideas from bad ones and develop the former; and Kay Mulligan, whose constant secretarial efficiency enables me to multiply the results of my labors. Finally, I dedicate this book to my many past and present colleagues at Real Estate Research Corporation. Their efforts, inspiration, and patience have been the *sine qua non* of the many challenging and tremendously varied activities we have undertaken together in the past fifteen years.

1
Alternative Forms of
Future Urban Growth
in the United States

For the past two decades, the prospect of further large-scale urban growth in the United States has evoked cries of alarm from many observers. In the early 1960s, the alarm focused upon the tremendous capital investment that appeared necessary to meet needs arising from future population growth. One frequent lament (the "Columbus Challenge") warned that we would have to build as many new homes, roads, schools, shopping centers, and the like, from 1960 to 2000 as we did from the time of Columbus up to 1960. A second widely publicized view urged America to build a large number of completely new, freestanding cities to cope with population growth and avoid continuing the supposedly chaotic horrors of urban sprawl. More recently, dismay concerning urban growth has centered upon its supposedly undesirable impacts upon the environment. Ecologists seeking to preserve rural landscapes decry the outward march of subdivisions on the edges of urban areas. They have been joined in a powerful "anti-growth" movement by suburbanites trying to prevent increases in housing density—and in lower-income residents—in mainly single-family home communities. In addition, many voices urge the United States to develop a "national urban growth policy" or a "national land policy" before we become submerged in "megalopolis."

Revised version of an article originally appearing in the *Journal of the American Institute of Planners* 36, no. 1 (January 1970): 3–11, by permission of the American Institute of Planners.

In my opinion, these and other similar views lack an adequate framework for viewing future urban growth and development as a whole. Such a framework should allow us to explore alternative ways in which future growth might occur and to design one or more effective strategies for shaping it.

This article sets forth a classification of alternative future forms of urban growth, some factors relevant to deciding which are most likely and which are most desirable, and some policy implications for influencing this growth. Limited space permits me to present only an overview and basic conclusions, rather than any detailed analysis justifying the many admittedly arbitrary judgments involved.

CLASSIFICATION OF GROWTH FORMS

Defining the most likely forms of future urban growth requires an inherently subjective and arbitrary selection of a few combinations of key factors out of thousands of possibilities. Urban development involves dozens of important variables, each of which could reasonably take on several different future values. Some of these variables are:

1. Location of new growth in relation to existing metropolitan areas.

2. Contiguity of new growth to smaller existing communities located beyond the continuously built-up portions of metropolitan areas (including outside such areas).

3. Type of planning control (such as unplanned and highly fragmented, planned-unit development, or citywide).

4. Level of quality standards required in new construction.

5. Degree of public control over new urban development.

6. Degree of public subsidy for new urban development.

7. Distribution of housing subsidies among various income groups.

8. Degree of social class integration.

9. Degree and nature of racial integration.

10. Mixture of transportation modes.

Just considering these ten variables, and several arbitrarily chosen values for each one, yields at least 93,312 logically possible combinations, each representing a potential form of future urban growth! Clearly, it is impossible to formulate practical policy analysis on the basis of so many alternatives; drastic reductions must occur.

I accomplished this by using only variables 1, 2, and 3 to form possible future growth alternatives, thereby shifting consideration of the remaining seven to other parts of the analysis. I further reduced the many possible combinations of values for these three variables by eliminating those which seemed either internally inconsistent, or unlikely to accommodate large-scale new growth. The remaining eleven combinations form my candidates for a standard classification of alternative forms of future urban growth in the United States:

1.   *Redevelopment* of older neighborhoods in central cities or older suburbs through clearance and rebuilding. It has three forms:
    a.   *Unplanned redevelopment* (by individual parcel-owners at a highly fragmented scale of control).
    b.   *Planned redevelopment* (at the planned-unit-development scale of control).
    c.   *New cities in-city* (at the scale of control of very large planned-unit-developments, or entire new communities, within existing cities).
2.   *Peripheral sprawl* with unplanned development control, either on the edges of the continuously built-up portions of metropolitan areas, or beyond those edges but still within commuting range.[1]
3.   *Planned peripheral growth* on the edges of the continuously built-up portions of existing metropolitan areas. It has two forms:
    a.   *Peripheral planned-unit-development* (under planned-unit-development type of control).
    b.   *Peripheral new cities* (under comprehensively planned, citywide type of control).
4.   *Satellite growth* beyond the continuously built-up portions of existing metropolitan areas but within commuting range of them. It has three forms:
    a.   *Scattered satellites* (under planned-unit-development type of control).
    b.   *Satellite new cities* (under citywide type of control but not contiguous to existing smaller communities).
    c.   *Satellite expanded cities* (under citywide type of control but contiguous to existing smaller communities).
5.   *Nonmetropolitan growth* beyond commuting range from any existing metropolitan areas. It has two forms:
    a.   *Nonmetropolitan new cities* (under citywide type of control and not contiguous to any existing communities).

---

[1] The second form of growth I have called *peripheral sprawl* includes another form that might be more logically called *satellite sprawl*. It is not on the edge of existing cities (hence peripheral) but away from that edge (hence satellite). Yet the term *satellite* implies a cluster of some type, rather than more scattered development. Moreover, *peripheral sprawl* is used by many observers to refer to *all* scattered development outside existing built-up areas, both on the edge and farther out but within commuting range. Thus, I have adopted this dual definition.

     b. *Expanded nonmetropolitan communities* under citywide scale of control but contiguous to existing communities.

Admittedly, it might be desirable to modify this scheme under some circumstances. For example, scattered development along interstate highways outside of metropolitan areas might be considered "nonmetropolitan sprawl." However, I believe the eleven basic forms of urban growth set forth above will form an adequate framework for most analyses of future urban development.

    Two important aspects of these alternatives should be emphasized. First, they are not mutually exclusive. All of them could occur simultaneously within a single state, and the first nine could even occur simultaneously within a single metropolitan area. Second, these alternatives are not equally probable. In fact, far more future urban growth is likely to be peripheral sprawl than all the others combined. Public policies can influence the relative likelihood of these alternatives, but they hardly start with even odds.

KEY FACTORS FOR URBAN GROWTH

Before any policy conclusions can be drawn concerning these alternative forms of future urban growth, it is necessary to understand certain key factors related to such growth. Brief discussion of these factors will form the basis for the policy implications set forth later in this article.

The Size of the "Urban Explosion"

Among urban futurists, one cause of alarm was the "explosion" of urban population they foresaw until very recently. Extreme estimates made in the 1960s indicated that total U.S. population would *double* from 1960 to 2000, rising from 180.7 million to 361.4 million. This gain of 180.7 million in forty years was derived from the U.S. Census Bureau's highest-fertility projection (Series A), which assumed fertility rates typical of the peak postwar years.[2] But, since 1957, U.S. fertility rates have plummeted 45 percent to the lowest level in our history. In fact, they have fallen far below the level assumed by what was once the Census Bureau's lowest-fertility projection (Series D), which indicates a gain of 105.3 million from 1960 to 2000. As a result, the Census Bureau

---

    [2] All data on official population projections are derived from U.S. Bureau of the Census, *Statistical Abstract of the United States: 1973* (94th Edition, Washington, D.C.: GPO 1968), pp. 6–7.

has stopped publishing its two highest-fertility projections (Series A and B) and added two others that assume much lower future fertility rates (Series E and F).

In a 1970 analysis of future population growth, I made a crude calculation based upon the assumption that fertility rates would continue to fall steeply for another decade, then level off until 2000. My rough approximation showed this would reduce the total population gain between 1960 and 2000 to 68.8 million. This would result in a total U.S. population in the year 2000 of about 250 million, almost exactly the same as the 250.7 million subsequently projected by the Census Bureau in its lowest-fertility estimate (Series F).[3] This coincidence convinces me that most current estimates of future population (which rarely use Series F projections) are too high. This error has caused most urban observers to exaggerate the magnitude, or at least the rate, of future urban population growth.

Another consideration centers on the definition of *urban.* The Census Bureau officially considers any place with 2,500 or more inhabitants as urban. I believe the word *urban* as used in popular and expert parlance really should be defined as "pertaining to metropolitan areas." In 1970, about 69 percent of all Americans lived in metropolitan areas. However, those areas captured about 86 percent of total U.S. population growth from 1940 to 1950, 84 percent from 1950 to 1960, and 84 percent again from 1960 to 1970. Assuming such areas receive about 80 percent of future U.S. population growth, Table 1-1 indicates future "urban" growth defined in terms of these metropolitan areas. The table shows the very large difference in projections of future urban

Table 1-1   "Urban" Growth, 1970–2000

U.S. Population Projection Used	Millions	As Percent Gain Over 1970
Census Series F	36.6	26.3%
Census Series C	76.4	54.8%

growth resulting from different assumptions about future fertility rates. Even though the Census Bureau has discontinued its highest-fertility projections (Series A and B), its highest remaining projection (Series C) indicates a total gain in urban population in the next three decades more than double that estimated by its lowest-fertility projection (Series F). Many public and private agencies use population projections based upon Series C or Series D fertility assumptions, especially in deriving local population estimates for states, metropolitan areas, and individual

---

[3] Ibid.

communities.[4] However, I think these estimates are wrong, and by a large amount, because I believe fertility rates will continue to fall far enough to make the Series F projection more accurate. Even so, future urban growth will hardly be trivial. A gain of 36.6 million persons from 1970 to 2000 is 46 percent larger than the total gain in metropolitan-area population during the 1950s, the great decade of suburbanization, and almost double the analogous gain in the 1960s. And future growth after the year 2000 will probably make even the Series C projection for 2000 come true several decades later. But the *rate* of such growth will clearly slow down. That fact has critical implications for the strain on our economy likely to result from meeting urban expansion needs.

Linking the Two "Urban Frontiers"

It is useful to simplify the incredibly complex welter of urban problems by viewing them as clustered around what I call two "urban frontiers." One is the *Frontier of Deterioration* in older central cities and suburbs, especially in ghetto areas. The other is the *Frontier of Growth* on the periphery of built-up portions of our metropolitan areas.

At present, most public policies treat these frontiers as completely separate from and totally unrelated to each other. One set of policies focuses almost entirely on improving central cities and ghettos as if they were hermetically sealed off from the suburbs. This includes most public housing, most urban job-training programs, most housing code enforcement programs, a great deal of the urban Aid-to-Families-with-Dependent-Children, and even many mass transit grants. The one apparent exception is the federal highway-aid program. Yet even its effect has been mainly to link downtowns and suburbs more closely, thereby making it even easier to bypass deteriorating areas within central cities.

On the other hand, plans for further suburban development deliberately exclude ways to use such expansion to help solve inner-city problems. Low-income housing is systematically blocked out of growth areas, even though suburban industrial firms are short of unskilled labor. Only token efforts are made to introduce minority group workers into suburban building trades, in spite of critical shortages of construction workers in many areas. Thus, "natural" ways to simultaneously alleviate inner-city unemployment and suburban labor shortages are ignored. Metropolitanwide plans drawn up by federally supported re-

---

[4] A common technique for making local estimates (such as for a given metropolitan area) is to estimate what percentage of the future total U.S. population the local area will contain as of a given date. This percentage is derived from past proportions of the U.S. population (or its growth) located in the local area. Hence, if the future estimate used for the entire nation is much too high, then any area estimates derived from it will likewise be too high.

gional planning agencies almost never contain any explicit consideration of where minority group members—especially blacks—will live in
the future. Yet the expansion of such groups provides the single most
important dynamic force in many big central city housing markets. But
it is "too hot to handle" for politically powerless metropolitan planning
agencies, who are often fearful of their segregationist suburban con-
stituencies.

We continue to ignore the need to use the dynamic economic expansion of suburban growth as a major input to solving inner-city problems. This bifurcation can only perpetuate the two racially separate
societies properly condemned by the Kerner Commission and the
myriad fiscally separate communities rightly criticized by the Douglas
Commission.

Moreover, even though these two frontiers are spatially separated,
they are in fact closely related parts of a single housing market in each
metropolitan area. New housing construction in the suburbs is linked
to the older housing inventory in the inner-city by the "trickle-down"
process that dominates U.S. urban development and by the "chains of
moves" that take place whenever households move into brand new
units.[5] On the average, each new suburban housing unit leads about
3.5 households to move—the one that occupies that new unit, the one
that moves into the home vacated by the first household, the one that
moves into the home vacated by the second household, etc. Furthermore, just under 10 percent of the households in these "chains" are
low-income households. They typically up-grade their housing by moving from relatively deteriorated inner-city units into better-quality
existing units located slightly farther out from the city center.

Thus, whenever new housing construction is large enough to exceed new household formation in a metropolitan area, the degree of
housing choice expands for almost *all* households there, not just for
those affluent enough to occupy the new units themselves. Most households then "filter up" through the inventory, improving the quality of
housing they occupy as much as they can. The result is often a net outward shift of population toward the newest and best-quality housing.
This shift can leave thousands of the oldest, worst-quality units in inner-
city areas vacant and abandoned. This is precisely what happened in
the very high housing production years from 1970 through 1973, which

---

[5] The data cited here on "chains of moves" come from John B. Lansing, Charles
Wade Clifton, and James N. Morgan, *New Homes and Poor People* (Ann Arbor: Institute for Social Research of the University of Michigan, 1969). The "trickle-down"
process of urban development is described in more detail in another article in this
volume. See "The Successes and Failures of Federal Housing Policy" (Chapter 5, pp.
87–110).

were also the years of greatest housing abandonment in inner-city neighborhoods.

Conversely, if new housing construction in the suburban fringe fell below the rate of new household formation in the metropolitan area, there might be an increasing shortage of available units in the market as a whole. This would increase competition for all decent-quality housing—including that in older neighborhoods. There would be an upward pressure on rents and property values in those areas and elsewhere. That is precisely what has happened in periods of "tight" housing markets, such as in World War II or immediately thereafter and in 1974.

This inherent linkage of the two urban frontiers is built into the very structure of U.S. metropolitan housing markets, even though most Americans do not realize it exists. Consequently, *a crucial determinant of conditions in inner-city housing markets is the rate of new housing construction in the suburbs.* The latter directly depends upon the total level of housing production in the entire economy. The more new housing units are built altogether, the more are built in suburbs, since a majority of all new units is located there. The more new suburban units are built, other things being equal, the greater their attraction for households now living in the central city, and the weaker the demand for the worst-quality housing in inner-city neighborhoods. Thus, ironically, the more successful the nation is in building new units to meet its total housing needs, the more likely it is to generate inner-city housing abandonment—at least under present institutional arrangements. Also, the future success of suburban "anti-growth" movements as a whole will have vital impacts upon inner-city housing conditions. If these movements become so widespread and powerful that they greatly reduce the nation's total annual production of new housing, a serious housing shortage might arise. One result would be rising rents and property values in older inner-city areas (and everywhere else, too). That would be financially beneficial to central-city property-owners and governments but hard on low-income renters.

This linkage also makes it extremely difficult for central-city governments and citizens to cope effectively with the causes of neighborhood deterioration within their own communities. Because of the fragmented nature of local governments in most metropolitan areas, central-city authorities have no influence over one of the most important determinants of housing conditions in their own neighborhoods: the rate of new housing construction in surrounding suburbs. On the other hand, outlying suburbs feel rising pressure to accept more residents when rapid growth of low-income or ethnically segregated groups within the central city "displaces" more middle-income households. Hence changes in conditions within the central city have profound impacts upon suburban housing markets, too. However, in spite of these two-way economic and social linkages that unite all parts of each metropolitan area into a single housing market, the area usually remains politically fragmented into myriad competing jurisdictions. This prevents either public or private groups from developing any effective overall housing strategy for meeting the needs of all the area's residents.

"Extra" Costs in New Cities

Accommodating future urban growth in new cities involves several real costs larger than the costs of alternative forms of development. These "extra" costs result from the following key characteristics which differentiate new cities from other forms of urban growth.

Comprehensive Planning at a Citywide Scale. This requires centralized control over land use and development in a very large area *before* anything is created on that land, so it generates the following added costs (as compared to growth at lesser scales of planning control):

1.   The added costs of assembling a large enough site to accommodate 100,000 people (or whatever number is considered to be "city-sized"), and holding parts of that site vacant during the first stages of development—which may last years.

2.   The cost of developing and operating new institutions for centralized planning and control of such a large-scale activity.

3.   The cost of overcoming the obstacles to new city development created by existing fragmented landownership and government institutions. A great deal of extra lobbying skill, waiting time, and money is needed to wrest comprehensive planning opportunities from them.

Distance from Existing Metropolitan Facilities. In nonmetropolitan new cities, where residents are beyond range of existing facilities, the following extra costs arise:

1.   The *initial* loss of return on, or initially inefficient operation of, facilities which must be built immediately with a capacity to handle a large population long before that population itself arrives. These facilities include public infrastructure (such as roads, sewer and water facilities, high schools, and public buildings) and private enterprises (such as shopping centers and industrial plants).

2.   The *total* costs of duplicating elements of existing metropolitan areas that now have enough excess capacity to serve many more people. Examples are some museums, universities, libraries, concert halls,

public buildings, theaters, and business firms. No new facilities like these would be required if growth occurred peripherally or in satellites not too far from existing central cities.

Housing Everyone and Everything in Brand-New Quarters. Not all households, business firms, or other institutions can afford brand-new quarters. But in a new city, everything is brand-new. Yet society cannot operate a large community without the services of many low-income households and many low-cost business firms. To enable these entities to survive in a new city, some form of public subsidy must be extended to cover the higher cost of their occupying new structures. This subsidy would not be required by peripheral growth. Then, such households and firms could occupy older quarters in the existing inventory of structures in each metropolitan area. Some subsidy for such entities might be required by satellite growth, but then many low-income workers could commute from lower-cost housing existing elsewhere. Moreover, these are not trivial costs. New housing is so expensive that over one-half the households in the U.S. cannot afford even to *rent* newly built, modestly designed, appropriately sized apartments without spending an inordinate fraction of their incomes on housing. So unless almost all residents of a new city are relatively affluent—which is impossible if the city is to operate efficiently—a large fraction of its residents will need subsidies to live there. The same is true of many businesses.

Some proponents of new cities argue that these costs should not be considered "extra." Either they are offset by extra benefits (such as lower air pollution), or we "ought to" bear them in *any* future growth (in particular, we "ought to" replace substandard housing with new units). Hence, they regard paying for these extra costs as a form of *social investment* that will pay off handsomely in the long run.

Measuring the net total costs of alternative ways to accommodate future urban growth is an extremely complex task beyond the scope of this article. Nevertheless, I believe there are three reasons why building new cities—especially nonmetropolitan ones—would definitely require extra public subsidies unnecessary if future growth occurred through peripheral or even satellite expansion. First, some of the extra costs cited above produce no offsetting benefits or reductions in other costs. This is true of duplicating existing facilities that now have excess capacity. Second, most of the benefits resulting from the extra costs cited above would be of the type for which no direct revenues could be collected. They are what economists call "external benefits" or "public goods." Hence, they are received directly by consumers without going through any market; so no prices can be charged for their use. Examples are reduced air pollution, lower traffic congestion, and improved aesthetic conditions. The private sector—including the beneficiaries themselves—will not voluntarily pay the extra costs of producing these benefits; therefore, the government would have to incur much larger expenditures for urban growth in new cities—especially nonmetropolitan ones—than in other forms. Third, it is not true that society would have to pay for upgrading many low-income households or businesses into brand new quarters if peripheral urban growth occurred. We could continue our traditional strategy of upgrading the poor by building new housing at the high-cost end of the market and relying on "trickling down" to open up adequate quarters for the poor in the older existing inventory. In part, this strategy has failed in the past because we did not build enough new units of any kind. But even if we decided to use large-scale housing subsidies to overcome this failure, the per unit subsidy cost would be lower if we still focused new subsidized construction on middle-income and upper-income households, rather than requiring *all* households to pay the high costs of new quarters—as in nonmetropolitan new cities.

Thus, to the extent that any future urban growth strategy emphasizes new cities, it compels society, early in the development process, to pay extra public expenditures as compared to peripheral or satellite growth. True, if those extra public expenditures are eventually offset by extra benefits and if public authorities own most of the land in new cities, then they may eventually recapture enough profits and land value appreciation to repay this large initial investment. This appears to be happening in Great Britain. Nevertheless, public authorities will still have to make some arrangements to pay the extra initial costs of new cities in order to bring them into being.

Lessons from European Experience with Growth Controls

For several decades, many European nations have been exerting significant controls of various types over their own urban growth. In my opinion, their experience indicates the following significant conclusions relevant to future policies affecting U.S. urban growth.

Any attempt to exert significant public influence over the nature, location, magnitude, or physical form of urban growth requires public ownership or other direct control of a significant part of the land in major metropolitan areas, especially on their growth peripheries. Leaving most of the control over land use in private hands, especially where private ownership is fragmented into thousands of small parcels, as in the U.S., makes it impossible to impose any real guided development policy on even one metropolitan area. This conclusion implies that creation of any overall "urban growth strategy" or "urban land policy" would involve radical *restructuring* of traditional land ownership and control arrangements in the U.S. Also, development of any significant number of nonmetropolitan new cities, or even peripheral or satellite new cities, will require *public* ownership of much of the land in those cities.

Creation of relatively independent nonmetropolitan new cities is an extraordinarily difficult achievement of dubious long-run value. In Great Britain, public agencies promoting new town development have for decades exercised financial and administrative powers vastly greater than any currently contemplated in the U.S. Yet after over 20 years of effort, only about 2.5 percent of all new housing construction in Britain occurs in new towns. Moreover, British government planners have virtually abandoned formation of additional nonmetropolitan new cities. They now favor peripheral new cities adjoining middle-sized metropolitan areas beyond commuting range from London or the big Midlands industrial centers. This policy shift is essentially an attempt to escape many of the extra costs of nonmetropolitan new city development described above. To the best of my knowledge, in Sweden and the biggest Soviet cities, all so-called new cities are either peripheral or satellite in nature.

A crucial determinant of the physical form which publicly controlled urban growth takes is the type of transportation serving new growth areas. The decision to plan such areas around public mass transit (as in Sweden and the Soviet Union) influences the physical form, density, and structure of the communities concerned—as does the universal decision to build them around automobiles in the United States. Swedish peripheral new cities linked to downtown Stockholm by subway feature very high-density residential areas clustered around each subway stop so that thousands of people can live within walking distance of transportation facilities. Huge shopping centers are built over each subway stop for the convenience of these pedestrian residents. This is in striking contrast to our own shopping centers built near expressway interchanges for the convenience of auto-driving residents scattered across low-density neighborhoods. Thus, public decisions about what kind of transportation systems should serve new growth areas exert profound influence over every facet of their development. Any decision to shift major emphasis to mass transit in U.S. urban growth areas would cause radical transformations in the patterns of development typical of such areas during the past twenty-five years.

Rapid construction of new urban facilities to accommodate large-scale growth cannot be achieved through clearance and redevelopment; it must be done on initially vacant land. Even in the Soviet Union, clearance and redevelopment of built-up areas takes much longer than construction on peripheral vacant land. In Paris, the huge *La Defense* urban redevelopment project had finished only 600 net new housing units (in addition to those needed for relocation) after ten years; whereas a single public housing project on suburban vacant land housed over 40,000 residents eight years after its inception. These facts simply reemphasize a conclusion long established by U.S. urban renewal experience: the average redevelopment project takes from six to nine years.

Deliberately slowing down the growth of major urban centers— especially the national capital—is extremely difficult. With all their powers, Soviet urban authorities have been unable to prevent the Moscow area from continuing to grow rapidly. Although British authorities have had some success in shifting growth out of the center of London, there is still pressure to locate more activities within the London metropolitan region. The economic, political, cultural, and psychological advantages of being "where the action is," or at least within easy range, strongly favor peripheral or satellite expansion, rather than nonmetropolitan growth.

Undoubtedly, many other significant lessons could be drawn from European experience in trying to impose a "national strategy" upon urban growth. I think they point to two basic conclusions. *First, the focal point of public concern should be urban growth in general, not just nonmetropolitan new cities.* In fact, the latter invariably encompass only a small fraction of total urban expansion. *Second, public policies regarding urban growth are severely constrained by many forces over which public authorities concerned with urban development have little effective control.* Achieving an "optimal" pattern of urban development is almost everywhere subordinated to other public policy objectives. The latter create formidable obstacles to formation and execution of rational urban growth strategies. This suggests that changes in long-established institutional structures or behavior patterns needed to improve urban development are not likely to be undertaken solely for that purpose. The more radical such changes are, the more they need to be linked with other public policy purposes, or with powerful forces unrelated to urban development, in order to be enacted.

SPECIFIC POLICY IMPLICATIONS FOR THE UNITED STATES

In our diffused political system, creating a rational urban development strategy is extraordinarily difficult, even within a single metropolitan area. My own experience on the National Commission on Urban Problems convinces me that certain specific policy objectives must be attained before we can create any such strategies. These objectives are aimed at expanding the possible forms of future urban development beyond peripheral sprawl, which now encompasses almost all urban growth. They do not form a single urban development strategy in themselves; rather, they are the foundations on which several such strategies might be built. Each of these objectives can be achieved through one or more tactics.

Maintaining High Levels of New Housing Production

The first key objective is *maintaining high levels of new housing construction*. In the years 1971, 1972, and 1973, total housing production in the U.S. (including mobile homes) reached all-time record levels of 2.6 million, 3.0 million, and 2.6 million units respectively. This was a three-year average of over 2.7 million new units per year. In fact, from 1968 through 1973, new housing production has far exceeded that in any previous period, as shown in Table 1-2.

Table 1-2   New Housing Construction, 1950–1973

Time Period	Millions of New Housing Units Produced (Including Mobile Homes)	Annual Average in Millions
1950–1959	15.965	1.597
1960–1968	14.550	1.616
1969–1973	11.953	2.391

Source: data from Anthony Downs, *Federal Housing Subsidies: How Are They Working?* (Lexington, Massachusetts: D. C. Heath and Company, 1973), p. 11; and U.S. Department of Housing and Urban Development, *Housing in the Seventies* (Washington, D.C.: U.S. Government Printing Office, 1973), p. 4-4.

Total housing production in the five years from 1969 through 1973 came quite close to the national goal of 2.6 million units per year set forth in the 1968 Housing and Urban Development Act. This was remarkable, considering that the housing goal called for a 62.5 percent increase in average annual production over the performance of the previous 19 years. The main reason for this surge in housing production was greatly improved availability of mortgage money and other housing financing. This was caused by the recession of 1970–1971 and by certain unusual developments in U.S. money markets in 1972 and early 1973. Also, direct federal housing subsidies increased rapidly after the 1968 act, reaching very high levels in 1970, 1971, and 1972.

However, new commitments under these programs were suspended by the Nixon administration in early 1973. Moreover, rising interest rates caused by both prosperity and inflation led to a sudden drop in mortgage availability in mid-1973, and another similar housing "credit crunch" in 1974. The result was a decline in total housing production in 1974 to about 1.75 million units (including mobile homes). This means the official ten-year target of 26 million new units will probably not be achieved.[6] Nevertheless, continued output of somewhere between 1.75 and 2.4 million units per year would still expand the supply enough to prevent any nationwide housing shortage from arising.

The most important tactic necessary to move toward this objective is creation of an *economic climate* conducive to continued high-level housing production. Such a climate would be marked by low interest rates, a low rate of inflation, a somewhat slack economy with relatively high unemployment, and high levels of spending for all aspects of housing, including planning and data gathering. Thus, there is a fundamental conflict between sustained large-scale housing production and sustained high-level prosperity. When the economy is booming, demands for capital surge upward. But many alternative uses of capital have traditionally paid much higher returns than investment in housing. Housing production tends to be choked off, or at least fails to rise very high. The only way to counteract this relationship would be to raise housing to a much higher level of national priority. This would justify using various subsidies to increase the rate of return on housing investment. I believe such a shift in national priorities will occur only if an emerging housing shortage becomes bad enough to inconvenience large numbers of middle- and upper-income households.

Providing Housing Subsidies to Low-Income Households

The second key objective related to future urban growth is *providing large-scale housing subsidies to low-income households* to encourage a more desirable economic mixture of income groups in new-growth areas than would otherwise occur. America's so-called "housing problem" really consists of three different maladies:

1. *Physically inadequate dwelling units* that are deteriorated, overcrowded, or do not have sufficient plumbing or other basic amenities. Most such units are in rural areas rather than cities. In both places, such units are occupied primarily by low-income households. The main cure for this malady is increasing the supply of decent-quality units through new construction and rehabilitation, mainly within metropolitan areas.

2. *Financial disparities* between the cost of decent-quality housing (kept high by our very high-quality standards) and the incomes of poor households. These disparities cause many such households to pay in-

---

[6] A detailed explanation of this belief is presented in "Moving Toward Realistic Housing Goals," Kermit Gordon, editor, *An Agenda for the Nation* (Washington, D.C.: The Brookings Institution, 1968), pp. 141–178.

ordinately high portions of their incomes (over 35 percent) for housing. The main cure for this malady is raising the incomes of the households concerned through either direct income support, job creation programs, or a housing allowance (which is largely indirect income support). Far more households suffer from this malady than from living in physically inadequate dwellings.

3. *Undesirable neighborhood conditions* caused by concentration of many very poor households together in the least desirable housing, inadequate provision of public services, and exploitative local merchants and other institutions. This is the most difficult malady to cure, because doing so would require reducing the concentration of poor households in old inner-city areas that arises from the "trickle-down" process of urban development. Yet the "trickle-down" process is favored by most metropolitan-area residents because it provides good-quality environments for them—partly by keeping the very poor out of their neighborhoods precisely through such concentration.

Housing subsidies enabling low-income or moderate-income households to live in newly built units are quite high because of the increased cost of new units meeting legally required quality standards. Hence such subsidies should form only part of the nation's overall housing subsidy strategy. An even larger part should consist of improving the incomes of the poor through one or more of the three programs mentioned above. Traditionally, we have concentrated our housing subsidies on middle-income and upper-income households by allowing them to deduct mortgage interest payments and local property taxes from their federally taxable incomes. This has certainly stimulated housing production, but it has aided low-income households only indirectly, and often ineffectively, through acceleration of the "trickle-down" process. Really improving access of the ill-housed or ill-financed poor to good housing would require providing them with direct housing subsidies, as noted above. Congress authorized this in the 1968 Housing and Urban Development Act, and high levels of direct subsidies were achieved until the 1973 moratorium on their use. What will happen concerning such subsidies in the future remains uncertain as of 1976.

Yet almost all forms of urban growth would benefit from placing at least some low- and moderate-income households in brand-new housing. This is necessary in order to avoid continued spatial segregation of poor- and lower-middle-income groups from wealthier Americans. The vast majority of all new housing is built on vacant land, which is normally at the edges of existing built-up areas. If only upper-middle-income and upper-income households can afford to live in newly built units (as is now the case), then growth areas will always be occupied only by such households. This would lead to economically and socially "unbalanced" new communities, especially if new growth took the form of peripheral new cities or satellites of any type. It would be extremely expensive to house *all* the low-income households related to a new community in brand-new quarters, as in nonmetropolitan new cities. Yet, for several reasons, at least *some* low- and moderate-income households ought to live in new-growth areas. First, they perform vital roles in the local labor force, so if they lived in the new-growth areas where they work, total commuting time and traffic congestion would be reduced. Moreover, they would have much better access to suburban job markets, where most of the new jobs are being created. Second, they provide class diversity in local schools and other cultural institutions, hopefully enriching the experiences of everyone and stimulating their own upward mobility. Third, this gives them a much wider set of housing options. Thus, *the degree to which Congress provides direct housing subsidies to low- and moderate-income households has crucial implications for the particular forms of urban growth likely to occur in the future.* The less such subsidies are provided, the more future growth will be "locked in" to peripheral or satellite forms that will perpetuate economic class segregation. The more such subsidies are provided, the greater freedom we will have to use other forms, especially new cities and nonmetropolitan forms.

Opening Up the Suburbs

The third key objective needed to widen our choice among future forms of urban development is *opening up the suburbs and outlying portions of central cities to new low- and moderate-income housing.* This is desirable not only for all the reasons cited above, but also because we cannot build large numbers of housing units for such groups within central cities. There is not enough vacant land there, and that which exists is needed for nonresidential uses. Creating new housing through relocation and clearance is impractical. It is time consuming, expensive, and simply defers the problem by compelling poor people to move somewhere else. Further, most new jobs are being created in the suburbs. So it makes sense to put housing for low- and moderate-income households there.

As noted above, this would require large-scale direct subsidies so that such households could live in newly built housing. Some of these subsidies would probably take the form of a "writedown" of land costs similar to that under urban renewal, but applied to vacant land. In addition, four other tactics would help attain this objective. The first is weakening the power of small local governments to block federally assisted housing of all kinds. This could be done by empowering central-city and countywide housing authorities to operate outside central cities and inside suburbs without obtaining local permission as long as they conformed to local zoning and other regulations.

A second tactic consists of escalating land use control powers to areas of wider jurisdiction. This would prevent small communities from blocking the entry of low-income households through large-lot zoning and other manipulations of local ordinances. It could be accomplished by shifting all zoning powers to large bodies such as counties or cities with 50,000 or more population, providing review and alteration powers over small town zoning decisions to such larger bodies or to the state itself, or having the state require all communities to zone a certain amount of their buildable land so it could contain low- and moderate-income housing.

A third tactic for opening up suburbs is increasing the ability of state governments to create low- and moderate-income housing. They could do so by means of state housing authorities and other organizations provided with federally financed incentives. A fourth tactic is tying many forms of federal aid to the prior provision of low-income housing by local communities. Such aid should include all federal funds distributed under the new community development block grant funding program.

Escalating the Level of Planning

A fourth key objective relevant to future urban development is *escalation of the level of planning so that "spillover effects," now ignored by most developers, will be effectively taken into account.* Most building is now done by owners of relatively small parcels. They do not, and cannot, pay much attention to how their own behavior affects their neighbors. They have very little control over their neighbors' projects except for that provided by zoning ordinances, which are vulnerable to court overthrow. This fragmentalized approach to new growth leads to "hodgepodge" development that is aesthetically disastrous and often inefficient. In order to achieve more fully integrated planning of urban growth, it is necessary to escalate the level of planning control to larger areas.

Several tactics would accomplish this. The first has already been discussed: shifting zoning and other land use control powers away from smaller communities to larger ones. No one in our fragmentalized system of local government simultaneously has both the overall interest of the entire metropolitan area at heart and sufficient power to influence critical decisions about the area's urban growth. But this tactic would widen the parochial legal and geographic horizons of planning bodies so that their actions would exhibit far more comprehensive scope.

A second possible tactic would be forcing developers in at least some parts of each metropolitan area to undertake action only at a certain minimum geographic scale. This is a means of "internalizing" within a single plan certain land use relationships which would be "external"—and therefore largely ignored—under our present fragmented land development. If development occurred mainly in large chunks, such relations could be fully taken into account by the one plan covering everything within the boundaries of each chunk. For example, assume that in some high-growth part of a metropolitan area, the state passed a law that no urban development could occur at a scale less than 1,500 acres, or under a single plan encompassing such an area. This would compel individual owners to get together somehow in a cooperative plan, or to sell out to larger developers. In order to avoid injustice, the state would have to develop some procedure for buying and holding the individual parcels of those owners who wanted to sell before any overall plan was developed. Such sales would occur at the price of the land before development, so this practice would not allow such owners to capture speculative land value gains. This tactic fits very well with the recent tendency of more and more developers to concentrate upon sizable planned-unit developments because of their superior marketing appeal and construction efficiencies. It is also consistent with rising local concern about environmental quality. It is both easier and more economical to incorporate more open space and higher-quality amenities into large developments than into tiny ones.

A third tactic for escalating the scale of planning is bolstering state planning powers and creating new institutions to carry out urban development at several scales. This would involve four different kinds of institutions. The first would be a *national framework organization* charged with creating and administering national policies toward urban development. It could be part of the Department of Housing and Urban Development or an offshoot of the Council of Urban Affairs. Its functions might include (1) developing national migration and population-growth policies; (2) coordinating all federal programs relevant to new cities; (3) coordinating land acquisition and disposition policies of all federal and some state agencies; (4) administering direct financial assistance to both state enabling organizations and actual developers of new cities; and (5) forming other national policies toward urban growth.

The second type of new institution would be *state or regional enabling organizations.* They would make it easier for private or public developers to overcome existing institutional obstacles to large-scale urban development. Possible functions for them include (1) creating statewide plans for shaping future urban growth (including selecting sites for new cities if any are built); (2) controlling the location of major public investments such as universities and highways; (3) granting franchises to developers to build new cities on specific sites; (4)

establishing multipurpose taxing districts to help finance public improvements needed in urban growth; (5) using powers of eminent domain to assemble large-scale sites or create land banks or buffer zones; (6) "writing down" the cost of assembled land with federal funds so some housing on it could be occupied by low-income households; and (7) suggesting needed changes in existing regulations concerning zoning, subdivision, building codes, and the like to improve urban growth patterns.

The third type of new institution would be *operating development organizations,* created to plan and build large-scale new developments. These could be fully public corporations (like New York's Urban Development Corporation), quasi-public organizations, or fully private organizations benefiting from special powers exercised by the state (as private developers benefit from the eminent domain powers of local urban renewal agencies). They would carry out most of the initial planning, land assembly, public infrastructure construction, and some residential and other construction required for large-scale new developments. Since it is impossible to select from the menu of different possible organizations for such development any one best way applicable everywhere, national legislation should be designed to encourage formation of many different kinds of enabling and operating development organizations.

The fourth type of new institution involving escalation of planning control would be mainly for redeveloping older neighborhoods, rather than initially developing vacant land. It would be some form of *collective neighborhood management organization.* Its purpose would be overcoming problems of property maintenance, security, and tenant-selection caused in part by the fragmented ownership of property in deteriorated inner-city neighborhoods. Since this article focuses mainly upon future urban growth rather than redevelopment, I will not grapple further here with the need for or nature of this type of organization.

Broader Financing of Local Governments

A fifth objective critical to expanding our choices among forms of future urban growth *is widening the financial base of most local governments.* We cannot expect narrowminded thinking to disappear from most small communities as long as existing local government financial structures provide strong incentives for parochialism. Suburban resistance to the entry of low-income residents is partly—perhaps even mainly—a matter of fiscal self-defense. When low-income residents move into a wealthier community, they generally bring many children. The added cost of educating them is larger than the added tax revenues produced by the housing in which the low-income families live. Thus, every new low-income family represents an instant deficit to the local government and instantly higher taxes on all existing residents. We can hardly expect rational citizens to disregard these conditions by welcoming more low-income neighbors at their own expense. Americans have also traditionally resisted mixing with "lower-class elements" after having escaped from those same elements themselves, so not all suburban hostility to low-income residents is fiscally motivated. Yet, we will never reduce that hostility unless we first remove its economic causes. I believe we must shift a large part of the financial burden for key local government activities—particularly schools and welfare—away from local property taxes to a much broader base. That base could either be much larger property taxing districts encompassing whole metropolitan areas, state funds, federal funds, or federal funds channeled through the states.

Other Objectives

Other key objectives that would expand our future choices among forms of urban growth include *reducing the diversity of existing building codes, zoning rules, and other local regulations, and reducing the cost of producing housing.* The first is necessary so that builders can capture more of the economies of large-scale production and marketing than in the past. At present, more than 8,000 legal entities in the United States issue building and/or housing codes. Almost all these codes are significantly different from each other. It is nearly impossible for housing developers of truly nationwide scope to come into being, since they must tailor their products to these immense local variations in requirements. We do not know what kinds of economies might possibly be achieved through mass production, and through creation of nationwide market acceptance for a single type of housing unit, or a small number of such types. If each state adopted a single building and housing code applicable everywhere within its boundaries, then there would be sufficient uniformity to encourage mass production, but sufficient diversity to test a variety of code elements. States will probably not do this unless strong federal financial incentives are available, and a single national testing facility exists to verify particular building technology innovations.

Reducing housing costs significantly would surely be desirable, but I doubt if it will happen. Most of the cost of occupying housing pays for land and financing, rather than for building the unit. In fact, technical innovations in construction will have to be incredibly significant just to keep the cost of housing from continuing to rise, given the acute shortage of skilled construction labor, rising land costs, and zooming interest rates. In my opinion, unless we drastically reduce the size and quality we require in newly built units, we will never have truly *low-cost* new housing. Hence new units for low- and moderate-income house-holds will still require major subsidies.

CONCLUSIONS

The following conclusions represent what I believe are the most impor-tant implications of the foregoing analysis:

1.   Future urban growth in the United States through the year 2000 will be much smaller than most official projections indicate, though it will still represent significant expansion of existing metropolitan areas.

2.   Peripheral sprawl will undoubtedly be the dominant form of future urban growth throughout the United States. Whether it will be almost totally dominant or just largely dominant will depend upon the extent to which the key policy objectives set forth here are actually achieved.

3.   Nonmetropolitan new cities or expanded communities are not likely to capture any significant fraction of the nation's future urban growth, in spite of their current vogue in planning literature. The extra costs of these forms of urban growth mean that peripheral or satellite alternatives to peripheral sprawl are far more likely to occur.

4.   The nature of future urban growth and its consequences for inner-city neighborhoods will be greatly influenced by the total amount of housing produced in the U.S. each year. Very high levels of housing production will expand suburbs significantly and continue to attract people out of older parts of central cities. Much lower production levels might re-create housing shortages and raise the level of demand for units in older central-city areas. Housing production tends to rise dur-ing and right after general economic recessions, and decline in periods of boom or inflation. Thus, the nature of future urban growth depends in part upon the general economic climate that prevails over the next two decades, on the average.

5.   Formulation of any one "national urban strategy" or "national land policy" is neither likely nor desirable. It is not likely both because of our diffused decision-making structure and because the necessary pre-conditions for real alternatives to peripheral sprawl do not yet exist. It is not desirable because diversity both within and among metro-politan areas makes a multiplicity of "urban strategies" better than just one.

6.   State governments are the best focal points for development of any overall strategies controlling future urban growth or even for in-creasing our choices among forms of future urban growth. They are the only institutions that combine metropolitanwide perspective, decisive

powers to override local governments, and sufficient local knowledge and local political roots to make use of such powers acceptable.

7.   The proper federal role in shaping future urban growth should probably be one of structuring effective financial incentives for state governments to assume major policy responsibilities, financing subsidies needed for socially and economically "balanced" new development, and continuing to sponsor innovative approaches to key urban problems.

8.   Developing effective alternatives to peripheral sprawl, or even mitigating some of its socially segregating effects, will require major changes in deeply rooted existing political and other institutions. These include local control over land use and zoning, local financing for schools, fragmented planning of new development, and the ability of individual landowners to engage in real estate speculation. The traumatic nature of these changes to many citizens can hardly be overestimated. In fact, they are likely to occur only if the failings of existing arrangements become far more pressing and obvious than they are now in most areas.

9.   The choices Americans make among alternative forms of future urban growth will ultimately depend upon the way they resolve certain key ambiguities among their own desires. On one hand is a widespread feeling that future urban growth could be improved through more comprehensive planning and less haphazard decision making. On the other hand is the traditional desire of individual Americans to control their own small parcels of land and their own small local governments, and to gain from speculating in land values. But more comprehensive planning and continued fragmentalized control over development are mutually exclusive; we cannot enjoy the benefits of both simultaneously. As Pogo said about racism, "We have met the enemy, and he is us."

2

Up and Down with Ecology—
The "Issue-Attention Cycle"

American public attention rarely remains sharply focused upon any one domestic issue for very long—even if it involves a continuing problem of crucial importance to society. Instead, a systematic "issue-attention cycle" seems strongly to influence public attitudes and behavior concerning most key domestic problems. Each of these problems suddenly leaps into prominence, remains there for a short time, and then—though still largely unresolved—gradually fades from the center of public attention. A study of the way this cycle operates provides insights into whether public attention is likely to remain sufficiently focused upon any given issue to generate enough political pressure to cause effective change.

The shaping of American attitudes toward improving the quality of our environment provides both an example and a potential test of this "issue-attention cycle." In the past few years, there has been a remarkably widespread upsurge of interest in the quality of our environment. This change in public attitudes has been much faster than any changes in the environment itself. What has caused this shift in public attention? Why did this issue suddenly assume so high a priority among our domestic concerns? And how long will the American public sustain high-intensity interest in ecological matters? I believe that answers to these questions can be derived from analyzing the "issue-attention cycle."

Reprinted from *The Public Interest* 28 (Summer 1972): 38–50.

THE DYNAMICS OF THE "ISSUE-ATTENTION CYCLE"

Public perception of most "crises" in American domestic life does not reflect changes in real conditions as much as it reflects the operation of a systematic cycle of heightening public interest and then increasing boredom with major issues. This "issue-attention cycle" is rooted both in the nature of certain domestic problems and in the way major communications media interact with the public. The cycle itself has five stages, which may vary in duration depending upon the particular issue involved, but which almost always occur in the following sequence:

1. *The pre-problem stage.* This prevails when some highly undesirable social condition exists but has not yet captured much public attention, even though some experts or interest groups may already be alarmed by it. *Usually, objective conditions regarding the problem are far worse during the pre-problem stage than they are by the time the public becomes interested in it.* For example, this was true of racism, poverty, and malnutrition in the United States.

2. *Alarmed discovery and euphoric enthusiasm.* As a result of some dramatic series of events (like the ghetto riots in 1965 to 1967) or for other reasons, the public suddenly becomes both aware of and alarmed about the evils of a particular problem. This alarmed discovery is invariably accompanied by euphoric enthusiasm about society's ability to "solve this problem" or "do something effective" within a relatively short time. The combination of alarm and confidence results in part from the strong public pressure in America for political leaders to claim that every problem can be "solved." This outlook is rooted in the great American tradition of optimistically viewing most obstacles to social progress as *external* to the structure of society itself. The implication is that every obstacle can be eliminated and every problem solved *without any fundamental reordering of society itself,* if only we devote sufficient effort to it. In older and perhaps wiser cultures, there is an underlying sense of irony or even pessimism which springs from a widespread and often confirmed belief that many problems cannot be "solved" *at all* in any complete sense. Only recently has this more pessimistic view begun to develop in our culture.

3. *Realizing the cost of significant progress.* The third stage consists of a gradually spreading realization that the cost of "solving" the problem is very high indeed. Really doing so would not only take a great deal of money but would also require major sacrifices by large groups in the population. The public thus begins to realize that part of the problem results from arrangements that are providing significant benefits to someone—often to millions. For example, traffic congestion

and a great deal of smog are caused by increasing automobile usage. Yet this also enhances the mobility of millions of Americans who continue to purchase more vehicles to obtain these advantages.

In certain cases, technological progress can eliminate some of the undesirable results of a problem without causing any major restructuring of society or any loss of present benefits by others (except for higher money costs). In the optimistic American tradition, such a technological solution is initially assumed to be possible in the case of nearly every problem. Our most pressing social problems, however, usually involve either deliberate or unconscious exploitation of one group in society by another, or the prevention of one group from enjoying something that others want to keep for themselves. For example, most upper-middle-class whites value geographic separation from poor people and blacks. Hence any equality of access to the advantages of suburban living for the poor and for blacks cannot be achieved without some sacrifice by middle-class whites of the "benefits" of separation. The increasing recognition that there is this type of relationship between the problem and its "solution" constitutes a key part of the third stage.

4. *Gradual decline of intense public interest.* The previous stage becomes almost imperceptibly transformed into the fourth stage: a gradual decline in the intensity of public interest in the problem. As more and more people realize how difficult, and how costly to themselves, a solution to the problem would be, three reactions set in. Some people just get discouraged. Others feel positively threatened by thinking about the problem; so they suppress such thoughts. Still others become bored by the issue. Most people experience some combination of these feelings. Consequently, public desire to keep attention focused on the issue wanes. And by this time, some other issue is usually entering Stage Two; so it exerts a more novel and thus more powerful claim upon public attention.

5. *The post-problem stage.* In the final stage, an issue that has been replaced at the center of public concern moves into a prolonged limbo—a twilight realm of lesser attention or spasmodic recurrences of interest. However, the issue now has a different relation to public attention than that which prevailed in the "pre-problem" stage. For one thing, during the time that interest was sharply focused on this problem, new institutions, programs, and policies may have been created to help solve it. These entities almost always persist and often have some impact even after public attention has shifted elsewhere. For example, during the early stages of the "War on Poverty," the Office of Economic Opportunity (OEO) was established, and it initiated many new programs. Although poverty has now faded as a central public

issue, many of these programs have experienced significant success, even though funded at a far lower level than would be necessary to reduce poverty decisively.

Any major problem that once was elevated to national prominence may sporadically recapture public interest; or important aspects of it may become attached to some other problem that subsequently dominates center stage. Therefore, problems that have gone through the cycle almost always receive a higher average level of attention, public effort, and general concern than those still in the pre-discovery stage.

WHICH PROBLEMS ARE LIKELY TO GO THROUGH THE CYCLE?

Not all major social problems go through this "issue-attention cycle." Those which do generally possess to some degree three specific characteristics. First, the majority of persons in society are not suffering from the problem nearly as much as some minority (a *numerical minority,* not necessarily an *ethnic* one). This is true of many pressing social problems in America today—poverty, racism, poor public transportation, low-quality education, crime, drug addiction, and unemployment, among others. The number of persons suffering from each of these ills is very large *absolutely*—in the millions. But the numbers are small *relatively*—usually less than 15 percent of the entire population. Therefore, most people do not suffer directly enough from such problems to keep their attention riveted on them.

Second, the sufferings caused by the problem are generated by social arrangements that provide significant benefits to a majority or a powerful minority of the population. For example, Americans who own cars—plus the powerful automobile and highway lobbies—receive short-run benefits from the prohibition of using motor-fuel tax revenues for financing public transportation systems, even though such systems are desperately needed by the urban poor.

Third, the problem has no intrinsically exciting qualities—or no longer has them. When big-city racial riots were being shown nightly on the nation's television screens, public attention naturally focused upon their causes and consequences. But when they ceased (or at least the media stopped reporting them so intensively), public interest in the problems related to them declined sharply. Similarly, as long as the National Aeronautics and Space Administration (NASA) was able to stage a series of ever more thrilling space shots, culminating in the worldwide television spectacular of Americans walking on the moon, it generated sufficient public support to sustain high-level congressional appropriations. But NASA had nothing half so dramatic for an encore, and repetition of the same feat proved less and less exciting (though a near disaster on the third try did revive audience interest). So NASA's congressional appropriations plummeted.

A problem must be dramatic and exciting to maintain public interest because news is "consumed" by much of the American public (and by publics everywhere) largely as a form of entertainment. As such, it competes with other types of entertainment for a share of each person's time. Every day, there is a fierce struggle for space in the highly limited universe of newsprint and television viewing time. Each issue vies not only with all other social problems and public events, but also with a multitude of "non-news" items that are often far more pleasant to contemplate. These include sporting news, weather reports, crossword puzzles, fashion accounts, comics, and daily horoscopes. In fact, the amount of television time and newspaper space devoted to sports coverage, as compared to international events, is a striking commentary on the relative value that the public places on knowing about these two subjects.

When all three of the above conditions exist concerning a given problem that has somehow captured public attention, the odds are great that it will soon move through the entire "issue-attention cycle" —and therefore will gradually fade from the center of the stage. The first condition means that most people will not be continually reminded of the problem by their own suffering from it. The second condition means that solving the problem requires sustained attention and effort, plus fundamental changes in social institutions or behavior. This in turn means that significant attempts to solve it are threatening to important groups in society. The third condition means that the media's sustained focus on this problem soon bores a majority of the public. As soon as the media realize that their emphasis on this problem is threatening many people and boring even more, they will shift their focus to some "new" problem. This is particularly likely in America because nearly all the media are run for profit, and they make the most money by appealing to the largest possible audiences. Thus, as Marshall McLuhan has pointed out, it is largely the audience itself—the American public—that "manages the news" by maintaining or losing interest in a given subject. As long as this pattern persists, we will continue to be confronted by a stream of "crises" involving particular social problems. Each will rise into public view, capture center stage for a while, and then gradually fade away as it is replaced by more fashionable issues moving into their "crisis" phases.

THE RISE OF ENVIRONMENTAL CONCERN

Public interest in the quality of the environment now appears to be about midway through the "issue-attention cycle." Gradually, more and more people are beginning to realize the immensity of the social and financial costs of cleaning up our air and water and of preserving and restoring open spaces. Hence much of the enthusiasm about prompt, dramatic improvement in the environment is fading. There is still a great deal of public interest, however, so it cannot be said that the "post-problem stage" has been reached. In fact, as will be discussed later, the environmental issue may well retain more attention than social problems that affect smaller proportions of the population. Before evaluating the prospects of long-term interest in the environment, though, it is helpful to analyze how environmental concern passed through the earlier stages in the "issue-attention cycle."

The most obvious reason for the initial rise in concern about the environment is the recent deterioration of certain easily perceived environmental conditions. A whole catalogue of symptoms can be arrayed, including ubiquitous urban smog, greater proliferation of solid waste, oceanic oil spills, greater pollution of water supplies by DDT and other poisons, the threatened disappearance of many wildlife species, and the overcrowding of a variety of facilities from commuter expressways to national parks. Millions of citizens observing these worsening conditions became convinced that *someone* ought to "do something" about them. But "doing something" to reduce environmental deterioration is not easy. For many of our environmental problems have been caused by developments which are highly valued by most Americans.

The very abundance of our production and consumption of material goods is responsible for an immense amount of environmental pollution. For example, electric power generation, if based on fossil fuels, creates smoke and air pollution or, if based on nuclear fuels, causes rising water temperatures. Yet a key foundation for rising living standards in the United States during this century has been the doubling of electric power consumption every 10 years. So more pollution is the price we have paid for the tremendous advantages of being able to use more and more electricity. Similarly, much of the litter blighting even our remotest landscapes stems from the convenience of using "throw-away packages." Thus, to regard environmental pollution as a purely external negative factor would be to ignore its direct linkage with material advantages most citizens enjoy.

Another otherwise favorable development that has led to rising environmental pollution is what I would call the democratization of privilege. Many more Americans are now able to participate in certain activities that were formerly available only to a small, wealthy minority. Some members of that minority are incensed by the consequences of having their formerly esoteric advantages spread to "the common man." The most frequent irritant caused by the democratization of privilege is congestion. Rising highway congestion, for example, is denounced almost everywhere. Yet its main cause is the rapid spread of automobile ownership and usage. In 1950, about 59 percent of all families had at least one automobile, and 7 percent owned two or more. By 1968, the proportion of families owning at least one automobile had climbed to 79 percent, and 26 percent had two or more cars. In the 10 years from 1960 to 1970, the total number of registered automotive vehicles rose by 35 million (or 47 percent), as compared to a rise in human population of 23 million (or only 13 percent). Moreover, it has been estimated that motor vehicles cause approximately 60 percent of all air pollution. So the tremendous increase in smog does not result primarily from larger population, but rather from the democratization of automobile ownership.

The democratization of privilege also causes crowding in national parks, rising suburban housing density, the expansion of new subdivisions into formerly picturesque farms and orchards, and the transformation of once tranquil resort areas like Waikiki Beach into forests of high-rise buildings. It is now difficult for the wealthy to flee from busy urban areas to places of quiet seclusion, because so many more people can afford to go with them. *The elite's environmental deterioration is often the common man's improved standard of living.*

OUR SOARING ASPIRATIONS

A somewhat different factor which has contributed to greater concern with environmental quality is a marked increase in our aspirations and standards concerning what our environment ought to be like. In my opinion, rising dissatisfaction with the "system" in the United States does not result primarily from poorer performance by that system. Rather, it stems mainly from a rapid escalation of our aspirations as to what the system's performance ought to be. Nowhere is this phenomenon more striking than in regard to the quality of the environment. One hundred years ago, white Americans were eliminating whole Indian tribes without a qualm. Today, many serious-minded citizens seek to make important issues out of the potential disappearance of the whooping crane, the timber wolf, and other exotic creatures. Meanwhile, thousands of Indians in Brazil are still being murdered each year—but American conservationists are not focusing on that human massacre. Similarly, some aesthetes decry "galloping sprawl" in metropolitan fringe areas, while they ignore acres of rat-infested housing a few miles away. Hence the escalation of our environmental aspirations is more selective than might at first appear.

Yet regarding many forms of pollution, we are now rightly upset over practices and conditions that have largely been ignored for decades.

An example is our alarm about the dumping of industrial wastes and sewage into rivers and lakes. This increase in our environmental aspirations is part of a general cultural phenomenon stimulated both by our success in raising living standards and by the recent emphases of the communications media. Another cause of the rapid rise in interest in environmental pollution is the "explosion" of alarmist rhetoric on this subject. According to some well-publicized experts, all life on earth is threatened by an "environmental crisis." Some claim human life will end within three decades or less if we do not do something drastic about current behavior patterns.

Are things really that bad? Frankly, I am not enough of an ecological expert to know. But I am skeptical concerning all highly alarmist views because so many previous prophets of doom and disaster have been so wrong concerning many other so-called "crises" in our society.

There are two reasonable definitions of "crisis." One kind of crisis consists of a rapidly deteriorating situation moving toward a single disastrous event at some future moment. The second kind consists of a more gradually deteriorating situation that will eventually pass some subtle "point of no return." At present, I do not believe either of these definitions applies to most American domestic problems. Although many social critics hate to admit it, the American "system" actually serves the majority of citizens rather well in terms of most indicators of well-being. Concerning such things as real income, personal mobility, variety and choice of consumption patterns, longevity, health, leisure time, and quality of housing, most Americans are better off today than they have ever been and extraordinarily better off than most of mankind. What is *not* improving is the gap between society's performance and what most people—or at least highly vocal minorities—believe society *ought* to be doing to solve these problems. Our aspirations and standards have risen far faster than the beneficial outputs of our social system. Therefore, although most Americans, including most of the poor, are receiving more now, they are enjoying it less.

This conclusion should not be confused with the complacency of some super-patriots. It would be unrealistic to deny certain important negative trends in American life. Some conditions are indeed getting worse for nearly everyone. Examples are air quality and freedom from thievery. Moreover, congestion and environmental deterioration might forever destroy certain valuable national amenities if they are not checked. Finally, there has probably been a general rise in personal and social anxiety in recent years. I believe this is due to increased tensions caused by our rapid rate of technical and social change, plus the increase in worldwide communication through the media. These developments rightly cause serious and genuine concern among millions of Americans.

THE FUTURE OF THE ENVIRONMENTAL ISSUE

Concern about the environment has passed through the first two stages of the "issue-attention cycle" and is by now well into the third. In fact, we have already begun to move toward the fourth stage, in which the intensity of public interest in environmental improvement must inexorably decline. And this raises an interesting question: Will the issue of environmental quality then move on into the "post-problem" stage of the cycle?

My answer to this question is: Yes, but not soon, because certain characteristics of this issue will protect it from the rapid decline in public interest typical of many other recent issues. First of all, many kinds of environmental pollution are much more visible and more clearly threatening than most other social problems. This is particularly true of air pollution. The greater the apparent threat from visible forms of pollution and the more vividly this can be dramatized, the more public support environmental improvement will receive and the longer it will sustain public interest. Ironically, the cause of ecologists would therefore benefit from an environmental disaster like a "killer smog" that would choke thousands to death in a few days. Actually, this is nothing new; every cause from early Christianity to the Black Panthers has benefited from martyrs. Yet even the most powerful symbols lose their impact if they are constantly repeated. The piteous sight of an oil-soaked seagull or a dead soldier pales after it has been viewed even a dozen times. Moreover, some of the worst environmental threats come from forms of pollution that are invisible. Thus, our propensity to focus attention on what is most visible may cause us to clean up the pollution we can easily perceive while ignoring even more dangerous but hidden threats.

Pollution is also likely to be kept in the public eye because it is an issue that threatens almost everyone, not just a small percentage of the population. Since it is not politically divisive, politicians can safely pursue it without fearing adverse repercussions. Attacking environmental pollution is therefore much safer than attacking racism or poverty. For an attack upon the latter antagonizes important blocs of voters who benefit from the sufferings of others or at least are not threatened enough by such suffering to favor spending substantial amounts of their money to reduce it.

A third strength of the environmental issue is that much of the "blame" for pollution can be attributed to a small group of "villains" whose wealth and power make them excellent scapegoats. Environmental defenders can therefore "courageously" attack these scapegoats without antagonizing most citizens. Moreover, at least in regard to air pollution, that small group actually has enough power to greatly reduce pollution if it really tries. If leaders of the nation's top auto-producing, power-generating, and fuel-supplying firms would change their behavior significantly, a drastic decline in air pollution could be achieved very quickly. This has been demonstrated at many locations already.

Gathering support for attacking any problem is always easier if its ills can be blamed on a small number of "public enemies"—as is shown by the success of Ralph Nader. This tactic is especially effective if the "enemies" exhibit extreme wealth and power, eccentric dress and manners, obscene language, or some other uncommon traits. Then society can aim its outrage at a small, alien group without having to face up to the need to alter its own behavior. It is easier to find such scapegoats for almost all forms of pollution than for other major problems like poverty, poor housing, or racism. Solutions to those problems would require millions of Americans to change their own behavior patterns, to accept higher taxes, or both.

The possibility that technological solutions can be devised for most pollution problems may also lengthen the public prominence of this issue. To the extent that pollution can be reduced through technological change, most people's basic attitudes, expectations, and behavior patterns will not have to be altered. The traumatic difficulties of achieving major institutional change could thus be escaped through the "magic" of purely technical improvements in automobile engines, water purification devices, fuel composition, and sewage treatment facilities.

FINANCING THE FIGHT AGAINST POLLUTION

Another aspect of anti-pollution efforts that will strengthen their political support is that most of the costs can be passed on to the public through higher product prices rather than higher taxes. Therefore, politicians can demand enforcement of costly environmental quality standards without paying the high political price of raising the required funds through taxes. True, water pollution is caused mainly by the actions of public bodies, especially municipal sewer systems, and effective remedies for this form of pollution require higher taxes or at least higher prices for public services. But the major costs of reducing most kinds of pollution can be added to product prices and thereby quietly shifted to the ultimate consumers of the outputs concerned. This is a politically painless way to pay for attacking a major social problem. In contrast, effectively combatting most social problems requires large-scale income redistribution attainable only through both higher taxes and higher transfer payments or subsidies. Examples of such politically costly problems are poverty, slum housing, low-quality health care for the poor, and inadequate public transportation.

Many ecologists oppose paying for a cleaner environment through higher product prices. They would rather force the polluting firms to bear the required cost through lower profits. In a few oligopolistic industries, like petroleum and automobile production, this might work. But in the long run, not much of the total cost could be paid this way without driving capital out of the industries concerned and thereby eventually forcing product prices upwards. Furthermore, it is just that those who use any given product should pay the full cost of making it—including the cost of avoiding excessive pollution in its production. Such payment is best made through higher product prices. In my opinion, it would be unwise in most cases to try to pay these costs by means of government subsidies in order to avoid shifting the load onto consumers. We need to conserve our politically limited taxing capabilities to attack those problems that cannot be dealt with in any other way.

Still another reason why the cleaner-environment issue may last a long time is that it could generate a large private industry with strong vested interests in continued spending against pollution. Already dozens of firms with "eco-" or "environ-" in their names have sprung up to exploit supposedly burgeoning anti-pollution markets. In time, we might even generate an "environmental-industrial complex" about which some future president could vainly warn us in his retirement speech! Any issue gains longevity if its sources of political support and the programs related to it can be institutionalized in large bureaucracies. Such organizations have a powerful desire to keep public attention focused on the problems that support them. However, it is doubtful that the anti-pollution industry will ever come close to the defense industry in size and power. Effective anti-pollution activities cannot be carried out separately from society as a whole because they require changes in behavior by millions of people. In contrast, weapons are produced by an industry that imposes no behavioral changes (other than higher taxes) on the average citizen.

Finally, environmental issues may remain at center stage longer than most domestic issues because of their very ambiguity. "Improving the environment" is a tremendously broad and all-encompassing objective. Almost everyone can plausibly claim that his or her particular cause is another way to upgrade the quality of our life. This ambiguity will make it easier to form a majority-sized coalition favoring a variety of social changes associated with improving the environment. The inability to form such a coalition regarding problems that adversely affect only minority-sized groups usually hastens the exit of such problems from the center of public attention.

All the factors set forth above indicate that circumstances are unusually favorable for launching and sustaining major efforts to improve the quality of our environment. Yet we should not underestimate the

American public's capacity to become bored—especially with something that does not immediately threaten them, or promise huge benefits for a majority, or strongly appeal to their sense of injustice. In the present mood of the nation, I believe most citizens do not want to confront the need for major social changes on any issues except those that seem directly to threaten them—such as crime and other urban violence. And even in regard to crime, the public does not yet wish to support really effective changes in our basic system of justice. The present administration has apparently concluded that a relatively "low-profile" government—one that does not try to lead the public into accepting truly significant institutional changes—will most please the majority of Americans at this point. Regardless of the accuracy of this view, if it remains dominant within the federal government, then no major environmental programs are likely to receive long-sustained public attention or support.

Some proponents of improving the environment are relying on the support of students and other young people to keep this issue at the center of public attention. Such support, however, is not adequate as a long-term foundation. Young people form a highly unstable base for the support of any policy because they have such short-lived "staying power." For one thing, they do not long enjoy the large amount of free time they possess while in college. Also, as new individuals enter the category of "young people" and older ones leave it, different issues are stressed and accumulated skills in marshaling opinion are dissipated. Moreover, the radicalism of the young has been immensely exaggerated by the media's tendency to focus attention upon those with extremist views. In their attitudes toward political issues, most young people are not very different from their parents.

There is good reason, then, to believe that the bundle of issues called "improving the environment" will also suffer the gradual loss of public attention characteristic of the later stages of the "issue-attention cycle." However, it will be eclipsed at a much slower rate than other recent domestic issues. So it may be possible to accomplish some significant improvements in environmental quality—if those seeking them work fast.

3
Racism in America and
How to Combat It

AMERICANS NEED TO UNDERSTAND RACISM

Racism is a dirty word in America—and a hotly controversial one. Calling somebody a "racist" is—and should be—a grievous insult. It implies that the person concerned is guilty of committing a serious injustice. Black Americans accuse the nation's ethnic majority of white racism; while many whites accuse some blacks of black racism.

What is racism anyway? What significance does it really have in American life today? Unfortunately, almost no one who uses this word defines it clearly or at all. And it is used in such widely varying ways that it hardly seems to have any commonly agreed upon meaning, except that nearly everyone believes racism is evil and un-American. The result is widespread confusion, uncertainty, and disagreement concerning the nature of racism. Even worse, practically any use of the word calls forth strongly emotional reactions. Rather than consider the subject reasonably, Americans of all colors usually adopt self-righteous and defensive views about it, even though racism is one of the most complicated and profoundly important issues in the nation's history.

Because racism is too important in the destiny of America to allow this confusion to continue unchallenged, this paper seeks to clarify its

Reprinted by permission of the U.S. Civil Rights Commission from Clearinghouse Publication, Urban Series No. 1, January 1970. The opinions expressed are the author's and do not necessarily represent the views of commission members or staff.

I am profoundly indebted to John McKnight of Northwestern University for his key contributions to this essay, including many of its central ideas.

meaning, to measure its true significance in American life, and to indicate some ways to combat it.

SIGNIFICANCE OF RACISM

Millions of Chicanos, Puerto Ricans, blacks, Indians, and other minority groups in our society suffer from severe deprivation and injustice, not only in the past, but now. Many widely varying factors cause this deplorable situation. They include historical development, economic and physical conditions, technical and population trends, long-established institutional structures and practices, political forces, and social and personal customs and attitudes. An additional factor, racism, is not always the most important one. Therefore, any reduction of deprivation and injustice must involve actions aimed at many things other than racism.

The harmful effects of racism upon American society are immense. These effects are especially injurious to members of certain minority groups, often in ways completely unrecognized by most Americans. Racism worsens the impact upon these minority groups of nearly all the other causal factors listed above. Therefore, no attempts to provide equal opportunities in our society, or to improve conditions among deprived groups, are likely to succeed unless we eliminate *or* counteract racism. Such success will not occur until most Americans—especially whites—understand racism well enough to recognize and counteract its pervasive forms in their own behavior and in the institutions around them.

The great significance of racism in American life received dramatic and widely publicized emphasis in the "Report of the National Advisory Commission on Civil Disorders" in March 1968. Among the most controversial findings in this report are:

What white Americans have never fully understood—but what the Negro can never forget—is that white society is deeply implicated in the ghetto. White institutions created it, white institutions maintain it, and white society condones it.

Race prejudice has shaped our history decisively in the past; it now threatens to do so again. White racism is essentially responsible for the explosive mixture which has been accumulating in our cities since the end of World War II.

These statements were controversial when they were first made because most white Americans did not believe that they had racist attitudes or that they exhibited racist behavior. After all, most whites are far removed from direct contact with what the National Advisory Committee on Civil Disorders called "the ghetto." So they do not see themselves as "deeply implicated" in creating, maintaining, or condoning it. Most of all, they cannot understand why they should be held "responsible for the explosive mixture which has been accumulating in our cities since the end of World War II." The overwhelming majority of whites do not understand how they can be blamed for riots and disorders among people with whom they have very little direct contact, and whose affairs have been—and still are—largely unknown to them.

The National Advisory Commission failed to clarify its accusations by explicitly defining "white racism" in its report. It did not directly link that term with the many examples of racist institutional practices set forth throughout the report. These omissions strengthened the initial antagonism of many whites to its findings. Moreover, events since the commission issued its report have further increased this antagonism, and even caused many whites who at first favored the commission's findings to change their views. Yet these same events have made it even more imperative for most Americans to understand the real nature and significance of racism in our society.

Racism is one of those words that many people use, and feel strongly about, but cannot define very clearly. Those who suffer from racism usually interpret the word one way while others interpret it quite differently. This ambiguity is possible in part because the word refers to ideas that are very complicated and hard to pin down. Yet, before we can fully understand how racism works or how to combat its harmful effects we must first try to define it clearly even though such an attempt may be regarded as wrong by many.

Perhaps the best definition of *racism* is an operational one. This means that it must be based upon the way people actually behave, rather than upon logical consistency or purely scientific ideas. Therefore, racism may be viewed as *any attitude, action, or institutional structure which subordinates a person or group because of his or her or their color.* Even though "race" and "color" refer to two different kinds of human characteristics, in America it is the visibility of skin color—and of other physical traits associated with particular groups—that marks individuals as "targets" for subordination by members of the white majority. This is true of blacks, Puerto Ricans, Chicanos, Japanese Americans, Chinese Americans, and American Indians. Specifically, white racism subordinates members of all these other groups primarily because they are not white in color, even though some are technically considered to be members of the "white race" and even view themselves as "whites."

This definition emphasizes that racism is not just a matter of attitudes: actions and institutional structures, especially, can also be forms of racism. An "institutional structure" is any well-established, habitual, or widely accepted pattern of action or organizational arrangement, whether formal or informal. For example, the residential segregation of almost all blacks in large cities is an "institutional structure." So is the widely used practice of denying employment to applicants with any nontraffic police record. This tends to discriminate unfairly against residents of low-income areas where police normally arrest young men for minor incidents that are routinely overlooked in wealthy suburbs.

Just being aware of someone's color or race, or even taking it into account when making decisions or in other behavior, is not necessarily racist. Racism occurs only when these reactions involve some kind of subordination. Thus, pride in one's black heritage, or Irish ancestry, is not necessarily racist.

Racism can occur even if the people causing it have no intention of subordinating others because of color, or are totally unaware of doing so. Admittedly, this implication is sure to be extremely controversial. Most Americans believe racism is bad. But how can anyone be "guilty" of doing something bad when he does not realize he is doing it? Racism can be a matter of *result* rather than *intention* because many institutional structures in America that most whites do not recognize as subordinating others because of color actually injure minority group members far more than deliberate racism.

The separation of races is not racism unless it leads to or involves subordination of one group by another (including subordination of whites by blacks). Therefore, favoring the voluntary separation of races is not necessarily a form of racism. However, it would become racism if members of one group who wanted to cluster together tried to restrict the locational choices of members of some other group in order to achieve such clustering; for example, if whites tried to discourage Chicanos from moving into all-white neighborhoods or if a group of black students forced other black students to live in a specific dormitory. Furthermore, separation of groups is one of the oldest and most widespread devices for subordination in all societies. It is particularly effective in modern urbanized societies because it is extremely difficult, if not impossible, to provide different but truly equal opportunities and conditions for separated groups within an economically integrated society.

Ways White Racism Appears or Works in American Society

White racism exhibits itself in hundreds of ways in American society and acts in hundreds of other ways that are not recognized by most citizens. Yet all of these can be usefully grouped into two basic categories: *overt racism* and *indirect institutional subordination because of color.* (For convenience, the second category will be referred to as just *institutional subordination.*)

Overt racism is the use of color per se (or other visible characteristics related to color) as a subordinating factor. *Institutional subordination* is placing or keeping persons in a position or status of inferiority by means of attitudes, actions, or institutional structures which do not use color itself as the subordinating mechanism, but instead use other mechanisms indirectly related to color. Institutional subordination is particularly difficult to define clearly in a few words. The very essence of institutional subordination is its indirect nature, which often makes it hard to recognize. Furthermore, there are so many different forms of institutional subordination that it is difficult to include all of them in a single definition. Therefore, these two categories of racism, and the relations between them, can best be clarified by discussing them rather than by further refining their definitions.

Historical Dominance of Overt Racism and Its Results

For more than 300 years, overt racism was a central part of American life, particularly in the South. During these centuries, thousands of overtly racist laws, social institutions, behavior patterns, living conditions, distributions of political power, figures and forms of speech, cultural viewpoints and habits, and even thought patterns continually forced colored Americans[1] into positions of inferiority and subordination. It took the bloodiest of all American wars to abolish the most terrible form of legal subordination—slavery—just 100 years ago. But many other overtly racist laws and institutions remained in force until well after World War II. These include legally segregated schools, restrictive covenants forbidding nonwhites to live in certain neighborhoods, laws prohibiting interracial marriages, required racial separation of public facilities like bus seats and restaurants, and denial of the right to vote.

In the past two decades, there has been important progress in striking down legal support for most of the forms of overt racism. The actual effects of many such forms of racism have been greatly reduced, too. Moreover, this type of conscious and deliberate subordination by color is now considered wrong by most Americans. As a result, many whites *believe* that overt racism—which is the only form they recognize—is disappearing from America.

Yet hundreds of forms of overt racism remain throughout most of

---

[1] The terms colored and nonwhite in the remainder of this paper refer to blacks, Puerto Ricans, Chicanos, Japanese Americans, Chinese Americans, and American Indians because this is how most whites really view and identify them.

the nation. Examples are the deliberate exclusion of blacks, Chicanos, and other colored persons from labor unions, law firms, school districts, all-white residential neighborhoods, college fraternities, and private social clubs.

Furthermore, the effects of more than three centuries of overt racism upon both whites and nonwhites cannot be overcome in just a few years. For many generations, millions of blacks, Chicanos, Indians, and other nonwhites have been treated as inferiors, given inferior jobs and legal rights, compelled to accept inferior schooling, forced to live in inferior housing and neighborhoods, made to use inferior public facilities, and constantly told that they were inferior human beings and had no chance to be otherwise. They have been—and still are—systematically excluded from most residential areas, most schools, most jobs, most social privileges, and most political opportunities—particularly the best of all these things. This treatment has had tremendous effects upon a whole range of conditions among nonwhites in America. These conditions include where they live, their incomes, their self-images and degree of self-confidence, the nature and stability of their families, their attitudes toward authority, their levels of educational and cultural attainment, and their occupational skills. Of course, not all members of each nonwhite minority group have been equally affected by these conditions. Yet, taken as a whole, Americans of color are still severely handicapped by the residual effects of past overt racism—plus the many forms of overt racism that still exist.

Relation of Residual Effects of Overt Racism to Institutional Subordination

The deeply embedded effects of overt white racism will not instantly disappear if the white majority suddenly reduces or even eliminates the use of color as an explicit factor in making decisions or influencing its actions. Many whites now say: "All right, we recognize the injustice of overt racism. So we will stop using color as a factor in making decisions. Instead we will use other factors which are clearly and reasonably related to the activities and privileges concerned." Examples of these other factors used in making decisions are skill levels in relation to jobs, place of residence in relation to school attendance, ability to score well on entrance examinations in relation to higher education, self-confidence and leadership of whites in relation to job promotions, and savings plus present income in relation to buying homes.

Usually, the use of such factors is free from overt racism. Hence, it constitutes great progress in relation to most of American history. Thus, most civil rights organizations have argued for years in favor of "merit employment" based upon skill and ability without regard to race or color. And achievement of true "merit employment" regarding hiring, promotion, wages, and salaries would be a great advance in most firms. Therefore, whites who succeed in this achievement can rightly feel proud of eliminating an important form of overt racism from their behavior.

Nevertheless, even "merit employment" programs can conceal many forms of indirect institutional subordination by color. In fact, we can use the example of such programs to illustrate how present elimination of overtly racist action does *not* destroy or even significantly weaken the continuing racist effects of *past* overtly racist behavior. This can occur because many of those effects are embedded in institutional structures that no longer appear related to race or color.

Consider an employer who needs workers to fill certain jobs that demand advanced carpentry skills. Naturally, he requires that applicants have such skills in order to be hired. But what if the local carpenters' union excludes all blacks and Chicanos as members? Then this very reasonable behavior of the employer has racist effects because of overt racism of another organization upon which he relies to carry out his own activities. Or what if unions accept minority group apprentices specially trained in local high schools, but the only high schools providing such training are in all-white neighborhoods, either too far from minority group neighborhoods for convenient attendance, or far enough to be placed in different school districts because all school district boundaries are based upon the "neighborhood proximity" principle? In this case, no decision-makers are using overtly racist principles. Yet the result clearly continues systematic subordination of minority groups by excluding them from important economic opportunities. Returning to the example, assume that the employer saves money by never advertising available job openings. Instead, he relies solely upon word-of-mouth communications from his present employees to their friends to find applicants—but all his present employees are white. This is an extremely widespread practice, since most workers find their jobs by hearing of openings from friends. Yet it has the effect of excluding nearly all minority group members from consideration for available jobs. Because of past overt racism, most whites have mainly white friends, particularly since they live in all-white neighborhoods.

Again, the employer is taking actions which are not overtly racist in either nature or intent—but which nevertheless have racist effects, that is, they subordinate people because of their color. In this case, these effects occur because the seemingly reasonable and "unbiased" behavior of the employer takes place in an institutional context that still contains profoundly racist elements remaining from three centuries of overt racism. If the employer had carefully examined his recruiting practices to see whether he was giving members of all groups an equal chance to compete for his job, he might have discovered this situation. But he was not engaging in any overtly racist behavior; so it never occurred to him that his customary practices might have indirect racist effects because of institutional subordination.

"Invisibility" of Much Institutional Subordination

This "invisibility" of institutional subordination is even more striking concerning those forms which result from *geographic exclusion* of minority group members from all-white areas, or *perceptual distortion* in the way people see reality. Overt racism, both past and present, is the main cause of the spatial separation of where most whites live from where most nonwhite minorities live. The major form of such racism is deliberate discouragement of black and other nonwhite families from buying or renting homes in all-white neighborhoods. Such discouragement is systematically practiced by white realtors, renting agents, landlords, and homeowners. This clearly racist behavior has become so well entrenched that many minority group members no longer even try to find homes in all-white areas because they fear they will "get the runaround" or receive hostile treatment from at least some neighbors. So the pattern of exclusion is continued, in spite of recent laws and court decisions to the contrary.

Yet dozens of other forms of institutional subordination are indirectly caused by the absence of nonwhites from white residential areas. For example, most new jobs are being created in suburban shopping centers, industrial parks, new office buildings, and schools or universities. But American suburban areas are overwhelmingly white in population (about 94 percent in 1970). So the suburban sources of new employment are usually far from where nonwhites live. This makes it very difficult for the latter to know when such job openings exist, to get transportation to look for them, and to commute to work once they are found. Even if they do get jobs in the suburbs, they have great difficulty finding housing near their work. This difficulty does not result only from overt racism; it is also caused by zoning laws which deliberately discourage any housing serving relatively lower-income groups or local actions which prevent use of federal subsidies for such housing. Such laws are usually defended on grounds of "maintaining high community standards" of housing and open space, or protecting the existing residents from tax increases that would be caused by building more schools to serve new low-income residents.

All these conditions discourage minority group members from even trying to get suburban jobs. This perpetuates their exclusion from all-white suburban areas. Yet many of the best quality schools, housing developments, recreational facilities, and general residential environments are found in the suburbs. So most minority group members find themselves cut off not only from the fastest growing sources of new jobs, but also from many of the best amenities in American society. This is clearly racism or "institutional subordination."

Moreover, this exclusion is accomplished by very few acts of overt racism carried out by a small number of people, supplemented by thousands of acts of indirect institutional subordination carried out by millions of white suburbanites. But most of the latter are completely unaware of the subordinating nature of their behavior. In fact, many sincerely avoid any actions they believe are overtly racist. That is why so many whites become righteously indignant at the claim that American society is "racist." They have carefully purged their own actions of overtly racist behavior, and they sincerely believe their own communities "have no race problems" because there are practically no minority group members there. The institutionally subordinating nature of the processes that cause this exclusion remains completely hidden from them.

This invisibility of institutional subordination occurs in part because minority group members themselves are "invisible" in the normal lives of most white Americans—especially white children. Most white children are brought up in neighborhoods where blacks, Chicanos, and other nonwhite persons are totally absent, or constitute an extremely small minority, usually engaged in menial jobs. These children form an unconscious but deeply rooted mental image of "normal" society as consisting only of white people, and of all colored persons as "strange" and "different" from "normal people." This image is further reinforced by the world they see on television. Until very recently, "normal" American society as depicted by television programs contained few blacks, Indians, Chicanos, or other nonwhites in positive or realistic roles. Members of these groups were seen only as villains, or professional athletes, or entertainers, or servants, or on newscasts engaged in crime or violence. Recent introduction of many more blacks into television commercials and some major roles is certainly an improvement. But television still depicts a largely segregated society, especially in the situation shows and cartoons which children watch, and particularly regarding such minority groups as Puerto Ricans and Indians. Moreover, this perception of whites as the only "normal Americans" was further reinforced for more than 100 years by the elementary and other textbooks used in almost all American schools. The exclusion of minority group members from such texts is one more way in which millions of Americans were—and still are—made both "invisible" and "strange" in the minds of the white majority.

The same distortions in perception that make whites unconsciously feel "normal" and superior in relation to nonwhite persons have exactly the opposite effects upon the latter. Most minority children also grow up in neighborhoods where they meet few people not in their own ethnic group. However, they learn from adults who must deal with whites that people in their own group have relatively little power and status in society. Television has devastatingly confirmed this impression because the world of "normal Americans" they see on the screen almost totally excludes them, or shows them mainly in inferior or marginal roles. School textbooks and other educational materials further confirm this view. It is, therefore, not surprising that many members of nonwhite groups unconsciously come to believe that perhaps they really *are* inferior. Otherwise, how can the pictures of reality which society shows them be explained? But once a person begins to believe he is inferior, he starts losing confidence in his ability to overcome any obstacles he may run into. This often causes him to reduce his efforts when confronted by such obstacles—which in turn produces failures that confirm the feelings of inferiority. So the individual's subordination is not only perpetuated, but becomes justified in the eyes of others by the individual's behavior.[2] Thus, geographic exclusion of nonwhites by whites, plus perceptual distortions in white-controlled mass media, combine to produce largely unrecognized psychological and behavioral effects upon both groups. These effects perpetuate the institutional subordination of nonwhites because of their color.

The pervasive nature of institutional subordination, and its continuance over long periods, is illustrated by the black quest for good quality education in American public schools. Obtaining quality educations for their children is a central concern of all American parents. But among black parents, this desire has been continuously thwarted by a series of white-dominated institutions. Each time blacks overcome or bypass the obstacles posed by one such institution, another blocks them with some new form of subordination.

As late as the 1940s, blacks tried to get good quality schooling within the legally segregated separate school systems which then prevailed. But experience proved that the education their children received was definitely inferior in quality to that received by whites. For example, the few blacks who managed to complete college in this inferior system discovered they could not earn incomes even as high as those of white

---

[2] The key idea of "black nationalism" is precisely to reverse this process by generating pride in being black instead of feelings of inferiority. Such pride is designed to lead to greater self-respect and self-confidence and, therefore, to more success in overcoming obstacles. This in turn is supposed to reinforce self-confidence and reaffirm initial pride in being black. "Black nationalism" and "black power" seek to create a positive counteridentity to offset the negative "loss of identity" felt by blacks as a result of the forces described above.

high school graduates, both because their training was inferior and because of discrimination in hiring.

In response, black civil rights organizations launched a long legal battle for racial integration in the public schools so they could share in the good quality education received by whites. The legal struggle was finally won in the Supreme Court's monumental 1954 decision striking down segregation. But then they found themselves confronted by a whole new series of white maneuvers and institutions preventing meaningful integration. In the South, most areas simply ignored the Supreme Court's command to integrate schools. Other areas engaged in token integration of just a few students or devised "voluntary selection" schemes that nullified integration. As of 1966—*12 years* after the Supreme Court decision—the proportions of black elementary and secondary school students in schools with white students were 4.4 percent in Alabama, 8.8 percent in Georgia, 3.4 percent in Louisiana, 2.5 percent in Mississippi, and 5.6 percent in South Carolina. In only four of the eleven southern states was this fraction more than 16 percent. However, it was more than 75 percent in five of the seven border states. So the strikingly low fractions in the deep South unquestionably resulted from deliberate white policy rather than any necessity stemming from high proportions of blacks in the total population.

In 1969, civil rights leaders won another unanimous Supreme Court victory requiring *immediate* desegregation of schools in Mississippi, over the combined opposition of the local, state, and federal governments. After that, physical desegregation, that is, simultaneous attendance of both blacks and whites at the same schools, proceeded rapidly in the South. Thus, by 1972, the proportions of black elementary and secondary students in schools with white students had soared to 83.6 percent in Alabama, 86.8 percent in Georgia, 83.0 percent in Louisiana, 91.5 percent in Mississippi, and 93.9 percent in South Carolina. This fraction was 80 percent or more in all eleven southern states and above 90 percent in six of them. These data show that a remarkable change had occurred in the South, although it took nearly two decades to accomplish after the 1954 Supreme Court decision. However, *physical* desegregation has not always produced *effective* desegregation, that is, true equality of educational opportunity, because black students are not always given equal treatment within physically desegregated schools. Furthermore, in many large southern cities, *resegregation* of schools has begun as white families withdraw to mainly white suburban districts to escape racially mixed schools.

Northern white resistance to school integration was also strong, but it employed different forms of institutional subordination. Overtly racist practices in real estate markets strongly discourage blacks from moving into most all-white neighborhoods in order to gain access to the better schools serving those neighborhoods. So black residential expansion necessarily remains focused on areas near the edge of massive all-black concentrations. But as soon as blacks begin moving into all-white areas, white residents cease moving in. Eventually, most whites withdraw, causing the neighborhood to rapidly become almost entirely black. This *de facto* residential segregation was linked to school segregation by the neighborhood school principle, that is, the concept of having all children attend schools near their homes.

To cope with this form of institutional subordination, blacks proposed busing students from where they lived to schools in other areas so as to achieve racially mixed student bodies in each school. This idea evoked two hostile responses from many of the white parents whose children were concerned. The first was an even stronger defense of the neighborhood school principle. This principle had originated mainly for convenience reasons, but now formed a useful instrument for continued institutional subordination. The second was opposition to *all* busing of students as inherently undesirable because of delays, child fatigue, added costs, and other ostensibly "technical" reasons. White parents even opposed schemes that did not move their own children, but involved only the busing of black children from overcrowded all-black schools to underutilized all-white schools. *Such opposition to all busing as undesirable is clearly racist in nature.* This is indicated by the high proportion of white students in rural areas, suburbs, and Catholic big-city school systems who have used buses for years to get to school—and still use them—without arousing any such complaints. Yet white opposition to publicly supported busing schemes aimed at integrating schools is still effectively stymieing this route to improved educational quality for many black children. It is one form of the adamant white refusal to integrate that has driven many blacks to abandon integration as a major goal and instead turn to black nationalism.

Still searching for ways to improve the quality of education received by their children, black parents and educators then began emphasizing the idea of community control over public schools. Recent statistical evidence proves conclusively that present school systems in our largest cities are failing to provide equal or even minimally decent educational opportunity to most black students. So blacks in some cities have urged that local school boards be set up in each neighborhood or group of neighborhoods with real power over the schools in each area vested in such school boards. These school boards wolud be dominated by members of the minority group living in the area and providing most of the students in its schools. Hopefully, such local minority group members will be far more sensitive to the educational needs of their own children than the professionals in giant citywide school bureaucracies have proved to be. Moreover, having black children realize that their schools are controlled by black people might add to their self-respect and sense of control over their own destinies. This could markedly improve their attitude toward learning, thereby raising their achievement levels. Finally, creating closer links between local schools and parents may affect the encouragement toward education which children receive in their homes. The whole concept of local community control is new within large cities. Therefore, whether these hoped-for benefits will actually result cannot be evaluated until this concept has been tried out in practice. However, it does not differ very much from the idea of local control of schools already used throughout most of white suburban America.

But this latest attempt by blacks to achieve good quality schools is already facing mounting opposition from several white-dominated institutions. Professional educators who control big-city school bureaucracies claim such decentralization may result in *lower* quality education because of lack of professional skill and training by those who would then control schools. Teachers' unions seem ready to fight delegation of any authority over their members to local groups more likely to insist on evaluating teacher performance than professional administrators do now. This battle is so bitter that it closed the giant New York City public school system for many weeks. And similar opposition seems likely in other big cities where decentralization is being seriously considered.

This series of moves by blacks seeking to give their children a decent education, and countermoves by white institutions preventing this desirable outcome, clearly illustrates why so many nonwhite Americans believe our society is permeated with racist institutions. No matter what course black parents have pursued, their efforts have been frustrated by white-controlled institutions using a wide variety of arguments and tactics. The result is often a refusal to allow blacks either equal access to good quality white schools or control over the schools to which they have been relegated. On the one hand, they are compelled to use predominantly black schools by the neighborhood school principle; but on the other hand, they are prevented from applying the same principle to control over those schools so they can try to improve them.

No doubt there is often some truth in the "technical" arguments used by white-dominated institutions to oppose each attempt by nonwhites to improve their children's education. But the same dual denial of either equal access to white facilities or self-control over the inferior facilities relegated to nonwhites exists in many other spheres, such as housing and politics. It is no wonder that nonwhites now look past the "purely technical" arguments advanced by whites to support each set of tactics, and instead see the terribly frustrating underlying pattern of institutional subordination. It is time that all Americans saw it and attacked it vigorously.

Summary of How Institutional Subordination Works

The above discussion illustrates how institutional subordination constantly produces racist effects from actions which are usually *not* overtly racist in either content or intention. This type of transformation occurs whenever apparently nonracist actions are:

1. *Directly linked to other actions that are overtly racist (such as basing employment policies on acceptance of unions that deliberately exclude black members).*
2. *Heavily reliant upon personal qualifications or skills which minority group members have not been permitted to achieve because of past overt racism (such as requiring passage of academically oriented tests for getting a job, or basing early ability groupings of children in public schools on tests administered only in English in areas where many children have been reared in Spanish-speaking homes).*
3. *Dependent upon institutional arrangements which embody the residual results of past overt racism (such as policies—like the neighborhood school policy—which mainly benefit persons living near facilities in all-white neighborhoods).*
4. *Likely to perpetuate any of the three causal factors cited above, that is, overt racism, low achievement among minority groups of key skills or traits, or residual institutional arrangements from past overt racism (as distortions of reality in mass media and textbooks do).*

These relationships between seemingly nonracist actions and other actions or institutions which involve either present or past overt racism are rarely recognized by most whites. They see only the nonracist actions in themselves, not the institutional context in which they are embedded. Moreover, there are almost always "sound" economic or other reasons why these seemingly nonracist actions—and all the institutional structures surrounding them—have been adopted. But such "soundness" has been calculated from the unconsciously restricted "white only" viewpoint that most Americans have been absorbing since birth. This viewpoint is simply not aware of the impacts of any action upon Chicanos, Indians, blacks, or other minority groups. So it normally does not consider such impacts at all in deciding whether or not any given action is desirable. In recent years, more whites have become conscious of overt racism. Yet they still do not realize how many of their everyday actions continue to indirectly subordinate minority group members in the ways described above.

Is Institutional Subordination Really "Racist"?

If institutional subordination is one of two basic types of racism, should people who engage in it be considered "racist," even if they do not realize the effects of their actions? How can someone be guilty of racism when he does not realize that his actions have racist effects? After all, guilt is a matter of intention as much as effect.

There are several reasons why it would be both wrong and harmful to consider persons who support institutional subordination as "racists" in the same sense as those who practice overt racism. For one thing, many actions which involve institutional subordination seem perfectly fair, reasonable, and "unbiased" to most Americans. An example is adoption of "merit employment." Accusing people who follow this policy and others like it of being "racists" contradicts common sense, as well as the longstanding policy of many civil rights groups. Moreover, such accusations might simply infuriate persons who were sincerely trying to eliminate overt racism from their lives. Their outrage at this seemingly unjustified insult might blind them to any understanding of institutional subordination at all. The proper ways of offsetting institutional subordination may not require changes in the policies of some of the people who cause it. For example, the way to get rid of the subordinating impacts of "merit employment" is certainly not to have all employers put unqualified workers in every job. Rather it is to eliminate unfair union practices or have society as a whole pay for extra training for certain workers, etc. So what good would it do to make supporters of "merit employment" feel guilty about a policy that was actually producing many benefits merely because it also produced costs which they could not remove themselves anyway? Finally, almost every white American supports some form of institutional subordination. Therefore, we might remove nearly all significant meaning from the term—or cause many people to reject our whole analysis—for they *know* they are not "racists" in the overt sense.

On the other hand, most white Americans *are* causing impacts that unfairly subordinate blacks, Chicanos, Puerto Ricans, Indians, and other colored Americans. To this extent, they are all "unintentional racists," even though they are certainly not guilty of the same kind of deliberate injustice as those who practice overt racism.

HOW RACISM PROVIDES BENEFITS TO WHITES

American racism probably originated in slavery, the most extreme form of subordination by color. That type of racism, and all other later types, came into being mainly because subordination of minorities provides definite benefits to those who do the subordinating. In fact, overt racism persists mainly because it still yields significant psychological, economic, and political advantages to millions of white Americans—and even to a few nonwhites.

Successful efforts to combat racism will necessarily reduce or eliminate these benefits, thereby imposing a significant cost upon people who now enjoy them. That is why attempts to combat racism have been so strongly resisted. Moreover, such resistance is far more widespread than most people realize because so many whites receive significant but only dimly realized benefits from the subordination of nonwhites. Even many whites who sincerely abhor racism in principle and openly combat overt racism, sometimes find themselves resisting clearly antiracist actions for "intuitive" reasons they do not fully understand. This usually means such antiracist actions threaten to reduce certain almost subconsciously perceived psychological benefits these whites have been gaining from living in a society where they are considered members of a "superior" group.

A necessary step in weakening this widespread but unexpressed support for racism is clearly identifying the benefits which whites receive from continued subordination of minority people. True, some whites will still resist losing these benefits even after they realize that such benefits result from unjust subordination. But, hopefully, many whites who are opposed to overt racism in principle will begin to see how they have been profiting unawares from either overt racism or institutional subordination or both and will therefore begin supporting the antiracist strategies set forth later in this analysis.

Economic Benefits Derived from Racism

Overt racism and institutional subordination provide the following economic benefits to a significant number of whites:

1. Reduction of competition by excluding members of certain groups from access to benefits, privileges, jobs, or other opportunities or markets. The ability to easily identify members of the subordinated group by sight is a key factor linking such reduction of competition to color. An example is the refusal of many hospital medical staffs to accept black or Chicano doctors as staff members.

2. Exploitation of members of the subordinated groups through lower wages, higher prices, higher rents, less desirable credit terms, or poorer working or living conditions than those received by whites. Where racial or color discrimination per se is illegal, such exploitation probably cannot be effectively carried out unless the subordinated groups are spatially segregated from the white majority. Then differentials in wages, prices, credit terms, and other policies actually based

upon color can be more easily concealed and even rationalized as based upon geographic differences.

3.   Avoidance of certain undesirable or "dead-end" jobs (like garbage collection) by creating economically depressed racial or ethnic groups which will be compelled by necessity to carry out those jobs, even though their potential skill levels are equal to those of other groups.

Political Benefits Derived from Racism

All the political benefits of racism involve receipt by whites of a disproportionate share of the advantages which arise from political control over government. Their share is disproportionate because they prevent nonwhites from receiving what the latter would get if true political equality prevailed. The benefits of political control over government include ability to control government actions and policies as well as jobs. Therefore, political racism is an extremely important device for maintaining other forms of racism.

The main ways political racism occurs are as follows:

1.   Manipulation of potential nonwhite voters in order to maintain exclusive white control over an entire governmental structure (such as a county government in the South), or some portion of such a structure (such as a ward in a northern city), which would be controlled by non-whites if all citizens enjoyed equal voting rights, since nonwhites are a majority of the potential electorate in that area.

2.   Manipulation of political district boundaries or governmental structures by whites so as to minimize the ability of nonwhite voters to elect representatives sensitive to their needs. This includes "gerrymandering" congressional districts, creating "at-large" electoral systems in big cities with significant nonwhite minorities, and shifting to metropolitanwide government when nonwhites appear likely to constitute a majority of voters in a central city.

3.   Exclusion of nonwhites from a proportionate share—or any share—of government jobs, contracts, and other disbursements through the decisions of white administrative officials.

4.   Maintenance of the support of nonwhite voters by either white or nonwhite politicians who fail to provide reciprocal government policy benefits and other advantages to the same degree as for white groups in the electorate. This can occur when nonwhites as a group feel themselves too subordinated in general to demand such benefits, when competitive parties are somehow excluded from effective operation in all-nonwhite areas, or when voters are so poor they can be influenced by small monetary rewards and favors.

5.   Voter refusal to support a politician who is clearly superior to his opponent merely because he is not a member of the same racial or color group as the voters themselves and his opponent is. This kind of racism can also occur among nonwhite voters in relation to a white politician. Even though basing votes on group solidarity is a long established American tradition, it must be considered racist if it subordinates any candidate solely because of race, color, or ethnic background.

Psychological Benefits Derived from Racism

Both overt racism and institutional subordination provide the following psychological benefits to many whites in America:

1.   Creation of feelings of superiority in comparison to nonwhites. These feelings are extremely widespread among whites, though not always openly expressed or even consciously recognized. Hence it is important to examine their true implications. All whites who gain ego support from feeling superior to nonwhites basically believe that non-whites are somehow inherently or biologically inferior because of their color. This is the "purest" form of racism. It is so blatantly "un-American" that few whites will admit they believe it—or even consciously accept it. Yet all whites who feel the least bit superior to nonwhites as persons—in contrast to believing they live in *environmental surroundings* superior to those of nonwhites—basically adopt such a "pure" racist viewpoint. This is true because the obviously inferior economic, political, and social *status* of nonwhites can result from only two factors. Either nonwhites *are* inferior as persons, or white racism has prevented their natural equality with whites from asserting itself in actual attainments during their more than 300 years in America. Therefore, whites who deny that overt racism and institutional subordination are essentially responsible for the currently lower status of nonwhite groups are basically implying that those groups are biologically or otherwise inherently inferior.

2.   Suppression in oneself or one's group of certain normal traits which are regarded as undesirable. This is accomplished by projecting an exaggerated image of those traits and "legitimizing" attacks upon them. For example, many American whites unjustly accuse blacks of laziness, sexual promiscuity, and general irresponsibility. These are exaggerated versions of normal human impulses. But they happen to be the very impulses which the Puritan ethic, long dominant in America, seeks to suppress in favor of extreme industry, sexual purity, and individual self-reliance.

3.   Promotion of solidarity and reduced tension among white nationality and social class groups. Racism enables them to focus the

inevitable hostilities and antagonisms which arise in modern life upon the subordinated colored groups, and to identify themselves together in contrast to those groups.

4.   Avoiding the necessity of adopting difficult or costly policies to solve key social problems by falsely blaming those problems upon "immoral behavior" by members of the subordinated groups. For example, many whites erroneously blame unemployment and high welfare costs upon laziness and sexual promiscuity among blacks. In reality, more than three-fourths of all unemployed persons are white, most persons on welfare are white, and more than 90 percent of all persons on welfare are incapable of supporting themselves because they are either too old, disabled, children, or mothers who must care for children. By falsely converting these problems into "the results of sin," such scapegoating provides a moral excuse for relatively affluent whites to reduce their economic support for the unemployed and the dependent poor without feeling guilty about doing so.

5.   Diverting one's own energies from maximum self-improvement efforts by claiming that white racism makes any significant self-help attempts by minorities ineffective and useless. Such "reverse scapegoating" occurs—often unconsciously—among many minority group members. It is possible only because white racism *does* seriously inhibit—though not entirely nullify—nonwhite self-improvement efforts. This phenomenon can lead to two opposite results: excessive apathy or suicidal violence. Thus, by helping to create such "reverse scapegoating," white racism encourages some nonwhites to exhibit two of the very characteristics that it often falsely attributes to all nonwhites: "laziness" and tendencies toward violence.

Reinforcement of Racism Because of Heightened Anxieties in Modern Society

Recent events have emphasized the rising level of tensions, anxieties, and other psychologically threatening factors in modern American life. These things result from a combination of rapid technological change; high economic productivity; instant and universal communication of problems, dissent, and prevailing affluence through television; and the inertia and rigidities of legal and social institutions. The ways in which these basic causes interact are too complex to explore fully here. But their net effect is to heighten the needs of many whites for precisely the kinds of psychological benefits that racism provides.

For example, since the late 1960s, television has focused great attention upon the new life-style espoused by "hippies." This style features drugs, hostility toward authority, sexual freedom, unorthodox styles of dress, rejection of work as a central value, and willingness to engage in violent protests and demonstrations. These traits pose power-ful psychological threats to many Americans. They are a direct threat because they imply that the values upon which most middle class fami-lies have built their lives are really worthless. Moreover, "hippie" values also threaten to "seduce" middle-class children, causing profound cleavages between them and their parents. These values are also an indirect threat because they appeal to the suppressed desire of every normal person to engage in such activities to some degree. Thus, they may weaken the adherence of middle-class citizens to their existing values.

Such psychological threats are bound to produce anxieties—both conscious and unconscious—among many of the middle-class Amer-icans who form the vast majority of our population. One way to cope with such heightened anxiety is to lean more heavily upon the psycho-logical benefits which can be derived from racism. This can take the form of more vociferously blaming social problems upon minority groups, or projecting traits one wants to suppress in oneself upon mem-bers of such groups, or gaining feelings of solidarity with other whites by uniting in greater antagonism against nonwhites, or emphasizing the inferiority of others so as to reassure oneself about one's own worth. Consequently, powerful recent trends in American life may be signifi-cantly increasing the dependence of many whites upon the psychologi-cal benefits they derive from racism, whether consciously or uncon-sciously. Unless the anxieties caused by these trends can be alleviated in other ways, it may be increasingly difficult to get these whites to give up such benefits. This suggests that antiracism strategies must include, or be linked to, policies that will help reduce the threatening nature of these recent trends to the white middle class.

The fact that overt racism and institutional subordination produce benefits for many whites does not mean that these benefits outweigh the costs of racism. In the first place, such benefits are wholly illegiti-mate, since they spring from an unjust subordination of others. Second, creation of these benefits imposes immense costs upon millions of nonwhite Americans. Finally, by preventing nonwhites from developing their maximum productive potential, racism also inhibits them from creating much greater economic, social, and cultural wealth than they do now. This makes all of society poorer than it would be without rac-ism, including the very people who benefit from racist behavior and institutions.

BASIC STRATEGIES FOR COMBATING RACISM

Racism in America is extremely complex and deep-rooted. Conse-quently, only an equally complex and profound set of actions can possibly eliminate or counteract it effectively. Summarized under nine basic headings, each of the kinds of actions involved describes a basic strategy which aims at one or both of two essential objectives: *changing the behavior of whites* so they will no longer consciously or unconsciously support racism; and *increasing the capabilities of nonwhite groups* so they can overcome the handicaps racism imposes.

The nine basic strategies can be briefly summarized as follows:

1. *Make all Americans—especially whites—far more conscious of the widespread existence of racism in all its forms, and the immense costs it imposes on the entire nation.* Most whites are completely unaware of the many kinds of institutional subordination they themselves support. A crucial task facing those who wish to combat racism is converting this "blindness" into acute consciousness of the many unrecognized ways in which white attitudes, behavior, and institutional structures continue to subordinate minority groups.

Economic costs, including the loss of national output due to holding minority group members below their maximum productive potential, the loss of markets because the incomes of these groups are kept low by institutional subordination, and large social costs of policies aimed at remedying conditions partly caused by subordination, such as poverty, crime, poor housing, and poor health.

Political costs resulting from tensions in national life caused by unjust subordination of minority groups. These include civil disorders, restrictions of individual freedoms and rights, tendencies toward a weakening of the two-party system, possible rising difficulty in gathering sufficient congressional support for *any* cohesive set of national policies, and decreasing respect for the United States abroad.

Social and human costs caused by the loss of human potential due to institutional subordination and by the distortion of values in the white majority necessary to sustain such subordination. The first kind of costs includes loss of personal self-respect, weakened family stability, widespread frustration and apathy, frequent resort to narcotics and criminal behavior, and a declining respect for authority among minority groups. The second kind includes excessive narrowness of viewpoint; defensiveness and hostile feelings; resistance to constructive change; lack of human sensitivity; and overly technological (rather than humane) orientation of social policies and activities.

It is impossible to quantify these costs in this analysis. But some future attempts should be made to measure at least the economic costs so as to show what giant losses are involved. For example, in 1972, if black families had received the same median income as whites, incomes received by all U.S. families would have been $26.4 billion higher.

The process of education necessary to change white perceptions will never work if it consists mainly of some people "lecturing" others.

Rather, it must involve intense participation by two types of people. First, various groups of whites must thoroughly examine their own behavior in order to uncover all the subtle and unconscious forms of racism embedded in it. This should be done by teachers concerning schools, by property managers and realtors concerning real estate practices, by personnel directors concerning employment practices, etc.

Second, whites must overcome their habitual exclusion of blacks and other minority group members in this process of self-examination. Whites, themselves, are not likely to discover all the forms of subordination they impose on others without the help of the latter. This may require planned confrontation of whites by blacks or others who deliberately take an accusing posture, or simply insightful advice from well-informed members of minority groups. But, in any case, unless white self-examination incorporates significant contributions from nonwhites, it will embody a form of racism in itself.

2. *Build up the capabilities of minority group members, and greatly strengthen their opportunities and power to exercise those capabilities, especially regarding public and private activities that directly affect them.* This strategy embodies one of the ultimate objectives of all the others: enabling presently subordinated groups both to achieve and to exercise their maximum potential. The capabilities and opportunities concerned therefore include all types: economic, political, social, aesthetic, and cultural. It is especially crucial to provide blacks and other minority group members with direct experience and power in designing, running, and evaluating both public and private programs and activities in their own neighborhoods. This will not only enhance the capabilities of many deprived minority group members, but also permit many others who already have such capabilities to demonstrate their skills and competence both to themselves and to the nation as a whole.

Four key observations are relevant to this strategy:

a. *An essential ingredient is expressing strong political support for key national policies concerning housing, education, civil rights, employment, welfare programs, tax reforms, and other measures with antiracist effects.* Many problems associated with racism cannot be effectively solved, or even attacked, by local or state governments. They are inhibited by lack of financial resources within their boundaries, or competitive pressures from other cities or states which force them to keep taxes down. Older central cities containing large black, Puerto Rican, or Chicano groups are especially incapable of supporting effective antiracism policies by themselves. The concentration within their boundaries of low-income groups requiring expensive services and the shift of most new growth to suburbs cause them to sustain rapidly rising costs while their real property tax bases stagnate or decline. Only the use of nationwide taxing powers can effectively shift resources from wealthier areas to where the problems associated with racism are now most concentrated.

Yet Congress has been reluctant to launch many of the programs suggested by the National Advisory Committee on Civil Disorders. So far, its members have perceived very little support for such programs among their white constituents. *Until such white political support is both created and forcefully expressed to congressional representatives, no effective nationwide attack on racism is possible.* Because the white middle class constitutes a large majority of the American electorate, no significant federal programs can possibly be adopted unless they are supported by a great many congressional representatives of that group. Therefore, however tiresome and unexciting it may seem, keeping informed about national legislation and writing one's local congressman to support appropriate measures comprise an essential strategy for combating racism. Equally significant is persuading other citizens—especially whites in areas where few nonwhites live—to do likewise.

b. *In primarily black areas, this strategy is closely related to the concepts of black power and black nationalism, but it need not involve support of geographic separatism.* Undoubtedly, one effective way to build up capabilities quickly among the most deprived members of the black population, and to enhance the self-respect of the already capable members, is for blacks to dominate most public and private activities in predominantly black neighborhoods. This includes the design as well as the execution of such programs. It also might involve voluntary transfer of many white-owned stores and firms in all-black areas to black ownership through some type of purchase plans, or creation of new black-owned facilities there.

These and other economic resources can be generated fastest if most blacks deliberately direct their consumer trade and other business to black-operated stores, banks, service firms, professional firms, restaurants, etc. Clearly, such behavior involves taking race and color into account in making decisions; hence some might consider it "black racism." But it can be more accurately viewed as a form of "black pride" analogous to the nationality-conscious behavior of many Irish, Italian, Polish, German, Czech, Jewish, and other citizens in earlier periods, which still persists in some cities. This kind of selective patronage is really a nonsubordinating exercise of free choice by blacks in an essentially white-dominated society. Therefore, even though it certainly involves discrimination by color, it is not truly a "reverse" version of the white racism that institutionally subordinates so many nonwhites.

c.   *One important device for developing black and other minority group business capabilities is the "third-party contract" for providing both public and private services.* For instance, if expanded government services concerning neighborhood maintenance were to be carried out, the local government could contract that function in mainly black areas to a black-owned and operated firm organized for that purpose, rather than enlarging the government itself. Similarly, white-owned firms procuring or providing services in mainly black areas should make every effort to use black-owned and operated firms, or black franchise operators, as intermediaries between them and their final customers. In some cases, it will take major efforts by the white firms concerned to help minority group members organize new firms and manage them successfully. These efforts are a key input which whites can contribute to the success of this basic strategy.

d.   *One of the objectives of this basic strategy is to equip blacks and other minority group leaders with much greater bargaining power in dealing with whites.* This would enable such leaders to more successfully persuade whites to carry out some of the institutional and behavioral changes necessary to eliminate racism. For example, a black mayor of a large city who can form a coalition with black councilmen to control local property tax rates is in a strong position to influence white-dominated employers there to alter discriminatory hiring practices. Similarly, a Chicano-dominated union of hospital workers might be able to persuade all hospitals to adopt nondiscriminatory policies toward Chicanos and other doctors and patients. Thus, *the more successful this strategy is in building black and other minority group capabilities, the more likely it is that conflicts will arise between these minorities and some or all of the white majority.* Consequently this strategy embodies significant risks of at least temporarily "back-firing" and generating antiminority sentiments. Whites who support this strategy should be well aware of these risks and be prepared to counteract such sentiment in themselves as well as others. Yet no efforts to combat racism in America can succeed without greatly building up the capabilities of presently subordinated minorities and actually transferring significant power to them, since prevention of such outcomes is the essence of racism.

3.   *Develop legislative and other programs which simultaneously provide benefits for significant parts of the white majority and for deprived or other members of nonwhite minority groups, so it will be in the immediate self-interest of the former to support programs which aid the latter.* Publicly supported programs which benefit the most deprived persons in society, regardless of minority, often have difficulty obtaining

vital white middle-class support. An example is the federal antipoverty program. Such programs provide benefits for a minority of the population by imposing taxes or inflation on the remaining majority. In reality, there are significant long-run benefits to the majority in thus aiding the minority. But these more distant benefits are not always obvious, whereas the immediate costs are clear. The same thing is true of programs which primarily benefit blacks or other ethnic minorities, such as housing programs concentrated in ghetto areas. (Actually, almost all public programs, including public housing and welfare, mainly benefit whites, but many whites do not realize this.) Consequently, major programs benefiting *any* group which is a minority of the population—whether ethnically or economically or in any other way—would have a much better chance of gaining the necessary political support if they also provided benefits for many members of the large white middle class majority. For instance, it might be easier to get Congress to aid poor female-headed households with children by passing a family allowance that assisted *all* families with children than by expanding welfare payments that assisted only the poorest such families.

This strategy seems especially significant now because of the apparent discontent of the "silent majority" comprised of lower-middle-income and middle-income whites. Recent political developments indicate that millions of these white Americans believe public programs in the past few years have unduly focused upon the problems of ethnic minority groups and the poor. Regardless of whether or not this belief is accurate, it constitutes a significant political force. Moreover, it is extremely relevant to whether or not Congress can be persuaded to adopt legislation with significant antiracist impacts. Chances for such legislation appear critically related to the ability of its sponsors to develop "program packages" that will appeal to the immediate self-interest of large portions of the white middle class, while simultaneously providing key benefits to minority groups who are deprived or discriminated against.

There are two important qualifications to this strategy. First, such programs will not improve the *relative* position of the minority groups concerned unless they provide larger benefits to those groups than to members of the middle-class majority they also aid. From the viewpoint of persons seeking to reduce or eliminate the effects of racism, this "gap-closing" aspect is vital. For example, high-level national prosperity tends to raise everyone's income to some degree. But if all incomes go up to the same degree, then the subordinating effects of racism are not counteracted. The incomes of subordinated persons are still artificially suppressed below the incomes of others. Certainly absolute improvements are important, especially to poor people. But the subordination inherent in racism is essentially a relative condition. Therefore, it is also important not to sacrifice all possibility of gaining relative improvements for deprived or subordinated minority groups in order to form an effective coalition with parts of the white middle-class majority.

This leads to the second qualification: it is virtually impossible to create programs which provide *net* benefits both to most severely deprived people and to most of the white middle-class majority. Any program which redistributes income to poor people must cause a net loss to some other group. The only group with enough total income to support a meaningful redistribution of this kind is the middle-income majority. So no program can cause *net* redistribution favoring all of the lowest-income group and all of the middle-income group simultaneously. However, programs can be devised which provide net benefits to most of the lowest-income group and to large segments of the middle-income group. The net expenses they create could fall on the remainder of the middle-income group and on most of the upper-income group. For example, certain federal-aid-to-education programs might help all families with children in both income groups at the net expense of all households without children in the middle-class group. Moreover, such "program packages" can be designed or promoted in ways that soften their negative impact upon those who bear it. For instance, they could be financed out of the "automatic" increase in federal income tax receipts which occurs because of economic growth without any increase in tax rates. Or they can provide net benefits to only part of the lowest-income group, along with part of the middle-income majority, so their net burden is not extremely large. Congressional supporters of minority-favoring legislation benefiting the wealthy have been successfully designing such "packages" for decades, as the urban renewal program illustrates.

4. *Insure that minority group members are in a position to contribute to the design, execution, and evaluation of all major social policies and programs. This will improve the quality of such policies and programs by introducing a certain sensitivity to human values which is too often lacking in the overly technology-oriented behavior of the white majority.* Persons who are outside "the established system" which dominates economic, political, and cultural life in America have an important contribution to make in improving the output and operation of that system. Without question, the American economic and political system has been an unprecedented success. It has created the highest material standard of living in world history in an atmosphere of great individual freedom and opportunity. Yet the very orientation toward efficiency and high productivity responsible for this success often overlooks, suppresses, or distorts important human values. *Racism itself is a stunning example.* Others include the dehumanizing routines required on high speed assembly lines, the shattering impacts on family life of

migration caused by farm mechanization, and the demeaning procedures incorporated in welfare programs. People who receive significant net benefits from "the system" which commits these dehumanizing acts tend to overlook them entirely or simply to regard them as a price society must pay for high output. In contrast, people who are essentially "outside the system" are far more acutely conscious of these effects. They suffer from such effects more often, and they are not given a strong incentive to accept them by receipt of other net benefits from the system. Such "outside" groups include not only the minorities subordinated by racist institutions, but also many university students, intellectuals, artistically oriented citizens, and even "hippie dropouts." Partly because they do not receive many material or other rewards directly from the dominant system, these "outsiders" tend to develop life styles centered on values that emphasize personal characteristics rather than technological efficiency or material success. These values include great sensitivity and openness to the personal expression, individuality, and needs of others—far greater than is typical of the behavior of many middle-class Americans incorporated within the system. Such heightened sensitivity is a potentially uplifting contribution to American society in general—indeed, to the operation of the very system in reaction to which it developed. But that contribution can only become effective if such persons can exert significant influence on the design, execution, and evaluation of most major social policies.

An example may help clarify this reasoning. For two decades, many urban highways were constructed through low-income neighborhoods, thus forcing thousands of poor families to move. No compensation was paid to those uprooted unless they owned their own homes, and even then it was grossly inadequate. No relocation services were provided; no alternative housing was built to make up for the destruction of thousands of units in the midst of a shortage of housing for poor people; and little thought was given to the losses caused by destroying local schools, stores, parks, and even whole neighborhoods. This striking insensitivity to the problems of poor people—most of whom were "outside the system"—resulted from the almost completely technological orientation of the highway engineers responsible for building roads. They were concerned solely with moving traffic from point to point in the technically most efficient manner.

Moreover, the middle-class majority which used the resulting roads did not want them to behave otherwise. Recently, however, there have been mounting protests from those threatened with displacement, most of whom are blacks. And local politicians have become far more sensitive to black demands, because of recent disorders. So in 1968, federal policies regarding highway construction were changed to include much more adequate compensation to displaced owners *and* renters, and the provision of relocation assistance and perhaps even new housing. This is a clear example of heightened sensitivity to human needs partly counteracting an overly technology-oriented social policy. Similarly increased sensitivity, particularly to the negative impacts of institutional subordination, should be introduced into other social policies of all kinds—including economic and political—and at all levels—including federal, state, local, and private. In this way, the dominant part of American society could benefit from the humanizing influence of those whom it has heretofore excluded from any significant power in relation to most major policies. The result should be a society that is different from, and superior to, both the presently dominant system itself and the alternative life style developed by those whom the system has made "outsiders." This is what Martin Luther King, Jr., meant when he insisted that blacks and other minorities did not simply want to become part of the white middle-class America as it is now. Rather, they want to help build a new society far more sensitive to certain human values than white middle-class America has proved to be in the past. Hopefully, it will combine the best of both worlds. But this ideal outcome will be possible only if minority group members are able to influence policy design, execution, and evaluation at all levels in all major social institutions. These include predominantly white institutions which have significant impacts upon both nonwhite and white Americans. Examples are federal government agencies, large insurance companies, state governments, local school systems, and nationwide retail firms.

Therefore, placing minority group members in real positions of power and influence within such organizations is not simply a matter of making more and better jobs available to them. It is also a key means of implementing this vital antiracist strategy in society as a whole.

5. *Influence local, state, and national policies and programs—both pubic and private—so they have certain characteristics which will reduce their possible racist effects.* Two such characteristics have already been discussed: heightened sensitivity to human values and "gap-closing" improvement of the most deprived or subordinate groups relative to others benefited by the same policies. Others include:

a. *Avoidance of any action or arrangement that unnecessarily produces, sustains, or emphasizes derogatory or stigmatizing forms of differentiation.* These could involve differentiation by race or color, or by social and economic class. For example, current public housing regulations require that all the families living in a public housing project have very low incomes. This tends to stigmatize such projects as undesirable, especially if they become dominated by unstable multiproblem households. Conceivably, public housing projects could contain a majority of stable moderate-income families who paid higher rents. Then such projects would not be stigmatized as for low-status households only. Similarly, locating all the public housing projects in a city (except those for the elderly) so that nearly all occupants are blacks has racist effects. This practice causes most whites to identify the need for public housing with race, even though over half of all low-income persons in U.S. central cities are white. Thus, simultaneous differentiation of any programs by *both* poverty and color causes several very undesirable results. First, political support for such programs often declines because racism leads many whites to oppose funding anything they believe mainly aids blacks. Second, this dual differentiation reinforces the erroneous belief among some whites that most blacks are dependent, and therefore inferior. Third, participants in such programs are exposed mainly to other deprived people, so their own sense of differentiation and inferiority is reinforced.

b. *Emphasis upon participation by, and within, the private sector rather than direct dependency upon government at any level.* In attacking problems of poverty, poor housing, unemployment, poor health, and other undesirable conditions in large urban centers, the natural tendency will probably be to rely on direct government action as the primary weapon. This is likely because the people suffering from these maladies usually cannot pay enough to support private remedial action. That is why they are not getting any now.

However, it is vital that society avoid creating low-income minority-group neighborhoods that are almost totally dependent upon direct public expenditures aimed at self-maintenance, rather than at producing services consumed by society as a whole. Such a position of primarily nonproductive dependency discourages initiative among residents, reinforces their feelings of inadequacy and inferiority, results in a very low standard of living because of legislative economizing, and tends to confirm existing stereotypes that the residents are lazy and incompetent. It could even lead to a permanent publicly maintained "under class" in slum areas differentiated by dependency, location, and color. Experience with American Indians conclusively demonstrates the failure of such "public reservations."

This means that as much direct participation by the private sector as possible should be encouraged in remedial programs for these areas. Such programs include education, job creation, training, housing, and even welfare administration. Moreover, as many persons as possible now dependent upon direct public support should be transferred to positions in the private sector. These positions could be in either the kinds of remedial programs mentioned above or truly self-supporting private activities.

However, two vital qualifications must be made. First, this emphasis on the private sector does not imply that positions in government are not productive or desirable. Instead it is simply a balancing counterforce to the natural tendency to use direct government action as the main way to attack these problems. Second, public subsidies will play an essential role in this entire process, even if private firms carry out many of the programs concerned. Training unskilled workers, teaching low-achieving students, or building housing and pricing it so that poor families can afford it all require public subsidies. They cost more than those who are benefited can either pay themselves or provide through their participation. These extra costs are the real costs of eliminating accumulated deprivation, poverty, ignorance, and racism. It is unreasonable and naive to expect private firms to bear these costs themselves, any more than they bear the costs of achieving other public objectives, such as building highways or putting a man on the moon. The purpose of encouraging private participation is therefore not primarily to reduce costs. Rather it is to tap the many talents in the private sector, to get more of its members personally "involved" in combating racism and poverty, and to reduce the ultimate dependency of those being aided.

c. *Use of a metropolitan areawide geographic focus whenever possible.* Carrying out housing, employment, health, and other programs on a metropolitanwide basis will both discourage the development of geographic separatism and encourage a realistic view of each metropolitan area as an economically interrelated whole.

At present, racial cleavages on a geographic basis within metropolitan areas are indeed striking. Taken together, the central cities within all 243 U.S. metropolitan areas were 20.6 percent black in 1970. But 84.8 percent of their population growth from 1960 to 1970 was black (and many of the largest lost white population). In contrast, the portions of metropolitan areas outside central cities were 94 percent white in 1970, and their population growth from 1960 to 1970 was 92 percent white. In many of the largest metropolitan areas, if these trends continue, central cities will contain black majorities within 10 to 15 years; whereas the surrounding suburbs will remain almost entirely white. This could lead to a political conflict between large central cities and their surrounding suburbs along racial lines. Such a conflict could in turn cause fiscal bankruptcy in the large cities, and could even lead to racial violence and suppression.[3] Conducting programs aimed at reducing racism on a metro-

---

[3] Discussed in chapter 16 of the "Report of the National Advisory Commission on Civil Disorders."

politanwide level will at least maintain communications between these two racially diverging areas, and may help to counteract emerging racial separatism.

However racially divergent central cities and suburbs become, they are still critically dependent upon each other economically and physically. Central cities contain a majority of the jobs in many metropolitan areas, to which millions of suburban commuters travel daily. They are also the nerve centers of many vital networks, including telephone systems, utility systems, water systems, sewage disposal systems, railroads, and highways. Most of the largest corporations in the nation, and many small firms, have their headquarters and many major plants in central cities. The nation's key financial institutions are located primarily in large downtown areas, and most cultural and entertainment activities take place in large cities. Most of the leading universities in the country have huge physical plants tying them to central cities. On the other hand, the suburbs supply many of the workers that operate these central-city facilities and contain most of the vital air transportation links in the nation.

In spite of these intimate interconnections, many white suburbanites are not aware of their dependence upon central cities. They rarely go into such cities, since the suburbs in larger metropolitan areas contain a broad spectrum of shopping facilities, hospitals, banks, entertainment facilities, and even jobs. So some white suburbanites may be led by their spatial isolation to think they can disregard the fiscal and other problems of central cities, especially as the latter become more and more occupied by minority groups. The development of antiracist policies and programs on a metropolitan areawide basis would help to counteract such erroneous views, particularly if it included educating suburbanites concerning their dependence upon central cities.

This conclusion does not contradict the earlier observation that adoption of metropolitan government could be a form of institutional subordination. It would be if it were aimed at preventing nonwhites from dominating a central-city government. But many antiracist policies other than local government itself can be carried out on a metropolitan areawide basis without creating such subordination at all. Examples are job training, housing development, educational enrichment, job placement, and transportation programs.

6.   *Create recognition among all Americans that overcoming the burdens of racism will cost a great deal of money, time, effort, and institutional change; but that this cost is a worthwhile investment in the future which both society as a whole and individual taxpayers can bear without undue strain.* There is no precise way to estimate the costs of

significantly reducing the impacts of racism in the United States. However, the recommendations set forth by the National Advisory Commission on Civil Disorders (NACCD) embody a program that would probably accomplish a major part of that job and would greatly reduce poverty and deprivation among whites, too. Rough cost estimates of this program indicate that its many components would add from $21 to $57 billion per year (in 1974 dollars) to the federal budget depending upon exactly at what levels certain programs (such as building new housing and raising support payments for poor, dependent families) were carried out. These costs are roughly equivalent to from 1.5 to 4.1 percent of our gross national product of about $1,400 billion in 1974.

To some extent, such costs could be financed through future increases in federal tax receipts that will occur without any rise in tax rates. Because federal tax structure is progressive (that is, it contains higher percentage rates for higher dollar incomes), federal tax receipts rise automatically as American families earn higher incomes. Moreover, these receipts go up *faster* than national income as a whole, unless federal tax cuts are enacted. However, a significant portion of this so-called "national dividend" will be spent on programs which have already been adopted with built-in future cost increases. Therefore, some increase in federal taxes might be needed to launch a major program against racism and deprivation along the lines suggested by the NACCD. A survey completed in 1968 by the NACCD indicated that more than half of all white adult respondents would be willing to pay 10 percent more in income taxes to carry out the kind of program set forth in the NACCD report. That would have yielded an added $12.9 billion in 1969 (including higher corporation taxes). Thus, although the money costs of combating racism and deprivation are very large, it would be possible to pay those costs without placing any overwhelming strain upon either the economy as a whole or most individual taxpayers.

But the costs of effectively combating racism are not limited to money alone. Most Americans would have to reexamine and change their own behavior patterns and many of the structures and practices of the institutions which serve them and in which they participate. This might impose significant psychological costs upon some people, especially those who now benefit either consciously or unconsciously from racism. Yet those costs would surely be tiny compared to the gain of eliminating all the *existing* costs imposed upon the nation by racism, as discussed earlier. More important, all the costs necessary to combat racism and deprivation are essentially investments in a greater future output. These investments would gradually increase the economic and other capabilities of millions of persons whose potentials are now inhibited by racism and poverty. Since there are more than 24 million black Americans and millions of other Americans in smaller minority groups, a significant increase in their economic, social, cultural, and political productivity would add immensely to future benefits shared by the entire nation.

7. *Search out and develop alliances of nonwhites and whites organized to obtain common practical goals, particularly in combating racism.* At present, white and black or other minority group communities in most American cities act almost completely independently of each other. This is true in nearly all social, economic, and other nongovernmental activities, though somewhat less so in relation to government. Even efforts to combat racism tend to be conducted separately by both communities. As a result, those efforts are frequently far less effective than they would be if members of each community shared the insights, experience, capabilities, and contacts of the other. Moreover, such nearly complete separation of whites and nonwhites breeds mistrust, fear, and hostility between these groups, and generates both rumors and stereotypes based upon ignorance. Leaders in both communities should therefore take the initiative in organizing and carrying out well-defined joint projects (perhaps of existing organizations) to reduce racism.

One effective type of project would link influential whites with members of low-income black communities. They could jointly support continuous surveillance and evaluation of the quality of various local and national programs in those communities. The programs involved could include everything from garbage collection to on-the-job training. The whites could bring their influence to bear upon local and national government and private officials, using information and insights furnished by black observers living in the affected areas. This would in turn greatly enhance the effective power of black residents and their influence upon the design of future programs.

8. *Create many more positively oriented contacts between whites and blacks and other minority group members, including personal contacts, intergroup contacts, and those occurring through mass media.* It is an unfortunate fact that most whites have few, if any, personal friends or even acquaintances who are black or Chicano or members of other minorities—and vice versa. The resulting dearth of "normal" contacts between people of different races and colors but of like interests and capabilities is one of the main reasons why erroneous prejudices and rumors continue to flourish in each community about the other. Moreover, many interracial contacts which do occur (such as those between white police and black citizens) are negatively rather than positively oriented. Therefore, persistent efforts in increasing positively oriented contacts between races should be made by private individuals, private groups, and the mass media (which have markedly increased such contacts in the past several years).

9. *Open up many more opportunities for minority group members*

in now predominantly white organizations (such as businesses), areas (such as suburban neighborhoods), or institutions (such as public schools), and encourage other arrangements where members of different groups work, live, or act together. This *strategy of integration* is implicit in many of the eight others. Discussing integration fully would require another long essay. However, I believe *integration* implies much more positive action than desegregation. The latter consists of removing discriminatory barriers so that all have equal access to opportunities in proportion to their existing abilities to compete "within the system." Hence, desegregation is a vital first step toward integration. But such removal of unfair barriers makes no allowance for the fact that the existing competitive abilities of many minority group members suffer the effects of prolonged repression. Until those effects have been overcome, true social justice in many situations will require positive supplementation of the impaired abilities of many minority group members. I believe the term *integration* should imply such a policy.

Any situation regarding two groups can therefore be considered *integrated* if all the following conditions exist:

Enough members of both groups are *actually present* so that everyone in the situation constantly perceives both groups in day-to-day experience.

Enough members of the minority group in that situation (who might be white) are present so that as individuals they do not feel isolated or lost within the majority group.

The minority group in that situation exercises power and influence at least proportional to its numbers there. In some cases, the average capabilities of the minority-group members will be lower than those of the majority-group members. Then minority-group power and influence proportional to their number will be more than proportional to their overall competitive abilities. That is where the majority might deliberately supplement the competitive abilities of the minority group, or the influence that group would wield based on such abilities alone. An example is providing special training for some black workers in mainly white firms.

Integration aims at achieving equality of access to the opportunities and benefits of society both immediately and in the long run. It also seeks to promote more daily intergroup experience so members of each group will learn to accept others fully as individuals. Such experience will not result from just *potential* equality of access by minority group members to facilities or areas now predominantly occupied by majority group members. Instead, it requires *actual mixing* of these groups on a daily basis. That is one reason why integration implies positive programs rather than just the removal of discriminatory barriers.

Effective integration of many kinds, including jobs and schools, is often inhibited because such a high proportion of blacks and other minority groups live in segregated areas. Thus, achieving significant integration implies much greater black movement into now predominantly white residential areas as the National Advisory Commission on Civil Disorders stated. At present, this seems out of favor with many minority group leaders seeking group solidarity and stronger political power through group concentration. Yet, as the NACCD concluded, significant integration is essential for true equality of opportunity in America—especially economic opportunity—because separate societies cannot be made equal.

The nine strategies described above are not mutually exclusive; nor do they exhaust all the possible ways to combat racism. Yet they encompass the key approaches that must be carried out over the next few years—and decades—if racism is to be reduced to an insignificant factor in America.

CONCLUSION

Americans seeking to combat racism should understand three additional points. First, racism in this country is the product of more than 300 years of systematic subordination of Indians and blacks by the white majority, plus later subordination of still other groups. The racist attitudes, behavior patterns, institutional structures, and cultural heritage built up over three centuries are profoundly embedded in our society. They cannot be eradicated overnight, or in just a few years. Therefore, effectively combating racism will require continuous and prolonged persistence by both whites and blacks. They must be deeply committed —indeed, dedicated—to this goal.

However, there are signs that many white Americans are already tired of hearing about "the race question." Because most whites conceive of racism only in its overt forms, they believe it is rapidly disappearing or has already diminished to an insignificant level. For example, in 1966, 70 percent of the national sample of whites interviewed by the Louis Harris organization thought that blacks were moving too fast toward integration.

This leads to the second point: the principal task of those white Americans combating racism lies within the white community, rather than within nonwhite communities. As pointed out earlier, no policies or programs aimed at improving conditions in black America or among Chicanos or other minorities can possibly succeed unless they are politically supported by a majority of whites. Such support is essential to obtain the money and institutional changes required to alter those conditions. Yet that support will not be forthcoming unless most whites significantly revise their present views concerning racism. Many whites, especially those living in suburbs, are almost completely isolated from any direct contacts with life in black ghettos or Puerto Rican neighborhoods or other minority group areas. Hence, they fail to perceive the compelling need for further remedial actions there. Moreover, they do not understand how institutional subordination works. Therefore, these whites think the plight of ghetto dwellers is largely their own fault, rather than largely the product of racism expressed by institutions controlled by whites.

Only two forces can change this dominant view. The first consists of the dedicated efforts of well-informed white leaders within white communities who understand all forms of racism, and why much more must be done to eradicate them. The second is development of greater capabilities and power within the black community and other nonwhite communities. By its very nature, this development must occur primarily through the efforts of nonwhite Americans themselves. Once such development begins, it will better demonstrate the true potentialities and abilities of those Americans, and give their leaders a stronger bargaining position from which to influence public and private policies. These changes may in turn persuade the white majority to devote more resources to the task of still further developing nonwhite capabilities, both in nonwhite communities and throughout society.

Thus the process of overcoming racism involves a continuous feedback between changing the views of the white majority and expanding the capabilities and power of nonwhite communities. It is clear that the most critical role in this process for whites fighting racism is influencing the opinions of other whites. Similarly, the most critical role for nonwhites is developing their own communities.

This conclusion certainly does not imply that no whites should work in nonwhite areas, or vice versa. In fact, such joint action is one of the nine basic strategies for combating racism. But the predominant efforts of whites in this combat should nevertheless involve those strategies focused upon the white community itself. For no one else can carry out those strategies—yet without them, the entire struggle is doomed.

Opposing racism is indeed a worthy objective for all Americans. It is the highest tradition of democracy to promote equality of opportunity and freedom of choice for all citizens in fact as well as in theory. But such equality and freedom cannot exist as long as racism continues to operate through long-established and pervasive institutional structures and behavior patterns. No other single issue in domestic affairs has more profound implications regarding America's success in achieving its own ideals, or the kinds of social changes that must be carried out to attain them. That is why a clear understanding of racism and how to combat all its many unrecognized forms, plus a strong dedication to doing so, is essential for every true American.

4

Housing the Urban Poor:
The Economics of
Various Strategies

Helping to provide decent housing for low-income households is a worldwide challenge to national governments, especially in countries where most citizens are adequately fed. However, it would be euphemistic to use the term strategies to denote public policies concerning the housing situation in most countries, particularly those dominated by free markets. Their governments simply do not have well-reasoned, realistic, long-range policies for coping with housing needs. Nevertheless, for purposes of analysis, it is useful to view the public efforts to improve the housing of low-income households in each nation as resulting from at least an implicit strategy.

KEY BACKGROUND FACTORS AND RELATIONSHIPS

The analysis requires understanding of the following key background factors and relationships.

Quality Standards for New Construction

I will arbitrarily define three different quality standards actually used by various nations to control new housing construction (as distinct from

Reprinted from the *American Economic Review* 56, no. 4 (September 1969): 646–51, by permission of the American Economic Association. Footnote and minor revisions added by the author.

those verbally professed). High standards are equivalent to the housing consumed by upper-middle-class families in terms of unit size, land per unit, quality of construction, and utilities. In the United States, all new urban housing construction (except mobile homes) must meet high standards. Moderate standards embody far more modest quality levels, but still qualify as decent housing. They govern new construction in most European nations. Zero standards mean that any type of new housing construction is allowed, including crude shacks built by squatters. Zero standards prevail in most of the world.

Relationships Among Housing Standards, Housing Costs, and Public Subsidies

The public subsidy necessary to enable the average low-income household to live in a newly built decent home is much larger if high quality standards are required than if moderate quality standards are required. (If zero standards are required, the housing units concerned are not decent in quality.) Therefore, requiring high standards means that (1) a higher proportion of households in the economy cannot buy new housing without subsidies; (2) fewer badly-housed poor households can be provided with "decent" new housing per million dollars of public subsidy; (3) the total cost of providing all presently ill-housed poor households with "decent" housing is vastly greater; and (4) among middle-class voters, political opposition to large-scale housing subsidies is greater, since many appear to be paying taxes to put poor people in housing better than their own. Also, the higher the standards required for new housing, the more citizens of all incomes must resort to debt financing in buying homes, therefore paying a higher fraction of the total cost for interest instead of direct construction. In contrast, zero standard housing can be paid for entirely out of current income without debt financing, especially because the land is often expropriated.

Effects of Rising Incomes and Rising Occupancy Costs

If real incomes rise faster than housing occupancy costs (which include land, interest, and construction costs), then most households upgrade their housing. They do so either by moving into higher quality units or improving the units they now occupy. Improvement without movement is most likely where: social class mixture and racial mixture in any given neighborhood are common and socially accepted; zero standard construction is common, so residents can gradually upgrade initially skimpy housing by adding improvements wholly financed out of current income; there is an acute overall shortage of housing; or housing is rationed by public authorities who control the supply, or at least control all new units. Where opposite conditions prevail, upgrading is usually accomplished by moving to a better neighborhood, as in the United States. If occupancy costs rise faster than real incomes, then little upgrading occurs, and the amount of subsidy required per household to put ill-housed families into decent housing rises.

The Impact of Population Growth and Migration upon Local Housing Conditions

In any given metropolitan area or neighborhood, the number of households can normally fluctuate much more rapidly, both up and down, than the total supply of "decent" quality housing units. Thus, rapid natural increase in population plus heavy in-migration can lead to an acute local housing shortage. This situation absolutely compels one or more of the following indecent housing conditions to result at least temporarily: overcrowding of existing "decent" units; division of such units into smaller, substandard units; construction of many new substandard units (or even zero standard units); or households living in the streets or in the open without housing. Public authorities may attempt to prevent such outcomes by prohibiting migration into a given metropolitan area. However, experience throughout the world, even in totalitarian nations, shows that such prohibitions are ineffective if strong pressures are driving people out of rural areas. Hence a critical factor influencing housing conditions in any locality is the pressure of population growth on the local housing supply. Where such growth occurs mainly among poor households, the only way to prevent the above indecent results from lasting a long time is through huge public housing subsidies, since the new households cannot afford to purchase new housing on the free market.

The Importance of Public Policies in Stimulating Total Housing Production

In any locality, the relationship between the total supply of decent housing units and the total number of households determines to what extent the indecent housing conditions described above will occur. Any rapid increase in total supply relative to total needs, even consisting solely of more new luxury units, tends to loosen the entire housing market, thereby eventually improving conditions for all households, even the poorest. Unless demolition offsets new building, the prices of all units decline relative to incomes, and more options are available to all households, though frictions may weaken this effect in poor areas. Thus, any public policies which stimulate total housing production tend to improve housing conditions among the poor to at least some extent, other things being equal. Clearly, the bigger the total direct public subsidy put into housing, the more new units will be built. In addition, because so much new housing employs debt financing, national monetary and fiscal policies that reduce interest rates can greatly increase the amount of new housing produced in free markets.

The Effect of Varying Public Housing Subsidy Distributions

Public housing subsidies have two effects which improve housing conditions among poor households: they always increase total housing output, thereby tending to loosen the entire housing market; and they may provide direct access to new housing for poor households if they focus upon aiding such households. But, the lower the household's income, the greater the per-household subsidy needed to close the gap between ability to pay and the cost of a new decent unit. Therefore, any given public housing subsidy can generate more new production of decent units if concentrated upon middle-income and upper-income groups than if concentrated upon the poorest groups. True, the frictions of the housing market mean that the immediate impact of such larger outputs upon the poorest households will be far less than a lower total output directly distributed to them. Yet focusing housing subsidies upon middle-income groups (as in the United States) enables the government to assist more households per million dollars of subsidy and therefore may be considered politically more efficient than direct housing aid to the poor.

Approaches to Second Best Solutions

In all nations and all historic periods, providing decent housing for every household has been far too expensive for society to achieve without sacrificing other objectives which it considers more desirable. Hence, a variety of second best solutions have been tried. Where the poorest groups are politically powerful, there is usually a combination of (1) allowing urban squatters to expropriate housing sites without payment, especially on publicly owned land; (2) allowing large amounts of zero standard housing to be built privately by poor urban squatters; and (3) building some publicly subsidized decent units for poor households in large cities. Where middle-income groups are politically dominant, there is more pressure to prevent squatting and zero standard new construction, and to shift subsidies to directly benefiting middle-income or high-income households.

The Location of Low-Income Households in Urban Areas

Throughout the world, most new urban construction occurs on vacant land at the edges of existing built-up areas. It is almost always much cheaper and faster to build on vacant sites than to acquire existing properties, relocate their occupants, demolish the buildings, and then rebuild on their sites. Also, where acute housing shortages prevail, it is politically difficult to destroy existing units because it is so hard to relocate their occupants.

The edge of most urban areas is relatively distant from the central business district. However, in some cities, more close-in areas have remained vacant because of undesirable features that caused earlier developers to bypass them. For example, in Caracas, close-in hillsides were skipped by early urban developers because of the high costs of building on steep slopes.

In societies which cope with rapid increases in low-income population by housing poor households in new units, the poorest people tend to live at these edges of the developed area, mostly on the periphery, but sometimes also on initially bypassed hillsides, public parks, or swamps. Since it is too expensive to provide decent new units for most such households, the majority usually live in zero standard shacks clustered around these outskirts.

In contrast, societies which prohibit zero standard new construction generally cannot afford to house all or even most low-income population growth in new units. Instead, poor households must concentrate in the lowest price existing units. These tend to be the most dilapidated and obsolete houses, which are usually the oldest in the area. Almost all cities were historically built up in concentric rings outward from their points of origin. Hence the oldest units are close to central commercial areas. Thus, prohibiting poor households from building new zero standard or low standard housing on vacant land radically shifts the spatial concentration of the poor from the outer periphery of a metropolitan area to the inner core, as in the United States. Conversely, in these societies, only relatively affluent families or those receiving public subsidies can afford to occupy the decent new units built on vacant land at the edge of the urban area. True, a few very wealthy households live close to the center in older units they rehabilitate, or new units created through clearance. But these are exceptions to the general rule that whoever lives in older units dominates the near-core area.

BASIC STRATEGIES FOR PROVIDING HOUSING FOR LOW-INCOME URBAN HOUSEHOLDS

Using the background factors and relationships described above, we can systematically analyze the basic strategies employed in various nations to provide housing for low-income urban households. Each such strategy occurs in a setting influenced by three key exogenous factors: the rate of population growth and population migration patterns; the rate of change of average real income per household; and the rate of change of occupancy costs per household for newly built decent housing units. Variations in these factors influence both the selection of particular housing strategies by public authorities, and the outcomes of whatever strategy is selected. Clearly, a myriad of other exogenous factors can influence these things too, but these three are especially critical.

For purposes of analysis, I will arbitrarily view each basic housing strategy as containing four main elements: the quality standards actually enforced regarding new housing construction, the degree of overall public stimulation of total new housing production, the total amount of public subsidy for housing, and the way this public subsidy is allocated among income groups. A huge number of possible combinations and variations of these elements can be conceived of. But I believe it is useful to narrow down these possibilities to the following three major types of strategies:

Filtering strategies involve strict enforcement of high or moderate quality standards for all new construction, and either (a) no public housing subsidies at all or (b) public subsidies focused mainly on middle-income or high-income households. Thus, nearly all new housing units are occupied by nonpoor households. Poor households receive decent units through filtering down of older units from higher income households.

Low-income subsidy strategies also involve strict enforcement of high or moderate quality standards (usually the latter) for all new construction, but include large-scale public housing subsidies allocated directly to low-income households. High standard versions require either larger total public subsidies or reach fewer poor households than moderate standard versions. The latter are better able to use the economies of mass produced or industrialized housing.

Minimal standard strategies involve only partial enforcement of any housing quality standards in urban areas, primarily in existing good quality neighborhoods. A great deal of the new construction under such strategies consists of zero standard units built by their occupants. Any housing subsidies employed can be either concentrated on the poor or spread over all income groups.

Additional variations of these strategies can result from differences in the magnitude of both total stimulation of housing production and total public housing subsidies.

THE LIKELY RESULTS AND EFFECTIVENESS OF THESE STRATEGIES

The key results and effectiveness of these strategies can be assessed in terms of their locational outcomes and how well they cope with large-scale migration of poor households to urban areas.

Their Locational Outcomes

Filtering strategies usually cause a concentration of low-income house-holds in or near the central cores of urban areas, because the oldest and most deteriorated units—and therefore the least expensive—are located there. True, in some cities, many older units retain their attraction for high-income households because of unique locational ameni-ties. Examples are waterfront views (as in Sydney and San Francisco), locations overlooking attractive parks (as in Paris and New York), or proximity to central shopping, entertainment, and offices (as in London and Chicago). Such high-amenity older housing may be maintained in good condition for centuries or periodically rebuilt by high-income occupants. Nevertheless, in societies that use filtering strategies, most centrally located neighborhoods do not have such advantages; hence the older units there eventually become occupied by low-income house-holds. Moreover, in such societies, poor households can gain more housing units only by taking over those formerly occupied by wealthier households. Therefore, if the low-income population in an urban area expands rapidly, it must progressively displace more and more some-what wealthier households through gradual outward expansion of the areas it occupies. This displacement or transition process causes sys-tematic instability in residential occupancy patterns. It also tends to generate antagonism between the poor newcomers and those groups pressured to leave their existing neighborhoods. If older parts of the urbanized area are under a political jurisdiction different from newer peripheral parts (as in the United States), the concentration of poor households in the older parts can cause major political and fiscal dis-parities between the core and periphery in the urbanized area.

In contrast, since the other two strategies provide new housing for poor households, those households become concentrated on the out-skirts of the urbanized area. Under a minimal quality strategy, nearly all poor households are located in shacks at least partially encircling older built-up areas. But under a low-income subsidy strategy, total subsidies are almost never large enough to house all badly housed poor urban households in new decent housing built on vacant land. Hence at least some poor households, often a large fraction of all those newly entering the urban area, must still concentrate in older existing units near the central core, as in a filtering strategy.

These locational variations have important social class impacts. Where all housing for low-income groups is provided through filtering (as in the United States), the poor are almost completely spatially sep-arated from middle-income and upper-income groups. The central core becomes dominated by the former, and outlying growth areas by the latter. An opposite pattern of spatial segregation occurs in minimal quality strategies, with the poor living outboard of middle- and upper-class groups. However, many households who start out in shacks may gradually improve them as their incomes rise, thereby remaining in a primarily poor neighborhood. But in low-income subsidy strategies (as in Sweden and the Soviet Union), the new units occupied by low-income groups are likely to be spatially close to or intermixed with those occupied by high-income groups.

Consequently, any attempt to introduce strong elements of low-income subsidy into what has long been a nearly "pure" filtering strategy (as the United States Department of Housing and Urban Development did from 1968 through 1973) requires moving from strong social class segregation (and in the United States, racial segregation) to much greater spatial mixture of social classes in peripheral areas. The political implications of this aspect of the strategy shift may be more important in determining its success than either the physical availability of sites or the cost of the required subsidies. For example, the political hostility of the American suburban middle class toward such increased social class mixture undoubtedly played a key role in causing the Nixon administration to denounce its own success in stimulating direct housing subsidies and to advocate a housing allowance program instead. The latter tends to accelerate the gradual "filtering-up" of poorer households through the existing housing inventory. In contrast, directly subsidizing new units occupied by the poor would place them in new-growth areas close to new nondirectly subsidized units occupied by middle- and upper-income households.

Coping with Large-Scale Urban In-Migration

Large-scale movement of low-income households from rural areas into urban centers has been a worldwide phenomenon in the past few decades. How well can these strategies cope with such movement, and what are the differences in their effectiveness?

During periods of really rapid inflow of poor people into a given urban area, none of the strategies can provide decent housing for all the newcomers, even in the wealthiest nations. Hence there is an inescapable surplus housing need which must somehow be met. If public authorities still prohibit construction of new zero standard or substandard units, this need is met through overcrowding or subdividing existing units. Sometimes public authorities themselves build new lower standard units on a temporary basis (such as the veterans housing at United States universities right after World War II). Where a minimal quality strategy is official policy (usually because the nation cannot afford any other), whole cities of new shacks spring up on the edge of existing urban areas.

No one really knows whether it is more desirable to overcrowd or subdivide existing units than to build new substandard ones. Therefore, it is hard to compare the effectiveness of these different approaches. However, low-income subsidy strategies are clearly far more effective than filtering strategies at remedying these conditions among low-income households per million dollars of total public and private investment in housing. This is true because the former provide new decent units directly to poor households. On the other hand, the resulting interference with free markets tends to spread the impact of the housing shortage to middle-income and upper-income groups too and to distort normal allocations of resources in the economy.

Some Tentative Policy Implications

Space limitations prohibit any extensive analysis of the strategies summarized above, or their many policy implications. However, two related policy suggestions can be tentatively derived from them. Both spring from the undesirable results of a society trying to require poor urban households to meet housing quality standards which are in reality beyond their capacity, or the society's, to achieve.

For example, in the United States filtering strategy, rigid prohibition of any new construction at less-than-high quality standards forces many poor urban households to live in overcrowded slum conditions. Thus, unrealistic insistence upon high quality in fact produces more low quality than is necessary. The low-income households concerned would be much better off if the United States allowed construction of new moderate standard units.[1] Then the limited subsidies voted by Congress for direct housing aid to poor households would generate far more units. Also, Congress might be willing to increase these subsidies because it would not seem to be putting poor people into better units than those occupied by the taxpayers providing the subsidies. The widespread insistence of poor households themselves upon very high standards for public housing thus requires them to endure miserable housing conditions longer than would acceptance of moderate quality standards. Some observers hope that Congress will provide large enough direct public subsidies to put every badly housed poor family in a high quality unit in the foreseeable future, or that the filtering process will

---

[1] The recent surge of mobile home sales in the United States is in part a response to this need for lower quality housing. Mobile homes are much smaller than conventionally built housing, occupy less land, and are built with less durability. Yet their sales soared to 21 percent of all new housing units by 1969, and have remained at about that fraction through 1974. This has occurred precisely because so many households want new units, but either cannot afford conventional ones or prefer to allocate more of their incomes to nonhousing activities. Thus, the market is in effect sneaking lower quality standards "through the back door" on a growing scale.

work well enough to do so without huge direct subsidies. In my opinion, these hopes are largely wishful thinking.

Many poorer nations could also benefit from similarly accepting lower-than-optimal housing quality standards because they produce better results than unrealistically seeking higher standards. Some governments concentrate upon production of a small number of moderate quality subsidized units for the poor, while thousands more zero standard units are built in completely unregulated fashion. The net result would be superior if more public attention were focused upon trying to achieve even extremely low level standards regarding all housing, including shacks. For example, public funds might provide minimum-sized lots for shacks in selected locations, with streets, water, and electricity available. This could help control the location of zero standard development so as to conform to urban planning, while allowing room on each lot for future upgrading and immediately providing minimal utilities for all residents.

Hopefully, other policy implications can be derived from the housing strategy model set forth above by examining the impacts of varying both key exogenous factors and the basic elements of each strategy.

5

The Successes and Failures of Federal Housing Policy, 1960–1974

To assess the effectiveness of federal housing-related policies in the 1960s and early 1970s, it is necessary to make some arbitrary distinctions, heroic assumptions, and controversial judgments. The first arbitrary distinction is to divide all federal housing-related policies into the following four categories:

1. *Indirect influences:* Actions influencing *housing production* through monetary, fiscal, and credit policies aimed primarily at maintaining prosperity or fighting inflation.
2. *Direct financial influences:* Actions aimed at affecting the *total supply* of housing through credit and institutional arrangements rather than direct financial aid. An example is the creation of the Federal Home Loan Mortgage Corporation to help establish an effective secondary market in mortgages.
3. *Direct housing subsidies:* Actions aimed at increasing the supply of housing directly available to low-income households. Examples are the Section 235 and 236 programs.
4. *Community-related programs:* Actions that affect the structure of urban areas and therefore impact housing markets and the neighborhood conditions incorporated in the everyday meaning of the term "housing." Examples are the Interstate Highway Program, urban renewal, and the Model Cities Program.

Reprinted from the *Public Interest* 34 (Winter 1974): 124–145.

The second arbitrary distinction consists of dividing the time under consideration into three periods: (1) low-priority period (1960 through 1965); (2) reassessment period (1966 through 1968); (3) high-production period (1968 through 1973).

Evaluating policies requires comparing their results with the objectives they were intended to achieve. Congress adopted in 1949 a national housing goal of "providing a decent home and a suitable living environment for every American family," and in 1968 Congress linked that goal to a production target of 26 million additional housing units from 1968 through 1978, six million for occupancy by low-income and moderate-income households. Since that basic goal conceals many ambiguities, I will make the heroic assumption—derived from congressional legislation, administration statements, and my observation of federal behavior—that federal housing-related policies were designed to achieve the following major objectives: (1) *High-level housing production*—encouraging private construction of enough new housing units to serve needs created by rising total population, rising incomes, demolition, and migration; (2) *Adequate housing finance*—providing a sufficient flow of mortgage and other funds to reduce the production described above; (3) *Reduced housing costs*—reducing the cost of housing occupancy (including costs of construction, land, financing, and operation) so that more households can afford decent units; (4) *Overall economic stabilization*—causing countercyclical changes in total housing production to help stabilize the overall economy; (5) *Stabilization of housing production*—insulating the home-building industry from large-scale fluctuations associated with the general business cycle. (This objective is diametrically opposed to the preceding one.); (6) *Attraction of private capital*—designing incentives to encourage private capital to finance most housing production, including that for low-income and moderate-income households; (7) *Housing assistance to low-income and moderate-income households*—enabling households living in substandard quality units to occupy decent units, and financially aiding households who pay inordinately high fractions of their incomes to occupy decent units; (8) *Increased home ownership;* (9) *Improved inner-city conditions*—helping large cities to upgrade deteriorating older neighborhoods and to prevent further decay in aging "gray areas"; (10) *Creation of good new neighborhoods*—helping private developers and local governments create desirable new neighborhoods in subdivisions and new communities.

Many other secondary objectives were also served by housing-related policies, but I have limited this enumeration to only the primary ones. The objectives listed above are not entirely consistent with each other. Overall economic stabilization, in particular, often conflicts with almost all the others, since it requires sharp reductions in housing production during upswings in the rest of the economy.

THE "TRICKLE-DOWN" PROCESS

To evaluate housing-related policies, it is necessary to understand the "trickle-down" or "filtering" process that dominates American urban development. All newly built U.S. urban housing (except mobile homes, which are not allowed in most parts of metropolitan areas) must meet the relatively high standards of size and quality set in local building codes and zoning regulations. The cost of meeting those standards is quite high. Consequently, less than half of all U.S. households can afford to occupy newly built housing without either receiving a direct subsidy or spending over 25 percent of their incomes on housing. Hence, only households in the upper half of the income distribution normally live in brand-new housing.

This pervasive exclusion of low-income and moderate-income households from brand-new units has profound impact upon our housing markets—and upon American society in general. Throughout the world, new urban housing is mainly constructed on vacant land around the edges of already existing neighborhoods. Therefore, all urban areas normally expand outwards. Most of the newest housing is always on the outer edge; most of the oldest housing is in the center; and moderately aged housing lies in between.

Outside the U.S., households of all income levels may be found at any given distance from the center of urbanization. Both poor and rich live in older housing near the center—the poor in deteriorated units, the rich in units they have maintained or rehabilitated. Similarly, both poor and rich live in brand-new housing on the urban periphery—the poor in low-quality shacks they have built themselves, and the rich in new units constructed to high-quality standards. Middle-income groups concentrate in the rings between the center and the outer edge, occupying "used" housing that is still of good quality.

In the United States, it is illegal both to build brand-new low-quality housing units and to allow older units to deteriorate into low-quality status. But the laws against these two types of substandard housing are not enforced to the same degree. Laws against *new* low-quality units are rigorously enforced in all urban areas. Therefore, only households in the upper half of the income distribution can afford to live in much of the urban periphery where new growth is concentrated. But laws against *older* low-quality housing are only moderately enforced in most older neighborhoods. They are almost totally ignored in areas where the most deteriorated units are found. This is not an evil conspiracy between local officials and landlords. Rather, it is a necessary recognition of the inability of many very poor households to pay for high-quality housing. No such recognition, however, is extended to the poor in newly built areas. There, local officials zealously exclude the poor by enforcing high-quality housing standards to the letter.

This process creates a major spatial separation of households by income group in U.S. urban areas. The most affluent urban households reside mainly around the suburban periphery; the poorest urban households are concentrated in the oldest inventory near the center (sometimes in older suburbs too); and middle-income groups live in between. Moreover, each neighborhood goes through a typical life cycle. When it is first built, the brand-new housing units there are occupied by relatively affluent households. Then, as these housing units age slightly, the most affluent households move on to still newer areas farther out. Other households move in who are somewhat lower in the *relative* income distribution, but still have good incomes. This "trickle-down" process continues as these housing units age. But they still provide excellent shelter as long as their occupants maintain them well.

Eventually, however, the income groups who move in are too poor to maintain these units—especially since maintenance costs have by then risen, and lending institutions are reluctant to risk funds in improving them. Then the housing deteriorates markedly and the neighborhood becomes a "slum." This life cycle normally takes from 40 to 60 years. (Some older neighborhoods never experience it because they are so well located that wealthy households remain and maintain the property in good condition.)

For the predominant majority of households in U.S. metropolitan areas, this "trickle-down" process works very well. It furnishes good-quality housing in neighborhoods free from the vexing problems of extreme poverty, since nearly all very poor people (except some elderly residents) are excluded. But for the poorest urban households, especially poor minority-group members, this process is a social disaster. It compels thousands of the poorest households to concentrate together in the worst-quality housing located in older neighborhoods near the urban center. This causes a "critical mass" effect that multiplies the impact of many problems associated with poverty. Such neighborhoods become dominated by high crime rates, vandalism, unemployment, drug addiction, broken homes, gang warfare, and other conditions almost universally regarded by Americans as undesirable. Most households with incomes high enough to have a choice of living somewhere else move out. So do many employers and retailers anxious to escape such conditions. This withdrawal of those with economic and other resources further weakens the neighborhood and removes many possible checks to the negative forces described above. Only a minority of the people living in these areas of concentrated poverty engage in destructive behavior; so the real victims are the nondestructive majority of poor residents there. They are prevented from moving out by the exclusionary barriers erected in most middle-income and upper-income neighborhoods. Thus, they must bear the social costs of providing the fine-quality neighborhoods enjoyed by the upper two thirds of the income distribution.

Yet prosperous households have strong arguments against opening up their neighborhoods to unrestricted entry by low-income households. They have observed the destructive environments in concentrated poverty areas, and they do not want such conditions where they live. They have no way of screening low-income households entering their areas to keep out destructive ones while admitting the nondestructive majority; so they prefer to keep *all* poor households out. This attitude is reinforced by their experience that nearly all nonpoor households stop moving into a neighborhood whenever many poor people enter. As normal housing turnover proceeds, the area inevitably becomes mainly poor, because only other poor households are willing to move in. This causes a temporary decline in property values that threatens the major investment residents have made in their homes. Thus, many powerful forces pressure middle-income and upper-income households to persist in exclusionary behavior—in spite of its unjust consequences for the nondestructive majority of low-income households "trapped" in concentrated poverty areas.

This explanation may seem far removed from evaluating federal housing-related policies, but understanding the "trickle-down" process is crucial for comprehending how those policies actually worked. In fact, the failure of federal officials to develop such an understanding caused them to be surprised by the many unexpected consequences of their actions, as will be explained below.

OTHER KEY BACKGROUND FACTORS

Before examining federal housing-related policies and actions, it is necessary to describe several additional background factors. First, there was an acute housing shortage during and right after World War II. But from 1950 onwards, the number of housing units built each year exceeded the number of new households formed, gradually easing the shortage. (Table 5-1 shows housing starts from 1950 through 1974). *An approximate balance was attained between total supply and total demand in most urban housing markets by 1960.* True, several million urban households were still in substandard or overcrowded units. But

Table 5-1   Annual Housing Starts by Type, 1950–1974

Year	Conventionally-Constructed Housing Starts*	Mobile Homes	Total Housing Starts
1950	1,951,648	63,100	2,014,748
1951	1,491,207	67,300	1,558,507
1952	1,504,520	83,000	1,587,520
1953	1,438,372	76,900	1,515,272
1954	1,550,445	76,000	1,626,445
1955	1,645,715	111,900	1,757,615
1956	1,345,739	104,800	1,450,539
1957	1,221,647	107,600	1,329,247
1958	1,375,588	100,400	1,475,988
1959	1,528,836	120,500	1,649,336
1960	1,272,137	103,700	1,375,837
1961	1,365,000	90,200	1,455,200
1962	1,492,400	118,000	1,610,400
1963	1,642,000	150,840	1,792,840
1964	1,561,000	191,320	1,752,320
1965	1,509,600	216,000	1,725,600
1966	1,195,900	217,000	1,412,900
1967	1,321,817	240,000	1,561,817
1968	1,545,500	318,000	1,863,500
1969	1,499,920	413,000	1,912,920
1970	1,466,759	401,000	1,867,759
1971	2,084,500	496,570	2,581,070
1972	2,378,500	575,900	2,954,400
1973	2,057,500	580,000	2,637,500
1974	1,352,300	371,350	1,723,650

Source: U.S. Department of Housing and Urban Development, Division of Research and Statistics; and Mobile Home Manufacturers Association.

* Conventionally *constructed* housing starts can be financed with either VA- and FHA-insured mortgages or *conventional mortgages.*

most urban households that could afford decent housing were living in such housing by 1960, except in racially segregated areas.

Second, until the late 1960s, *housing production had a natural tendency to move in a countercyclical pattern in relation to general economic activity.* Most buyers of new or existing homes borrow large fractions of the total cost and finance it over long time periods. Hence the amount they must pay each month is strongly affected by the interest rate. When interest rates rise, therefore, many households who could formerly afford to buy new housing can no longer do so. Conversely, when rates fall, many more households can afford to buy homes. Developers of rental apartments also borrow heavily and are therefore similarly affected. But short-term borrowers of money for other purposes—such as consumer loans or business investment in plants and equipment—are less sensitive to changes in interest rates. When the economy moves from a recession into general prosperity, there is rising competition for funds, and interest rates of all types go up. Because a slight rise in mortgage interest rates cuts down the number of borrowers sharply, lenders shift their funds into nonhousing channels where they can get higher rates without losing volume. Housing starts therefore decline because of inability to finance mortgage loans. When a general recession occurs, other demands for funds slack off, and more money becomes available for mortgage loans. Mortgage rates drop and terms (length of loan and amount of down-payment required) improve, so housing production rises.

Third, *the single most dynamic force in the housing markets of most large metropolitan areas in the 1960s was the rapid growth of the black and Spanish-speaking populations in central cities.* The resulting "massive" transition of whole neighborhoods from mainly white to mainly nonwhite occupancy did not reduce housing segregation, but it greatly improved the amount and quality of housing available to minority-group members. Moreover, it generated large-scale movement of white households into outlying suburbs.

THE LOW-PRIORITY PERIOD: 1960–1965

In the early 1960s, housing was not regarded as a high-priority item of domestic concern by Congress or the executive branch. The general goal of providing "a decent home and a suitable living environment for every American family" had been stated in 1949, but no specific production targets had been adopted by Congress. Federal housing policy was vested in the Housing and Home Finance Agency (HHFA), which did not enjoy departmental status. Major housing-related policies and actions in this period can be summarized under five principal headings.

1. *Total housing production was still viewed by federal economic policy makers as a countercyclical force useful in stabilizing the economy as a whole.* Hence, the monetary and fiscal conditions dominating housing production were oriented toward nonhousing objectives, with their impact upon housing treated as a residual rather than a controlling or central factor.

2. *The preferential tax and mortgage insurance treatment provided to homeowners continued to stimulate ownership as a preferred form of tenure during this period, although apartment construction began rising toward the middle of the decade.* Homeowners who occupy their own dwellings can deduct their mortgage interest and local property taxes from their federally taxable incomes. This tax saving provides a hidden

housing subsidy that accrues mainly to households in the upper half of the income distribution. Even in the early 1960s, this hidden subsidy to the relatively affluent was far larger than all direct subsidies to poorer households combined. Moreover, mortgage insurance provided by the Federal Housing Administration made home ownership possible for more and more Americans. By 1960, 61.9 percent of all occupied housing units were owner-occupied, as compared to 55.0 percent in 1950, and 43.6 percent in 1940. Homeownership held its own in the 1960s but did not expand much. This resulted from the rise in multi-family units (mainly rental units) to around 33 percent of total starts in the mid-1960s and 40 percent in the early 1970s.

3. *Federally financed highway construction and urban renewal programs were designed in part to bolster central-city economies, but they actually stimulated rapid population growth and job expansion in the suburbs.* Urban expressways were supposed to help downtown centers maintain dominance over their surrounding areas. Urban renewal was intended to remove blight and to promote economically self-sustaining redevelopment. These programs succeeded in aiding many downtowns —as evidenced by the surge of major downtown investments in private office buildings and public facilities in the late 1960s. But such programs also produced the following unforeseen "side effects" that heavily counteracted their positive achievements:

a. Thousands of small industries and retail businesses displaced by highways and urban renewal simply went out of business, and even more displaced industries and retail operations moved to newer, larger, and more efficient suburban sites.

b. Hundreds of thousands of low-income households displaced by urban renewal and highway clearance shifted into older housing in nearby once-stable neighborhoods. Hence, blight was often just moved rather than eliminated.

c. Radial and circumferential expressways made outlying locations more convenient than congested near-in locations; so many warehouse and distribution facilities moved away from central-city sites.

d. Commuting between relatively distant suburban homes and downtown or other in-city jobs became much easier; so millions of households shifted from central-city housing into growing suburban subdivisions.

e. Since the worst urban blight was in concentrated poverty areas, urban renewal efforts focused upon removing blight-created vacant sites in such areas. But most firms and households with enough money to support self-sustaining redevelopment would not locate there, because those sites were still surrounded by concentrated poverty.

f. Highway routes and urban renewal projects were often deliberately located in poor, minority-group neighborhoods to force relocation of groups regarded as undesirable by the local power structure. This tactic created unfair hardships for those displaced, and merely shifted minority-group occupancy to other nearby neighborhoods.

Why did the private interests, federal officials, and congressmen who designed these programs fail to anticipate such consequences? First, very few of them understood the nature of urban areas or the dynamics of the "trickle-down" process. Second, each major federally funded policy was initiated for rather narrowly conceived reasons by a specialized group with no responsibility for coping with its broader consequences. For example, highway engineers and the automobile industry promoted giant urban expressways in order to move traffic and increase road capacity, but they had little comprehension of, or concern for, the likely impact upon the local tax base or the fabric of urban life. Third, there was no effective way to coordinate all these specialized programs at the local level, since no one local government had overall responsibility for an entire metropolitan area. These three factors resulted in a complete inability to "orchestrate" specialized federal programs into a unified theme—or even to achieve minimal coordination among them.

4. *Production of directly subsidized housing for low-income and moderate-income households was kept at very low levels during this period by small-scale congressional appropriations and local resistance to such housing.* From 1960 through 1965, only 283,610 directly subsidized housing units for low-income and moderate-income households were started. That was 3.2 percent of all conventionally-constructed housing built during this low-priority period. Rising black occupancy of large high-rise public housing projects in big cities was generating increased local resistance to construction of any public housing except that occupied by the elderly. After the 221(d) (3) program was passed, some subsidized units for moderate-income households were created. However, federal officials responsible for promoting subsidized housing tended to measure their performance against past low levels of such output, rather than against any quantified concept of "national needs."

5. *In spite of low production of subsidized units directly available to the poor, housing conditions in most urban areas improved for all income groups because total production, less demolitions, exceeded net household formation.* Hence, the "trickle-down" process had some positive effects. From 1960 to 1965, the number of U.S. households rose by 4.452 million, according to Census Bureau estimates. But total housing starts (including mobile homes) equalled 8.161 million units. Subtraction of 600,000 demolitions per year yields a net increase of 5.161

million units—or 709,000 more than the increase in households during that period. This "surplus" should be reduced somewhat to allow for needs generated by migration. Nevertheless, subsequent data have shown that housing quality was improving in most urban areas from 1960 through 1965.

THE REASSESSMENT PERIOD: 1966–1968

A number of dramatic events from 1965 to 1968 caused a nationwide reassessment of the low priority the federal government had been placing upon meeting housing needs. Most striking were the civil disorders that occurred in over 150 cities from 1965 through early 1968. In the summer of 1967, President Lyndon Johnson appointed a National Advisory Commission on Civil Disorders to investigate the causes of and possible remedies for these disturbances. By March 1968, the commission had produced a report setting forth its major findings. It recommended massive expansion of the production of directly subsidized units for low-income and moderate-income households to 600,000 units in the next year, and six million units in the next five years.

A second crucial event was the severe "credit crunch" in housing mortgage markets in 1966. In 1965, just as the economy was recovering from its slight slump in 1963, rapid escalation of the Vietnam conflict required large federal outlays. Combined with ongoing prosperity, as well as spending on the space program and Great Society programs, this caused an extraordinary expansion in overall economic activity. By 1966, the Federal Reserve Board decided to sharply curtail the growth of the money supply to reduce inflationary pressures. This produced a sudden jump in interest rates, which in turn resulted in a startling reduction in available mortgage funds. Nonsubsidized conventional housing starts dropped 22.3 percent from 1.446 million in 1965 to 1.124 million in 1966—the lowest level since before 1950. In Southern California, the nation's largest housing market, total starts plunged to one third of the all-time record level attained in 1963, and the local building industry was decimated. Leaders in both home building and savings and loan associations began lobbying to insulate mortgage credit more completely from cyclical changes in general credit availability. This led to the creation of nonbudgetary agencies capable of borrowing funds in the nation's bond markets to support mortgages when cyclically tied sources of funds dried up. Moreover, a new form of security backed by mortgages was developed, but in a form more attractive to pension funds and other large-scale investors. Consequently, mortgage markets became considerably more insulated from the general business cycle than they had been in the past—though by no means fully insulated.

A further stimulus to the reassessment of housing priorities came from two reports by federally appointed commissions. The National Commission on Urban Problems, headed by former Senator Paul H. Douglas, was appointed by President Johnson in 1967 in response to a 1965 congressional directive. The commission held public hearings in many cities, commissioned dozens of fact-finding studies, and presented a final report entitled *Building the American City* in late 1968. This report urged the federal government to measure its housing programs against some estimate of "national housing needs," rather than against past levels of performance. The commission also recommended that 2.0 to 2.25 million housing starts be undertaken every year, including at least 500,000 units for low-income and moderate-income households other than the elderly. The second commission was the President's Committee on Urban Housing, a group of prestigious citizens headed by industrialist Edgar F. Kaiser. Appointed by President Johnson in June 1967, it focused on methods of making housing available to American households at lower cost than in the past. The Committee's final report, *A Decent Home,* recommended that Congress adopt a ten-year production goal of 26 million additional housing units, including at least six million for lower-income families. Still another major event contributing to the reassessment of housing priorities was the elevation of the former Housing and Home Finance Agency to Cabinet status in 1965 as the new Department of Housing and Urban Development.

The culmination of all these events was passage of the Housing and Urban Development Act of 1968. This landmark bill set an official housing production target of 26 million additional new and rehabilitated units to be built from 1968 through 1978, including six million units available to low-income and middle-income households. Toward this end, it created two new, generously funded housing-subsidy programs for moderate-income households that combined an interest subsidy, depreciation tax shelter, and some features of a housing allowance. These were the Section 236 program for rental housing, and the Section 235 program for ownership housing. Also included among the act's provisions were the creation of secondary mortgage market instruments to help insulate mortgage credit from the business cycle; liberalization of credit terms on market-rate mortgage loan insurance for households in high-risk areas, or with relatively poor credit, or making very small down-payments; expanded funding for public housing, and an emphasis on creating scattered-site, low-rise units to avoid excessive poverty concentration; guaranteeing of privately-issued bonds to finance new communities; and changes in the urban renewal program emphasizing

shorter-range, more comprehensive actions and requiring more housing for low-income and middle-income households on renewal sites.

This bill, plus the major appropriations for it passed by Congress,
signaled a dramatic rise in the status of housing and housing-related
problems on the nation's priority list. Combined with the Model Cities
Act passed earlier, the Housing and Urban Development Act of 1968
created a whole arsenal of housing and community development tools
that—in theory—were capable of responding effectively to many of the
physical and social problems plaguing urban areas.

THE HIGH-PRODUCTION PERIOD: 1968–1974

Before the Democratic administration responsible for the Housing and
Urban Development Act of 1968 could carry it out, it was replaced by a
new Republican administration in 1969. As a result, there was an almost
total turnover of top-level personnel in HUD, the Bureau of the Budget,
and the White House. But even if the Democrats had stayed in power,
a major turnover would probably have occurred in accordance with the
"Law of Inescapable Discontinuity": *High-level federal personnel
change so fast that almost no major federal program is ever initially
conceived of, drafted into legislation, shepherded through Congress,
and then carried out by the same officials.* Therefore, no program is
ever perceived in the same way by those who put it into effect as by
those who invented it.

Another important determinant of the behavior of federal officials is
the "Law of Compulsive Innovation": *Newly installed administrators
have a strong desire to reject what their predecessors have started and
to emphasize programs they create themselves so they can claim full
credit for whatever success results.* Consequently, they tend to ignore
the lessons their predecessors have learned from experience. It was
difficult, however, for the incoming Republicans to start over completely, since the massive Housing and Urban Development Act of 1968 had
just been passed and funded. So HUD's new managers expressed their
originality by emphasizing housing production and technology as the
keys to urban problems, and de-emphasizing other facets of urban development. Unfortunately, as Secretary Romney soon discovered, this
partial approach to solving urban problems ignored the perplexing social difficulties that had become visible in the reassessment period.

A corollary of the "Law of Compulsive Innovation" had an even
more drastic impact upon HUD's behavior: *Whenever one party re-
places the other in the executive branch, the newcomers have a compulsive desire to reorganize nearly every agency.* Since all human organizations are imperfect, and large bureaucracies are especially subject

to inertia and malfunction, it is always easy to justify reorganization as "required" to improve performance. HUD and FHA were subjected to several overlapping reorganizations that involved both reshuffling functions in Washington and creating a whole new decentralized layer of regional offices. The internal confusion generated by these reorganizations had a devastating impact upon HUD's capabilities.

The new team at HUD charged off in pursuit of technical improvements in housing production by launching Operation Breakthrough. This was to be a three-phased movement encouraging more mass-production of housing in factories to meet large aggregated markets, thereby achieving economies of scale that would reduce housing costs. The first phase was to design new ways to build housing industrially; the second phase was to demonstrate those new methods by constructing such housing on a number of prototype sites; and the third phase was to serve large-scale markets with those systems that appeared most successful.

Meanwhile, however, a series of other developments stimulated the most massive housing production in American history. The Nixon administration's response to inflation in 1968 and 1969 was to induce a nationwide recession through flattened federal spending and tight monetary policy. Hence builders had difficulty obtaining adequate mortgage credit in 1970 for conventionally financed units. But Section 235 and Section 236 financing was available, so thousands of builders shifted to the new direct-subsidy programs. Non-directly-subsidized housing starts fell from 1.382 million in 1968 to 1.036 million in 1970— the lowest total since before 1950. But subsidized starts shot upward from 163,360 in 1968 (the record high before the new programs were available) to over 430,000 in both 1970 and 1971. Thus in 1971 the number of directly subsidized housing units started was *nine times* as great as the annual average in the low-priority period.

At the same time, the number of non-child-oriented households was rising rapidly in the late 1960s, and many wanted to find relatively inexpensive housing even if it did not meet the high-quality standards required of conventionally built new units. Therefore, consumer acceptance of mobile homes escalated dramatically. From 1955 through 1961, around 100,000 mobile home units were shipped annually. But from 1962 onwards, annual shipments rose steadily, reaching over 500,000 units by 1972. In fact, since 1969, one out of every five new housing units created in the United States each year has been a mobile home.

Moreover, in 1971 there occurred the usual huge movement of financial resources into housing right after the low point in a general recession as savings flows into savings and loan associations reached all-time highs. This traditional surge of mortgage credit was augmented by the flight of investment funds from the stock market. Although the stock market recovered sharply from its 1969–1970 down-slide during 1971 and 1972, by 1973 it was well below its 1965 and 1966 levels. In the past, major controllers of many investment funds had always avoided real estate as too risky and specialized. But now they compared this long-term stagnation in stock values with the steady and seemingly endless rise in land values and real property prices during the same period, and consequently, pension funds, bank trust departments, and large corporations began to put billions into real estate from 1970 through 1973. Moreover, dozens of real estate investment trusts (REIT's) issued stock in equity markets and used the billions so raised to invest in real estate. The result was a flood of credit into real estate markets unprecedented in both size and duration. This flood was responsible for the sudden escalation of nonsubsidized conventionally built housing starts from the postwar low of 1.035 million units in 1970 to 2.028 million in 1972—almost a doubling in two years. Millions of 95-percent loans greatly expanded the market for housing ownership, helping to support these enormous production levels without any great rise in vacancies. By 1972, rising prosperity offered another such support as the economy moved into a traditional upswing. But real estate credit did not soon decline as in past upswings.

The consequence of these various developments was a rise in total housing starts to a plateau of about 1.9 million units annually from 1968 through 1970—a total exceeding any previous annual production level except the 2.0 million units in 1950. Then, in 1971, 1972, and 1973, housing starts shot up to 2.6 million, 3.0 million, and 2.6 million units respectively.

THE DARK SIDE OF HIGH PRODUCTION

The massive levels of housing production generated a number of major consequences wholly unexpected by the federal government, and quite disruptive to its housing policies:

1. The ability of the supposedly obsolete housing industry to produce 3.0 million units in a single year—including 2.4 million "stick-built" units (i.e., not factory-built like mobile homes)—proved that industrialized housing was not necessary to reach the nation's housing goals, as Operation Breakthrough had supposed. Operation Breakthrough did persuade many states to adopt statewide building codes for industrialized housing, but it failed to produce housing units at lower cost than traditional methods or to aggregate markets that were large enough to absorb truly mass-produced factory housing.

2. HUD and the Congress had assumed the nation had a housing

shortage when they established the 10-year goal of 26 million additional units in 1968. They failed to recognize that many of the worst-quality units to be replaced were in rural areas—but most new housing production was in urban areas. Hence, the total number of housing units available in many large metropolitan areas shot up well above the number of households there. This accelerated the entire "trickle-down" process. Millions of white households moved out of central cities to new suburban units, and black and Spanish-speaking households moved out of the worst housing into the units thus made available. *The stunning success of HUD's efforts to increase total housing production—actually produced largely by factors beyond HUD's control—thus generated the unexpected and undesirable result of rising abandonment and vacancy in the concentrated poverty "ghettos" of many large cities.*

3.   The new direct-subsidy programs shifted the initiative in creating housing for low-income and moderate-income households to private builders rather than government bureaucrats. These programs also funded large numbers of such units and created strong tax-shelter incentives for private investment in them. As a result, HUD's new area offices were swamped with applications to create and purchase new and rehabilitated subsidized units, and high-level officials pressured the area offices to speed up processing. This occurred in the midst of the personnel disruptions caused by HUD's reorganizations, and thus led to a breakdown in HUD's administrative controls in many areas. Thousands of poor households were bilked by unscrupulous speculators. A few outright corrupt practices by FHA officials were uncovered in some cities, and the resulting scandals shocked Secretary Romney and FHA leaders into denouncing their own programs.

4.   HUD began experiencing the high costs of emphasizing housing production without paying much attention to neighborhood conditions. Many poor families bought housing units at full market interest rates under programs that allowed tiny down-payments or accepted poor credit risks. The majority of such purchases successfully enabled low-income households to benefit from homeownership for the first time, but a significant number resulted in defaults and HUD repossessions. These defaults were concentrated in big-city poverty areas at the bottom of the "trickle-down" process. The number of units across the nation repossessed by FHA rose from its normal level of about 50,000 at any one time to over 200,000 by 1973. HUD officials regarded this not as a costly if unavoidable result of rapid escalation of housing aid to the poor, but as a "disaster."

5.   The high annual cost of directly subsidizing large numbers of new housing units over the lifetimes of their mortgages began to dawn on HUD officials (although it had always been readily calculable). This

cost might escalate to $7.5 billion per year by 1978 if all six million sub-sidized units are built by that time. True, $5.7 billion per year was al-ready being spent in 1971 on *indirect* subsidies through homeowner deductions of mortgage interest and property taxes. But those subsidies mainly to the affluent did not appear in the federal budget, so adminis-tration officials ignored them in calculating costs.

6. Other difficulties began appearing in the direct-subsidy pro-grams. Where many subsidized new units were clustered together—as in many public housing projects—the "flooding" of the neighborhood with low-income and moderate-income households often led to general deterioration in the surrounding area. Some subsidized units were of poor-quality construction; many were occupied by households who were not "truly poor," such as young married graduate students with temporarily low incomes. Furthermore, the rising number of directly-subsidized units placed in middle-income suburbs began to alarm the administration's political constituents. Finally, many middle-income households began complaining when they saw poorer households liv-ing nearby in better units than they enjoyed themselves, thanks to sub-sidies they were helping to pay for.

These developments led the administration to declare a moratorium on further approvals of directly subsidized units after January 1973—both to cut costs and to reassess alternative subsidy policies. HUD also stopped all federal community development programs (urban renewal, sewer and water facility construction, open space support, Model Cities, and public facility construction) for one year. It proposed that Congress shift future funding for them into a special revenue sharing fund to be distributed directly to cities and states in accordance with a fixed for-mula. This proposal amounted to abdication of any specific responsibil-ity for these activities by the federal government. Apparently, the administration thought that categorical aid programs had failed to im-prove urban conditions, or it wanted to pass the political "hot potato" of making decisions concerning these touchy matters to someone else, or both.

EVALUATING FEDERAL HOUSING-RELATED POLICIES: 1960–1973

Because both federal housing-related policies and their objectives are so complex, there is no simple way to evaluate those policies. As a means of assessing them, I have prepared the *evaluation matrix* (Table 5-2). This table presents my evaluations of the relative effectiveness of all four types of housing-related policies (shown in the first four col-umns of the matrix) in achieving all 10 primary objectives (shown in

Table 5-2 Evaluation Matrix: Types of Federal Housing-Related Policies

Objec- tives	I Indirect Influ- ences[1]	II Com- munity- Related Programs[1]	III Direct Financial Influences[2]	IV Direct Housing Sub- sidies[2]	V All Types Con- sidered Together
1) High-Level Housing Production	++	NR	++	+	++
2) Adequate Housing Finance	++	NR	++	+	++
3) Reduced Housing Costs	— —	NR	— —	— —	— —
4) Overall Economic Stabilization	++	NR	—	—	+
5) Stabilization of Housing Production	—	NR	++	—	—
6) Attraction of Private Capital	++	+	++	++	++
7) Housing Assistance to Low- and Moderate- Income Households	— —	— —	—	+	+
8) Encouraging Home Ownership	+	—	++	+	+
9) Improved Inner-City Conditions	— —	—	—	—	— —
10) Creation of Good New Neighbor- hoods	++	+	++	+	++

[1] Assessed for period 1960–1973
[2] Assessed only for period 1968–1973

the rows). The matrix also contains a fifth column that shows my opinion concerning the *overall effectiveness* of *all* federal policies in achieving each objective. In each of the 50 cells of this matrix, policy effectiveness is "scored" on a five-position scale: very effective $(+ +)$, moderately effective (+), moderately ineffective (—), very ineffective (— —), and not relevant (NR). These ratings represent my subjective judgments, based upon the points set forth throughout this paper.

I have assessed the performance of both *Indirect Influences* and *Community-Related Programs* (columns I and II) over all three time periods (that is, from 1960 through 1973). I believe these policies were applied throughout all three periods to about the same degree of intensity in relation to their maximum potential. In contrast, I have assessed the performance of both *Direct Financial Influences* and *Direct Housing Subsidies* (columns III and IV) only during the high-production period—that is, from 1968 through 1973. I believe these policies were not applied with sufficient intensity during the two earlier periods to provide a fair test of their effectiveness. A second qualification is that the entire evaluation matrix applies only to the effectiveness of these policies in metropolitan areas. Most federal housing-related policies have not been aimed at rural areas and small cities; hence, they have been very ineffective in those places. This summary evaluation indicates that, in my opinion, federal *urban* housing-related policies of all types considered together were:

1. *Very Effective* in generating high-level housing production, providing adequate housing finance, attracting private capital into housing, and creating good-quality new neighborhoods.
2. *Moderately Effective* in promoting overall economic stabilization, providing housing assistance for low-income and moderate-income households, and encouraging home ownership.
3. *Moderately Ineffective* in stabilizing housing production.
4. *Very Ineffective* in reducing housing costs and improving conditions in deteriorating inner-city neighborhoods.

ADDITIONAL CONCLUSIONS

Some additional conclusions can be drawn from this analysis and from other data not included here. First, neither the executive branch nor Congress has developed any clear, accurate, widely accepted conceptual "model" of how housing markets and the dynamics of urban development really work. This lack has resulted in the adoption of federal policies that generated theoretically foreseeable—but in fact unforeseen—adverse consequences. I believe the description of the "trickle-down" process presented in this article provides a basis for such a model.

Second, the level of total housing production crucially affects nearly all aspects of federal housing-related policy. When really high-level production is attained (as from 1968 through 1972), metropolitan area housing markets "loosen" as net additions to supply exceed the additional demand generated by population increases and rising incomes. Most of the newly built units are located in suburban areas, and their availability tends to draw moderate-income and upper-income households out of older and less desirable central-city and near-in suburban neighborhoods. This allows all income groups—including the poorest—to improve their housing, because it increases the housing choices available to them. But it may also result in abandonment of the worst-quality units, a spreading of concentrated poverty into adjacent neighborhoods, and falling property values in older areas. Hence it can be fiscally and socially damaging to central-city governments. Conversely, when total housing production remains moderately low, as it did in the early 1960s, metropolitan area housing markets tend to "tighten"; and when total production falls drastically—as it did in the 1940s—acute housing shortages may develop. Such conditions generate rising rents and home values (unless they are constrained by rent and price controls). These conditions aid central-city governments fiscally, but reduce the housing choices available to all income groups, especially the poorest.

Third, although high-level housing production aids low-income households through the "trickle-down" process, their housing conditions are improved to a much greater extent when large numbers of good-quality units (either new or existing) are made available to them through direct housing subsidies—as was done from 1968 through 1972. Consequently, providing adequate housing aid to such households requires a high level of direct federal housing subsidies, as well as high-level total housing production.

Fourth, housing production in the United States is much more strongly affected by indirect financial influences—especially federal monetary policies—than by federal policies aimed specifically at housing. Hence the federal government's key housing policies are still determined more by its attempts to influence the general level of prosperity than by its attempts to affect housing in particular. Moreover, improving housing conditions clearly has a lower national priority than maintaining general prosperity. The "natural" countercyclical forces in housing markets make the deliberate varying of housing production levels a relatively easy and effective way to help maintain general prosperity. Since (1) the vast majority of Americans are already well housed, (2) the poor as a group receive much greater benefits from high-level prosperity than from federal attempts to improve their housing, and (3) the housing industry exhibits amazing flexibility of output (though with some serious internal costs), at least some subordination of housing improvement to the maintenance of general prosperity seems reasonable.

Fifth, the most serious urban housing problems involve many factors other than physical dwelling units, including income poverty that prevents millions of households from being able to pay for decent housing; high-quality local housing standards that exclude the poor from living in more prosperous areas; destructive personal behavior patterns exhibited by a small percentage of the residents in concentrated poverty areas that make their neighborhoods undesirable places in which to live; and middle-class withdrawal that takes place in and near concentrated poverty areas. Experience proves that attempts to combat the most serious urban housing problems are certain to fail unless they respond effectively to these factors, as well as to needs for physical dwelling units.

However, governments at all levels (federal, state, and local) almost never adopt policies that adequately respond to *all* the relevant factors. Instead, they tend to make partial, selective policy responses focused mainly upon physical production or construction, rather than social factors, because the former are both more visible and much easier to control than the latter. Governments are not likely to take actions that would upset the basic institutional structures supporting the entire "trickle-down" process, or the established behavior patterns involved in that process. The "trickle-down" process depends institutionally upon fragmented local government jurisdictions, plus spatial separation of lower-income households (especially those containing minority-group members) from middle- and upper-income households. Hence federal policies rarely challenge these established arrangements—at least not intentionally. Another class of policies that governments usually avoid are those requiring considerable time between inputs (which cost money) and outputs (which generate political support); the timing of recurrent elections gives most political leaders short-run perspectives. These biases make federal policies far less effective in dealing with the needs of low-income households in areas of concentrated poverty than in dealing with the needs of middle-income and upper-income households on the urban periphery.

Finally, despite the intractability of urban "housing problems," a major change in federal housing-related policies in the mid-1960s greatly increased their effectiveness in dealing with those problems. Instead of continuing to measure the performance of federal housing-related policies solely in relation to what they had achieved in the past, the federal government reassessed its priorities and began measuring that performance against a quantified conception of "national needs." Moreover, that conception was based upon the almost utopian goal of completely eradicating substandard housing in the United States in a single decade. This radical shift of perspective was accompanied by a sharp escalation in the resources devoted to housing production, and outputs of both total housing units and directly subsidized units shot up so high that many unexpected adverse consequences began to appear. This led to the current pause in direct federal subsidies (and probably a slowdown in total production), which may be accompanied by another reassessment and a new perspective.

LOOKING TOWARD THE FUTURE

As was noted earlier, housing problems are closely interrelated with poverty, business cycles, the nation's financial structure, inner-city decay and crime, and many other social issues. Therefore, it is almost impossible to answer the question of what future federal housing-related policies should be without going into the nation's entire range of social and economic policies. The best I can do here is discuss what I believe federal policy ought to be toward certain key housing variables.

Total housing production. To meet the needs of future population growth plus replacement of deteriorated dwellings, annual total production of new units over the next decade ought to average much more than in the 1960s—say, about 2.6 million units including mobile homes. (It is inescapable and probably desirable, however, that housing production fluctuates countercyclically to at least some degree; thus this high average level would not be attained in every year.) Because most new units will be built in the suburbs, such high-level production could run into two serious problems. First, it will stimulate continued withdrawal of middle-class households from central cities. This will cause spreading abandonment and neighborhood decay unless we devise new methods of managing older neighborhoods and fund significant urban renewal efforts there. Second, rapid extension of suburban development is already generating tremendous resistance in the form of a burgeoning "anti-growth movement" all across the nation. Activists in this movement range from ecologists rightly worried about environmental damage to selfish suburbanites trying to evade their share of metropolitan costs and to exclude the poor. Because of their combined efforts, future urban growth will be accompanied by stricter public controls and regulations aimed at upgrading the quality of urban development. This is clearly desirable, but it will probably raise development costs and may make sustaining high-level production difficult.

Community development and land use planning. Instead of wastefully "throwing federal money" at tough domestic problems like these, the Nixon administration proposes to throw federal money at state and local governments and let them worry about such problems. This "hot potato" policy involves minimum federal guidelines and therefore only a small chance of achieving any national objectives across the country. It will, however, probably result in special statewide or regional regulation of proposed land development with large-area impacts—big shopping centers, airports, power plants, expressways, and environmentally fragile sites like beaches or wetlands. It would be desirable for the federal government at least to sponsor the formation of some model standards for setting ground rules within which private developers must operate and passing judgment on their proposed projects. But to achieve any national goals like forming well-planned, economically integrated "new cities," it will also be necessary either to maintain federal categorical subsidy programs, or to sneak tougher federal guidelines back into revenue sharing.

Providing housing for low-income and moderate-income households. The Nixon administration has proposed permanently cutting back the annual level of newly constructed subsidized units for low-income and moderate-income households. Instead, it would eventually assist such households through a nationwide housing allowance. Undoubtedly, we need to supplement the incomes of the poor through improved income maintenance and job creation programs even more than we need to improve their housing. Since a housing allowance is mainly a form of general income maintenance, it is sensible to adopt one as long as Congress will not adequately fund direct income maintenance. Moreover, providing aid to such households on the demand side (by *either* direct income maintenance or a housing allowance) would stimulate their greater use of the existing inventory of older housing, which is more efficient than building new units for them. Yet we also need to construct significant numbers of new units for such households. This would (a) expand the supply available to them and thereby avoid the inflationary effects of just increasing demand (as happened with Medicare); (b) allow some economic integration in new growth areas where 50 million more Americans will reside in the next 25 years, but where there is no existing inventory; and (c) create certain types of units not provided by private builders (such as large ones for big families). Thus, *both* demand-side and supply-side subsidies—funded at significant levels—are required to meet the housing needs of low-income and moderate-income households.

Combating inner-city decay. The greatest *urban* housing deficiencies are in the decaying environments of inner-city "crisis ghettos" and nearby areas. Paradoxically, I believe the intractable social problems of these areas cannot be resolved without creating many subsidized housing opportunities for poorer households in suburban and other nonpoverty neighborhoods. In the long run, reducing the poverty concentrations produced by the "trickle-down" process is essential to either upgrading existing inner-city populations or redeveloping their neighborhoods with "balanced mixtures" of households from all income groups. And such reduced concentration of the poor can occur only through their voluntary dispersal into housing scattered outside inner-city areas. Middle-class resistance to such a dispersal strategy is so powerful, however, that few politicians dare to confront it. In the absence of any significant start toward dispersal (which had begun on a small scale through the Section 235 and 236 programs stopped by the moratorium), the best federal policies toward such areas would include: improved income maintenance and job opportunities, rather than direct physical investment in housing; reform of the criminal justice system to produce at least a minimal degree of security in these areas; experimental testing of new methods of centrally managing entire inner-city neighborhoods to combat abandonment and decay; and requiring that a certain fraction of special revenue sharing funds be used to cope with inner-city problems.

Financing future housing. Two big factors in financing the recent high level of housing production have been the big shift of institutional investors into real estate from the stagnant stock market, and the requirement that savings and loan associations must invest most of their assets in mortgages. If the recent dual devaluation of the dollar stimulates a boom in U.S. manufacturing and agriculture, and thereby creates a rising stock market, institutional funds may not flow into housing so strongly. Also, if some financial reformers have their way, savings and loan associations will be freed from ties to mortgages in return for giving up rate ceilings on the interest they and banks can pay to depositors. These developments could prevent a return of the easy mortgage money conditions that stimulated record housing production from 1971 up to the tight-money period in late 1973. In that case, either future consumers would have to pay higher fractions of their incomes for housing, or production totals would remain at 1960s levels, causing possible market shortage conditions in many areas. Ironically, the best way to insure good financing for housing is to keep the U.S. economy in a near-recession condition—or at least to keep the stock market from rising. What federal policy should be in this thorny matter is hard to discern, since every alternative produces serious negative results. But in any case, considering these potential financing difficulties, the rising costs to builders of wages, material, and land, and the increasing environmentalist resistance to suburban growth, the chances are great that in the future housing will absorb a higher percentage of the average consumer's income than it does today.

Clearly, diagnosing the past is easier than prescribing for the future with confidence. Yet housing is not a pressing concern for most Americans because they are better housed than ever before. Hence it is not likely that future federal policies will place a very high priority on removing the ever-diminishing—but still large—complex of social conditions erroneously known as America's "housing problem."

6

Alternative Overall Strategies for Coping with the Nation's Housing Needs

BASIC STRATEGY ISSUES

What type of housing subsidies to use, how many units to subsidize, and who should occupy those units all depend upon what overall strategy the nation adopts regarding its housing needs.

1.   In the past, the nation's overall housing strategy has been arrived at almost accidentally. It has been the net result of many policy decisions made by different people without any single guiding plan. This analysis seeks to provide a framework for such a plan, or at least for understanding the implicit plans we are already following.

2.   Developing such strategies is a fantastically difficult task, because housing affects everyone in society in so many different ways. We have approached this task by dividing strategy formation into seven key issues, considering each separately, then examining their

---

This article originally appeared as Chapter 6 in *Federal Housing Subsidies: How Are They Working?* (Lexington, Mass.: Lexington Books, D. C. Heath and Company, 1973). It was part of a larger analysis of the entire federal housing subsidy program as it existed in late 1972. Therefore, the chapter contains some allusions to detailed discussions of other aspects of federal housing subsidies presented elsewhere in that volume. In most cases, I have included brief summaries of these other discussions in this revised version to make it relatively self-sufficient. Also, since the analysis was based upon data mainly from 1970 and 1971, some of the specific numbers are now outdated. However, both the basic approach and the major substantive assertions and conclusions contained herein still apply as of early 1975.

interrelations. These seven issues are set forth in Table 6-1. The following sections present our main conclusions about them.

NATIONAL PRIORITIES ISSUE

1. A preponderant majority of American households are well housed and are not suffering from any housing-related problems. Hence, they are not under any strong pressure to make housing a high priority national issue. In this respect, housing differs from such other issues as need for medical care, increased environmental pollution, rising property taxes, and inflation.

2. Nevertheless, for a relatively small—but absolutely large—

Table 6-1   Basic Issues in Formulating Alternative Overall Housing Strategies

- *National Priorities Issue*
  To what extent should the creation of additional housing units, or other provision of housing-oriented aid, be given high national priority in relation to other possible use of federal funds?

- *Income Maintenance Issue*
  To what extent should we devote resources used in helping the poor to improve their physical dwelling units, as opposed to raising their incomes so they can afford better housing, along with better everything else?

- *Spatial Location Issue*
  To what extent should we use housing subsidies to influence the spatial location of low- and moderate-income households in relation to other households? Specifically, should such subsidies be used to counteract the concentration of poverty caused by the "trickle-down" process of urban development?

- *Level of Insertion Issue*
  At what level in overall distribution of incomes should federal housing subsidies have their primary impact? Should they concentrate upon middle- and upper-income households, moderate-income households, low-income households, or some combination of income groups?

- *Total Cost Issue*
  How much money do we want to spend on all federal housing subsidies—direct and indirect—both annually and over the next few decades?

- *Administrative Centralization Issue*
  Should there be one agency responsible for allocating federal housing subsidies to specific locations within each metropolitan area? Or should such allocation result from the separate decisions of many different builders, sponsors, consumers, and other "actors" as it does now?

- *Form-of-Subsidy Issue*
  What specific forms of housing subsidies should be used, and to what degree?

Source: Real Estate Research Corporation.

group of Americans, inadequate housing is a critical deficiency. It is part of a cluster of deficiencies in their lives associated mainly with poverty. Creating the political support required in our majority-oriented system to help these households overcome their housing deficiencies is part of the fundamental social dilemma of removing poverty and poverty-related maladies in our society.

3.   Other than poverty in general, the potentially most serious housing-related problems are those connected with deteriorating neighborhood environments in older urban areas. Adequate public policy responses to problems of neighborhood decay must involve far more comprehensive actions than subsidies aimed at improving physical dwelling units. Yet significant amounts of housing subsidies will also be required.

4.   Housing is already receiving more total public assistance than most Americans realize. Few citizens or political leaders now consider either tax deductibility benefits or housing welfare benefits as comparable to direct housing subsidies. Nevertheless, we strongly believe they are indeed comparable.

The actual distribution of all housing subsidies among income groups varies strikingly from what most Americans believe it to be. Both the middle- and upper-income groups and poor households on welfare receive more public housing-related assistance than most people realize; whereas nonwelfare low-income households and all moderate-income households receive a far smaller share of all such assistance than is generally believed.

5.   The official national housing strategy stated in the Housing and Urban Development Act of 1968 called for creation of 26 million additional housing units in the decade from 1968 through 1978. This ten-year target was set high enough to simultaneously meet housing needs generated by population growth, replace all the physically substandard or overcrowded units in the nation as of 1968, and add enough units to vacancy to create a relatively "loose" overall housing market in most metropolitan areas. Thus, the official national strategy involved a long-range "flooding of the market" with new housing units, as related to future increases in demand. Metropolitan areas would become especially "flooded" with new units, because most physically substandard units were in rural areas, but their replacements would be in metropolitan areas, thus creating relative housing surpluses there. This basic strategy was designed to keep prices of the existing inventory from rising and to depress prices of older units so sharply that many would be abandoned and eventually demolished.

a.   The effectiveness of this strategy from 1968 through 1973 was illustrated by the high levels of total housing output attained in that period, especially from 1971 through 1973, when 8.2 million new units were built (including mobile homes)—an average of 2.7 million per year.

b. Other indications of the *initial* success of this strategy were the removal of about 700,000 units per year through demolitions and rising housing abandonment in many large cities. Such abandonment was indirectly caused by expansions of the total supply so large that even the poorest households could find alternative locations and therefore could move out of the worst-quality units.

6. However, effective pursuit of the nation's official housing production goals was disrupted in 1974 and 1975. This was caused by both a federal moratorium on direct housing subsidies for low- and moderate-income households, and general financial conditions adverse to large-scale mortgage availability. Total housing production levels fell sharply in 1974 and 1975 well below the high levels attained from 1971 through 1973, and directly subsidized units declined in number even more drastically. These decreases made it almost impossible for the nation to reach the official goal by the initial target date of 1978. Essentially, the federal government decided to place much lower social priority upon housing in 1974 and 1975 than in the preceding years, mainly as part of our struggle against inflation. This dramatic change proves that the social priority awarded to housing problems at any given moment depends upon how serious the nation believes those problems are *relative* to the other major problems it then perceives as most pressing. Hence, changes in the perceived intensity of other social problems can greatly alter the social priority given to housing problems, even when the absolute size and nature of housing problems has not changed at all.

THE INCOME MAINTENANCE ISSUE

1. Since most of the nation's *financial* housing needs arise from poverty rather than deficiencies in housing quality, one way to meet those needs would be with higher *general* income maintenance not specifically related to housing.

a. This would avoid the administrative red tape and difficulties associated with housing programs. It would also provide greater freedom for consumers to choose their own housing and set their own spending patterns.

b. Some critics of recent housing programs—and of other public assistance "tied" to specific commodities, such as food stamps—advocate such an "incomes policy" approach.

2. Categorical aid programs "tied" to specific goods or services —such as medical aid, food stamps, school lunch programs, and pub-

lic schools—have several important advantages compared to "pure" income maintenance.

    a. The American public is apparently willing to support greater total aid to the poor through several different "tied" programs than through direct income maintenance alone.

    • "Tied" aid programs give weight to *taxpayer* preferences about how low-income households ought to spend assistance funds, as well as to the preferences of those households. Taxpayers seem more willing to support aid going to things they believe are important than to general income support.

    • "Tied" aid programs also attract political support from industries that produce the goods or services involved.

    b. An expanded nationwide income maintenance program sufficient in scope and funding to replace existing "tied" aid programs would require a large administrative bureaucracy; hence, it might not reduce administrative costs of existing categorical programs.

    c. Adverse impacts upon work incentives are likely to be smaller for a set of diverse "tied" aid programs than for one large direct income maintenance program.

    d. Exploitation of the poor by unscrupulous operators of all types is easier when aid is provided directly in cash.

    e. Many objectives of "tied" aid programs are related to the specific goods or services produced, and might not result from larger income maintenance. Examples concerning housing are improving deteriorated neighborhoods, and encouraging home-ownership.

    f. When the industry producing some specific and widely used good or service does not respond rapidly by increasing the supply available to the poor, a rise in the general purchasing power of the poor will cause rapidly rising prices if there is no easily available substitute for that good or service. Rising prices are very likely to occur concerning housing if expanded income maintenance is enacted—as experience with welfare housing allowances clearly shows. Hence, much of the aid would be dissipated in windfall benefits to landlords, rather than improved housing quality for low-income occupants.

3. Moreover, the federal government is already spending large amounts for income maintenance of various types. It spent $46.9 billion for all cash grants in fiscal 1970, $73.9 billion in fiscal 1973, and an estimated $98.2 billion in fiscal 1975.

    a. This includes social security, retirement benefits, unemployment compensation, and aid to families with dependent children.

    b. The federal government also provided extensive funding to help people buy essentials other than housing. Federal outlays on such programs as Medicare, Medicaid, food stamps, and higher education student aid totaled $12.6 billion in fiscal 1970, $19.1 billion in fiscal 1973, and an estimated $28.7 billion in fiscal 1975.[1]

4. For the above reasons, we believe that some form of subsidy "tied" to housing should definitely be continued in the future, even if an expanded income maintenance program is adopted. However, we also believe the latter should have high priority as a means of combating poverty in general.

5. There are two basic forms of categorical subsidies "tied" to housing: direct supply expansion and direct demand expansion.

a. *Direct supply expansion subsidies* tie the subsidy to creation of a new or rehabilitated housing unit, although they may also add to demand at the same time. They initially flow through the housing production industry and benefit consumers by (1) reducing the occupancy cost of those living in the new units, and (2) adding to the total supply, thereby putting downward pressure on the prices of all existing units.

● These subsidies require complex administration because they deal with *both* housing suppliers and housing consumers.

● Examples of direct supply expansion subsidies are the Section 235 and Section 236 programs, the conventional and turnkey public housing programs, and the rent supplement new construction program.

b. *Direct demand expansion subsidies* tie the subsidy to a household, which then uses "normal" housing markets to meet its needs. They initially flow through consumer households, benefiting their recipients through reduced occupancy costs.

● These subsidies affect total housing supply indirectly by raising prices and thereby calling forth more total output in the long run (including better maintenance of existing units).

● These subsidies are much easier to administer than direct supply expansion subsidies if they do not require any periodic checks on the quality of housing occupied by the recipients. If such checks are required, they are probably almost as hard to administer as direct supply-oriented subsidies, though they can be put into effect faster.

● Examples of direct demand expansion subsidies are the income tax deductibility subsidy, a housing allowance paid to the occupants, and the public housing leasing subsidy applied to existing units.

c. Two key factors relevant to determining which of these

---

[1] Barry M. Blechman, Edward M. Gramlich, and Robert W. Hartman, *Setting National Priorities: The 1975 Budget* (Washington, D.C., 1974), p. 168.

forms of categorical aid to housing is superior in a given situation are the degree of housing shortage for low-income households, and the likely responsiveness of the housing supply industry to greater demand by low-income households.

- Where there is a marked shortage of units available to low-income households and a relatively unresponsive housing supply industry, large-scale use of direct demand expansion subsidies will produce rapidly rising prices without much improvement in housing quality for those aided. This will injure other households not receiving the aid by raising their prices too.

- Where there is an ample supply of existing housing units (as indicated by relatively high vacancy or abandonment rates) but maintenance is poor because of low cash flows to owners, then direct demand expansion subsidies can increase effective use of the existing inventory without dissipating too much aid as rising prices.

- Thus, local housing market conditions should have an important influence upon which form of housing related categorical assistance is used in any specific area.

d.   Another important consideration in selecting which type of housing subsidy to use is that direct supply expansion subsidies can involve *new construction* of units for low- and moderate-income households; whereas direct demand expansion subsidies probably cannot.

- Congress would probably not support direct demand expansion housing subsidies with large enough per-unit amounts to allow low- and moderate-income households to occupy brand new units—unless those subsidies were highly restricted to a few areas. The total cost of making such large per-unit subsidies available to *all* income eligible households would be too great.

- Thus, only direct supply-expansion subsidies can provide the five major benefits of *building new units for low- and moderate-income households* rather than improving their ability to pay for existing units. The key advantages of such newly built units are as follows:

  - They expand the total housing supply so as to keep housing prices from rising. In contrast, subsidies only in the form of income supplements or housing allowances to low- and moderate-income households tend to raise housing prices, even if they ultimately generate additional new housing construction.

  - They can achieve some economic integration in new-growth areas, where only newly built units are available.

• They can provide added numbers of certain types of units not in the existing inventory and not likely to be created through direct demand expansion subsidies, but needed by low-income households. These include units with many bedrooms and those especially designed for the elderly.

• They are more effective in stimulating increased activity in the construction industry, since very little of their impact is dissipated as higher prices of existing housing units.

• They can provide more dramatic, large-scale upgrading of older deteriorated areas than rehabilitation or upgrading of the existing stock. New construction can help create a wholly new environment in such areas, or demonstrate strong social concern for persons residing there.

● Our conclusions and recommendations concerning the use of new-construction-oriented subsidies vs. use of a housing allowance are as follows:

• The housing program mix should contain both new-construction-oriented subsidies and subsidies oriented toward more intensive use of the existing inventory.

• Although the program mix used in 1972 did contain both types, emphasis had up to then been much stronger on the new-construction-oriented subsidies. Therefore, it was then more desirable to move toward relatively greater emphasis upon subsidies using existing units. This could have been done either by expanding the latter more than the former, or contracting the latter less than the former, depending upon what is determined about the overall scale of housing subsidies.

• Already utilized subsidy programs capable of performing this function should have been given relatively high priority for expansion—especially the public housing leasing program. (However, the use of new-construction-oriented subsidies dropped to a very low level during 1974; so both types would have to be expanded as of 1975 in order to achieve a proper balance between them.)

• Experiments testing a housing allowance program that are underway in 1975 should be continued, and given high priority attention. However, no full-scale version of such a program should be undertaken until more is known about its likely effects, if then. Past experience with welfare rent allowances shows that price rises are likely to absorb such allowances with little improvement in housing quality if no provisions are made to expand the supply directly available to the low-income households concerned.

• Experiments should also be conducted to test a new program allowing low- and moderate-income households to rent single-family homes repossessed by FHA.

• Adequate funds should be made available to provide counseling services for households using all these subsidies.

• Requirements for specific local government approval prior to use of the public housing leasing program (or the later Section 8 program) should be removed. Central-city public housing authorities and state housing agencies should be empowered to lease units within their own metropolitan areas but outside central city boundaries, so long as they do not concentrate many such units together.

• Although any final decision should be postponed until the results of the above described experiments are obtained, we do not now believe that a nationwide housing allowance program providing assistance to all households eligible on the basis of low income alone would be desirable for the following basic reasons:

— Most of the money spent in such a program would really be general income maintenance, not housing assistance. We believe the proper vehicle for such general assistance is an expanded income maintenance program.

— Adoption of a nationwide housing allowance might cause Congress to reduce construction-oriented subsidies too far on the grounds that the nation's housing needs were "adequately taken care of" by the housing allowance. We believe there will continue to be a strong need for large-scale subsidies of newly built units, for the reasons set forth above.

— The bigger the housing allowance program, the greater the upward pressure on the prices and rents of existing units. We believe it would be desirable to confine such a program to areas where the existing stock needs such a "shot in the arm" because of high vacancy rates, rather than creating such inflationary pressure throughout the nation.

THE SPATIAL LOCATION ISSUE

1. The present urban development process inherently generates major problems in older central-city neighborhoods by concentrating large numbers of low-income households there. It also separates such households from the rapidly expanding economic opportunities caused by population and economic growth in suburban areas.

a. An important aspect of any overall housing strategy is formulating and evaluating alternative means of coping with these dual deficiencies. We believe the major alternative choices facing society about *where within metropolitan areas* to invest future resources for this purpose can be summarized in terms of seven different options for locational emphasis. These are shown in Table 6-2.

b. Suburban dominance of both population and economic growth is almost sure to continue in the near future. Therefore, all

Table 6-2   Alternative Options Concerning the Location and Intensity of Future Urban Development Activities Responsive to Public Policies and Funding

Short Title	Brief Description in Terms of Key Variables
1. Contained Decay	Continued exclusion of low- and moderate-income households from most suburbs; no large-scale investment of either income maintenance or physical improvements in inner-city decaying areas.
2. Noncapital Enrichment Only	Continued exclusion and no large-scale investment in physical inner-city improvements, but adoption of large-scale income maintenance and related social service delivery programs.
3. All-Out Enrichment Only	Continued exclusion, but large-scale investment in both physical improvement and income maintenance and other social service delivery systems in inner-city decaying areas.
4. Decay Plus Dispersal	No major investment in inner-city areas, but adoption of major program to provide low- and moderate-income housing on sites throughout metropolitan areas outside of inner-city decaying areas.
5. Noncapital Enrichment Plus Dispersal	Large-scale income maintenance and social service delivery programs in inner-city decaying areas, plus major dispersal programs, but no physical improvement of inner-city decaying areas.
6. Noncapital Enrichment, Dispersal, and Delayed Physical Redevelopment	Same as (5) above, except major physical improvement programs launched in inner-city decaying areas *after* interim period while values decline there, making acquisition less costly.
7. All-Out Enrichment Plus Dispersal and as Rapid Physical Redevelopment as Possible	Combines large-scale income maintenance and social service delivery in inner-city decaying areas, major dispersal programs in remainder of metropolitan areas, and gradual physical improvement of inner-city areas launched at same time as noncapital enrichment, proceeding as fast as possible.

Source: Real Estate Research Corporation.

seven of these options assume continued major investment of both public and private resources in all types of suburban facilities and activities.

c. The main variables among these options concern the degree to which each will involve:

- Large-scale income maintenance and social service delivery programs aiding inner-city residents (*noncapital enrichment*).

- Large-scale physical capital investment programs upgrading inner-city neighborhoods (the second ingredient in *all-out enrichment*).

- Major programs aimed at dispersing low- and moderate-income households throughout each metropolitan area—or at least in many locations outside areas where they are now concentrated, including suburban locations.

d. These alternatives incorporate six of the eight combinations possible if each variable is conceived of as having two potential values: yes or no. The two combinations omitted as unlikely are those calling for major physical renewal of inner-city decaying areas without any large income maintenance or social service delivery programs there.

2. We believe present policies (as of early 1975) amount to something between the *contained decay* and *noncapital enrichment only* options. Some income maintenance and social service delivery are now going into inner-city decaying areas—although not enough to be full-scale noncapital enrichment. There is also very little physical improvement there, or dispersal elsewhere.

a. Key factors to consider in deciding which of these options society should choose include the following:

- Continued growth of the central-city low-income population, plus more abandonment of neighborhoods in some cities, will cause a constant future expansion of urban decay in older central cities if present policies remain unchanged. Hence, "Contained Decay" really means constantly expanding decay.

- Continued concentration of poverty in older central-city neighborhoods will undermine the effectiveness of any physical improvements made there. Thus, we believe some type of dispersal policy is essential to any long-range upgrading of the quality of life in these areas.

- Dispersal into new growth suburban areas requires subsidies that allow low- and moderate-income occupancy of brand new units. Therefore, *the greater the social policy emphasis on dispersal as part of any strategy, the more important the role of new construction-oriented housing subsidies.*

• Housing subsidies alone will probably not cause much direct outward movement from inner-city poverty areas into dispersed locations without specific incentives tied to such movement.

• Strictly voluntary dispersal of at least some low- and moderate-income households throughout each metropolitan area would provide the following benefits:

• Easier access of such households to expanding suburban job opportunities.

• Greater opportunities for such households to upgrade themselves by escaping from the destructive environment of concentrated poverty areas.

• Improved quality education for the children from such households.

• A higher probability that the nation would reach its official housing goal of six million additional subsidized units by 1978 (though the probability would still be rather low as of 1975). Achievement of that goal would require building many such units on vacant suburban land.

• Fairer geographic distribution of the fiscal and social costs of dealing with metropolitan-area poverty. These costs are now disproportionately loaded onto central-city residents.

• A reduced probability that the United States will develop two separate and unequal societies within its metropolitan areas, as feared by the National Advisory Commission on Civil Disorders (the "Kerner Commission").

• Large-scale physical improvement of inner-city decaying areas would be extremely expensive, unless it was delayed until land prices fell very low because of advanced abandonment, or some type of low-cost public acquisition process was developed.

Existing repossession laws need to be radically changed, at least as applied to certain designated decaying areas. Public authorities need to be able to occupy physically vacant units with payment delinquencies almost immediately; otherwise, vandals render them useless for shelter purposes.

• Some new mechanism for *neighborhood management* is needed to provide for a more orderly quality of life in inner-city decaying areas, whatever future strategy is adopted toward them. These areas contain fragmented property ownership, plus very low incomes, plus very low levels of personal and physical security. As a result, social and personal problems spillover from one household or housing unit to others nearby. No local resources are available to respond with either stronger social controls or compensating investments. This is what causes abandonment to spread from dilapidated units that deserve to be demolished to sound units nearby that could be preserved and furnish good housing to those who need it.

• *The most crucial single improvement in urban affairs would be effective local surveillance or other arrangements providing high level personal and property security in these decaying urban neighborhoods.* This in turn requires radical reform in the existing system of criminal justice, which simply does not work in such areas.

3. Specific uses of housing subsidies that might encourage dispersal include spreading out subsidy allocations over more communities in each metropolitan area, tying other federal aids to acceptance of subsidized housing, providing greater counseling to inner-city households to aid them in finding dispersed housing, and creating "impact" subsidies for communities accepting low- and moderate-income households.

LEVEL OF INSERTION ISSUE

1. Overall housing strategies can be differentiated by the *levels* in the income distribution at which they insert both new housing units and housing subsidy aids. For example, conventional public housing involves the insertion of some new units at a low level in the income distribution by focusing housing subsidies there.

2. The present overall structure of housing laws, regulations, and subsidies in the United States encourages predominantly middle- and upper-level insertion of new housing units. This occurs both because legally enforced high quality standards prohibit low-cost new units (except mobile homes) and because the largest housing subsidy—the income tax deductibility subsidy—goes mainly to middle- and upper-income homeowning households.

    a. It is not very likely that this built-in bias towards relatively high level insertion will be altered in the near future. Both high quality laws and the income tax deductibility subsidy are probably too popular to be significantly changed, since about 64 percent of all American households own their own homes.

    b. Whenever direct housing subsidies supporting low- and moderate-level insertion are at low funding levels (as was always the case until about 1965, and became so again in 1974 and 1975), the primary source of housing for low- and moderate-income households is the "trickle-down" process. The basic built-in bias towards middle- and upper-level insertion further reinforces the dominance of the "trickle-down" process.

Although about 2.3 million directly subsidized housing units had been created in the United States by the end of 1971, there were about 5.9 million households in metropolitan areas in 1970 with incomes low enough to be officially classified as "poor" (including both families and unrelated individuals). Even excluding all moderate-income households, it is therefore clear that the "trickle-down" process is still the dominant source of housing for most low-income households.

3.   The net cost/benefit "efficiency" of any housing subsidy strategy is affected by the levels of insertion it emphasizes, both directly and through the "chains of movement" generated by every new housing unit created.

a.   New units inserted at relatively high levels in the income distribution start longer "chains of movement" than those inserted lower. But those chains affect a lower percentage of low- and moderate-income households.

• Expensive new homes start chains in which an average of as many as 3.8 households upgrade their housing. But only about ten percent of those households have low incomes—based on the sketchy data compiled on this subject to date.[2]

• Direct housing subsidies that cause low- and moderate-income level insertions start shorter chains—probably averaging around 2.0 households—but nearly all households involved have low and moderate incomes.

b.   Traditionally, high level insertion has been considered a far less expensive method of providing housing for the relatively poor —in terms of costs to the public—than lower level insertion created by direct housing subsidies, since high level insertion appeared to have no subsidy costs. But when both indirect subsidy costs (mainly the income tax deductibility subsidy) and chains of movement are taken into account, directly subsidized lower level insertion can be just as efficient in terms of the total subsidy cost per low- and moderate-income household aided. Moreover, lower level insertion allows those households to live in brand new units rather than older ones.

c.   On the other hand, middle-level insertion without direct subsidies benefits more *total households* at all income levels per dollar of subsidy cost than either high level or low level insertion.

d.   To illustrate these variations, we have set forth in Table 6-3 some rough estimates based upon plausible assumptions about

---

[2] John B. Lansing, Charles Wade Clifton, and James N. Morgan, *New Homes and Poor People* (Ann Arbor: Institute for Social Research of the University of Michigan, 1969).

Table 6-3 Estimated Comparative Total Subsidy Costs per Household Aided by Unit Types, Taking Account of all Subsidies and Moves (1972 Cost Levels and Dollars)

Type of New Housing Unit	Development and Construction Cost	Forms of Subsidy Involved: Direct	Forms of Subsidy Involved: Indirect	Estimated Average Annual Subsidy Size Per Unit*: Direct	Estimated Average Annual Subsidy Size Per Unit*: Indirect	Total Number of Moves**	Estimated Percentage of Moving Households with: Low Incomes	Estimated Percentage of Moving Households with: Moderate Incomes	Total Subsidy Cost Per Household Aided: For All Households Aided	Total Subsidy Cost Per Household Aided: Low- and Moderate-Income Households Only	Total Subsidy Cost Per Household Aided: Low-Income Households Only
1. Section 235 New*	$21,000	Interest Reduction	Tax Deductibility	$731	$370	3.0	16.7%	83.3%	$367	$367	$2,202
2. Section 236 New*	$17,500	Interest Reduction	Accelerated Depreciation	$765	$127	2.0	25.0%	75.0%	$446	$446	$1,784
3. Section 236 New* plus Rent Supplement	$17,500	Interest Reduction and Income Aid	Accelerated Depreciation	$1,773	$127	2.0	100.0%	—	$950	$950	$950
4. Public Housing—Conventional plus Operating Cost Subsidy	$20,000	Debt Service Payment plus Income Aid	Reduced Property Tax	$1,316	$300	2.0	100.0%	—	$808	$808	$803
5. Public Housing Leasing	—	Leased Fee Payments	None	$1,056	—	2.0	100.0%	—	$528	$528	$528
6. Nondirectly—Subsidized Unit, New and Owner-Occupied	$24,000	None	Tax Deductibility	—	$326	3.0	10.0%	25.0%	$109	$310	$1,087
7. Same as above	$33,000	None	Tax Deductibility	—	$573	3.8	10.0%	26.3%	$151	$415	$1,508
8. Same as above	$60,000	None	Tax Deductibility	—	$1,629	3.5	10.0%	28.6%	$465	$1,206	$4,654

* Maximum interest subsidy assumed. * Average per year over first seven years. ** Including household moving into new unit.

Sources: Real Estate Research Corporation; movement chain data drawn from several studies.

several different types of housing units inserted at different levels, taking into account all subsidies and chains of movements.

4. We have formulated seven alternative options concerning the appropriate mixture of income maintenance and housing production choices, with variations concerning the following key variables:

a. The relative emphasis placed upon "pure" income maintenance, direct demand-expanding housing subsidies (presumably some type of housing allowance), and direct supply-expanding housing subsidies (especially those involving new construction).

b. The levels of insertion where most new housing units are placed. These seven strategy choices are depicted in Table 6-4.

Table 6-4 Alternative Options Concerning the Proper Mixture of Income Maintenance and Housing Subsidies, Types of Housing Subsidies, and the Levels of Their Insertion

Short Title	Brief Description
1. "Trickle-Down" Plus Minimal Anti-Poverty	High level insertion with only tax deductibility subsidies, complete reliance on "trickle-down" to house poor, very little income maintenance directly to poor.
2. Pure Anti-Poverty	High level housing insertion as in (1) above, but massive income maintenance to poor at bottom of the income distribution.
3. Accelerated "Trickle-Down"	Maximized high level insertion with "normal" quantities of housing units produced, augmented by favorable monetary and fiscal policies; *both* large-scale income maintenance and a large-scale housing allowance program to counteract poverty; no low level insertion of *new* directly subsidized housing.
4. Accelerated "Trickle-Down" Marginally Augmented	Same as (3), but with *some* insertion of *new* directly subsidized housing to achieve limited dispersal and other objectives best served by such new construction.
5. All-Out New Construction With Minimal Anti-Poverty	Large-scale insertion of new housing at all levels similar to (6), but very little emphasis upon income maintenance, and no housing allowance.
6. All-Out New Construction Plus Anti-Poverty	*Large-scale* insertion of *new* housing units at *all* levels (high, middle, moderate, and low) through relevant indirect and direct subsidies. No housing allowance, but big income maintenance.
7. Mixed Options	Significant insertion of new housing units at all levels using appropriate subsidies though less massive than in (6) above. Income maintenance at significant scale, plus some use of housing allowance, but not on nationwide basis.

Source: Real Estate Research Corporation.

5.   These choices represent only seven of the twelve logically possible combinations if income maintenance and housing allowances are each conceived of as having two potential values (yes or no) and housing construction three values (high level only, high level plus some at other levels, or high level plus large amounts at other levels). Most of the five combinations we omitted seem implausible because they involve no income maintenance. All seven choices are assumed to continue major emphasis upon high level insertion of new units because of the built-in bias described above.

6.   We believe the situation in the United States in 1971 and 1972 could most accurately be characterized as lying somewhere between options five and six. It was marked by large-scale insertion of new units at all levels, with both indirect and direct subsidies, relatively modest income maintenance, and no housing allowance program per se (although several then-existing subsidies had some of the qualities of a housing allowance).

7.   By 1974, the housing situation in the United States had radically changed to resemble none of the seven alternative options shown on the accompanying chart. As a result of HUD's moratorium on new directly subsidized units, starts of such units fell to 47,000 in 1974—a drop of 89 percent below the peak level of 433,480 in 1971. At the same time, conditions in nondirectly subsidized housing markets shifted dramatically, mainly because of an acute shortage of mortgage funds throughout most of 1974. So total housing starts of all types fell 35 percent from 2.638 million in 1973 to 1.724 million in 1974 (including 1.352 million conventionally constructed units and 0.371 million mobile homes). This situation differs from all the strategy options on the chart because it embodies relatively low-level total housing production in comparison with the official national goal of 2.600 million new units per year (as adopted in the Housing and Urban Development Act of 1968). In contrast, *all strategies designed to help "solve" the nation's key housing problems necessarily involve relatively high-level total housing production.* High annual production is essential so the total supply of housing will expand fast enough to keep housing prices from rising rapidly. Then the average cost of housing occupancy will rise more slowly than consumer incomes, and nearly all households will have greater housing choices available to them. In contrast, when total annual production is low in relation to the growth of demand, the cost of occupying both new and existing units tends to rise faster than consumer incomes. This narrows the housing choices available to most households, especially the poorest, thereby intensifying the nation's housing problems rather than helping "solve" them.

8. Key factors to consider in deciding which of the options in Table 6-4 society should choose include the following:

a. Experience indicates that sole reliance upon the "trickle-down" process to provide adequate housing for the poor does not produce satisfactory results. It generates excessive concentrations of poverty in older inner-city areas and takes too long to get housing down to the poorest households.

b. Experience also indicates that combating poverty through programs that isolate assistance to the poor from assistance to more affluent citizens usually causes Congress to hold down the assistance to the poor—even though they need it most. This indicates that income maintenance alone may not be an adequate anti-poverty weapon.

c. Major stimulation of the demand for housing at low- and moderate-income levels through either income maintenance or housing allowances could produce excessive increases in housing prices and rents if not accompanied by a significant amount of new construction inserted at those same levels.

d. The factors cited above indicate that Options 1, 2, and 3 on Table 6-4 ("Trickle-Down" Plus Minimal Anti-Poverty, Pure Anti-Poverty, and Accelerated "Trickle-Down") are not very desirable.

THE TOTAL COST ISSUE

1. The housing subsidy programs used from 1968 through 1973 involved very large annual expenditures as well as legally enforceable long-term commitments to future spending over as many as forty years. How much should the nation spend on these or other housing-related programs?

a. This broad question can best be considered by examining six specific issues, which are set forth in Table 6-5 as additional questions.

b. The results of our efforts to answer these questions are presented below.

2. We believe future costs of housing subsidy programs and all other programs should be discounted before being compared with present dollars or with other future costs. This is consistent both with prevailing investment practices in the private sector and with congressional tendencies to weight near-future benefits more heavily than distant-future costs.

a. The reality of congressional discounting is illustrated by the use of interest reduction subsidies rather than capital grants. The

Table 6-5   Key Questions Regarding the Total Amount That the Nation "Ought to" Spend on Housing and Housing Subsidies

—Should future dollars be discounted before being compared with present dollars?

—Is the important cost the one that enters the federal budget, or the one that measures the total amount of resources actually consumed by housing?

—Is the important cost the annual level of spending, or the total lifetime amount, or some other measure?

—Can total lifetime costs be accurately forecast for programs that have many variable-cost features and last up to forty years?

—Is future spending that is required by contractual arrangements of greater significance than future spending that is likely to occur but is not contractually required?

—With what should total spending on housing subsidies, however calculated, be compared to determine whether it is a large or small amount? Should it be compared to gross national product, or the federal budget, or specific subsidies for other activities, or what?

$624 per year rent saving from the interest reduction subsidy on a $17,000 Section 236 unit has a "lifetime" cost of $24,978 if the maximum subsidy lasts for forty years. The same reduction in rents could be produced by an initial $9,092 capital grant with a market rate mortgage for the remaining cost—or a "lifetime" subsidy cost only 36 percent as large. However, the interest rate reduction subsidy produces far more units *immediately* per million dollars spent: 1,602 vs. 110 for capital grants. Although the capital grant approach would *eventually* produce more units over forty years of one-million-dollars-per-year spending (4,400 vs. 1,602), it would take 14.5 years to build as many units as the interest rate subsidy provided in the first year. Congress has consistently rejected the capital grant approach in favor of interest reduction subsidies because Congress implicitly discounts future costs and benefits in relation to present ones—as we believe it should. Capital grants also produce a much larger immediate budgetary impact per unit than interest reduction subsidies, but that is another way of saying the same thing as above.

   b.   Simply "running out" program costs over forty years, and then adding up the results without discounting, produces estimates of future costs (or benefits) that are mistakenly perceived as equivalent in importance and probability of occurrence to the same number of current dollars. This causes false impressions about the real costs involved. It tends to create "alarmist" views of housing programs as compared to other programs for which no such future estimates are made.

Almost all significant programs have alarming sounding total costs if their present annual levels are projected forward over forty years and then added without discounting. For example, Table 6-6 shows the total forty-year cost of various federal programs calculated as though their annual levels remained exactly the same as in 1972 for the next forty years. Because inflation will raise those annual levels in the future, the forty-year totals will actually be much larger than the figures in Table 6-6.

c. Discounting also allows more meaningful comparisons of programs with very different future timing of costs and benefits.

d. It is not clear whether the most appropriate discount rate is (1) the federal borrowing rate, (2) the marginal private rate of return representing what taxpayers sacrifice, or (3) the ten percent calculation rate now required by the Office of Management and Budget (when discounting is used). We believe the last rate is too high and suggest calculations using both the first two for comparison.

3. Costs that do not appear in the federal budget directly—but still must be paid by taxpayers—should certainly be included in calculating total subsidy costs. Moreover, it is desirable to distinguish between *income transfers* and *real consumption of resources* in certain types of calculations (although we have not done so in this article).

a. We believe it would be extremely misleading to ignore non-budgetary subsidy costs, especially since they form nearly two-thirds of all housing subsidy costs.

b. When a new Section 236 unit costing $17,500 was built, the total *subsidy cost* was $892 per year (including both interest rate reduction and accelerated depreciation subsidies), but the total *resource cost* of creating the unit was $17,500. We believe both types of cost should be taken into account, but for different purposes.

● The total resource cost should be used in determining whether sufficient capital is available to meet programmed production, what the employment effects will be, and whether

Table 6-6 Projected 40-Year Costs of Selected Federal Nonhousing Programs

Program	1972 Annual Spending— Billions	Projected 40-Year Total at That Level— Billions
Defense	$75.8	$3,032.0
Net Interest on Debt	$14.4	$ 576.0
Medicare and Medicaid	$12.4	$ 496.0

Sources: Real Estate Corporation projections.

reaching any specific production target is likely to produce inflationary impacts.

• The subsidy cost should be considered when weighing the cost of alternative subsidy programs to achieve a given housing production goal. However, most subsidies represent income transfers from one group to another, rather than real absorptions of resources.

4. Both annual and "lifetime" costs should be considered in making housing subsidy decisions. However, it is very difficult to forecast "lifetime" costs of many recent federal housing subsidies, or a housing allowance, because of uncertainties inherent in their design.

Many recent federal housing subsidies, and others proposed, are *income "gap" tied*. That means the amount of subsidy paid to each household depends upon the size of the "gap" between some "standard" fraction of the household's income and the cost of occupying the housing unit concerned. An example is a housing allowance. The other major form of housing subsidy is *debt tied*. The size of each such subsidy is related to the size of the debt incurred in initially constructing the housing unit concerned. Income "gap" tied subsidies have several specific advantages and disadvantages as compared with debt tied subsidies (Table 6-7). The future size of all income "gap" tied subsidies depends upon how fast consumer incomes rise in relation to housing costs. When consumer incomes rise faster, the size of the "gap" declines, and therefore the annual subsidy amount falls too. But when housing costs rise faster, the size of the "gap" rises, and so does the annual subsidy amount. Yet it is extremely difficult to forecast future rates of increase of both consumer incomes and housing costs as far ahead as the thirty to forty years for which legal commitments are made in these subsidy programs.

5. We believe it is unrealistic to regard *contractual* commitments for future spending as somehow more binding than *noncontractual* commitments which, once made, would be extremely difficult to eliminate for political reasons. For example, once a nationwide housing allowance program was adopted, it would be very difficult politically to halt it—even though no contractual commitments beyond one year would be involved. Hence, it is just as important to examine future costs of such a program over a long period as it is to examine those contractually required by mortgage loans.

6. How much public money a nation "ought to" spend on housing and housing subsidies altogether is a relative question. The answer depends in part upon its general standard of living, the importance of housing in the lives of citizens, and what it is spending on other activities or services of comparable importance. Perspective on this ques-

Table 6-7 Relative Advantages and Disadvantages of Income "Gap" Tied Housing Subsidies (Compared with Debt Tied Subsidies)

Advantages	Disadvantages
—They focus benefits more strongly on low-income households.	—They have no built-in cost limits per household.
—At the program scale required to provide aid for *every* eligible household, they involve lower subsidy costs per household aided.	—They do not have declining real costs per household as inflation increases over time.
—They involve no risk of federal involvement in repossession.	—They have no predetermined end-point in time; hence once established, they are likely to become permanent (like welfare).
	—They create little incentive for the household or the housing supplier to economize on housing costs.
	—They would probably require continuous administrative monitoring of both household income and housing unit quality.
	—They could have inflationary impact upon housing prices.
	—Much of the money spent on them would simply increase the general purchasing power of the recipients, rather than improve their housing quality per se.

tion is best obtained by making several different comparisons, as shown below.

a. Regarding total resource costs expended on housing, the share of gross national product devoted to housing in the recent past has not been as large as in earlier parts of the post–World War II period. The highest modern share of GNP devoted to housing was 5.5 percent in 1950. From 1965 through 1974, the share ranged from a low of 3.2 percent (in 1967) to a high of 4.7 percent (in 1972).

b. Other industrialized nations spend as much or more of their gross national product on housing as the United States. Fractions of gross national product spent on housing in the highest-fraction and lowest-fraction years from 1956 to 1966 for six industrialized nations are shown in Table 6-8.

c. The capital resources required to meet present national housing goals could be supplied without placing excessive strain

Table 6-8   Percentage of Gross National Product Spent on Housing Between 1956 and 1966 in Six Nations

Nation	Highest Year	Lowest Year
United States	5.5%	3.4%
West Germany	5.9%	4.8%
Sweden	5.9%	5.1%
Netherlands	5.2%	3.8%
France	6.7%	4.3%
United Kingdom	3.7%	2.8%

Source: Howard R. Moskof, "Foreign Housing Subsidy Systems: Alternative Approaches," paper submitted to Subcommittee on Housing Panels, House Committee on Banking and Currency, 92nd Congress.

on the economy. The *Second Annual Report on National Housing Goals* estimates that the total nonland capital could be supplied by devoting a maximum of 4.3 percent of gross national product to housing in the period from 1970 through 1978, and only 3.79 percent in 1978. This is more than the average in recent years, but far less than the postwar high in 1950, and also less than in either 1972 or 1973 (the two highest housing production years in U.S. history).

• Determining whether the other resources required—such as labor, construction materials, and land—could be supplied without inflationary effects is beyond the scope of this study.

• However, it is our general opinion that present national housing goals cannot now be met by 1978. This inability is not caused by resource constraints, but by the low levels of housing production in 1974 and 1975, due mainly to adverse financial conditions.

7.   Comparison of federal housing subsidies with other than federal subsidies provides useful perspective concerning how much should be spent on housing subsidies. Table 6-9 sets forth estimates of all federal subsidies for fiscal 1970 and fiscal 1975 made by the staff of the Joint Economic Committee of Congress in its report, *Federal Subsidy Programs*, dated October 18, 1974.

a.   This table includes allowances for savings of imputed rent by homeowners, which amounted to $3.0 billion in fiscal 1970 and $3.9 billion in fiscal 1975.

b.   According to these data, total federal subsidies in fiscal 1970 were $64.4 billion, equivalent to around 6.7 percent of gross national product. In fiscal 1975, total federal subsidies were $95.1 billion, or about 6.6 percent of gross national product.

c.   Housing subsidies totaled $11.7 billion in fiscal 1970, and $15.7 billion in fiscal 1975. These totals amounted to 18.2 percent

Table 6-9 Total Federal Subsidy Costs, Fiscal 1970 and 1975 (in billions of dollars)

Area of Activity	Cash Payment Subsidies		Tax Subsidies		Credit Subsidies		Benefit-in-kind Subsidies		Total Order of Magnitude	
	1970	1975	1970	1975	1970	1975	1970	1975	1970	1975
1. Agriculture	4.4	0.6	0.9	1.1	0.4	0.7	—	—	5.7	2.5
2. Food	—	—	—	—	—	—	1.5	5.9	1.5	5.9
3. Health	0.8	0.6	3.2	5.8	—	—	4.6	10.2	8.6	16.6
4. Manpower	2.0	3.3	0.6	0.7	—	—	0.1	0.1	2.6	4.1
5. Education	1.9	5.0	0.8	1.0	0.1	0.1	0.4	0.4	3.2	6.5
6. International	0.1	—	0.3	1.5	0.6	0.9	—	—	1.0	2.4
7. Housing	0.1	1.7	8.7	12.9	3.0	1.1	—	—	11.7	15.7
8. Natural Resources	0.1	0.1	2.0	4.1	—	—	0.1	0.1	2.1	4.4
9. Transportation	0.3	0.6	—	0.1	—	—	0.2	1.7	0.5	2.3
10. Commerce	2.0	0.3	14.1	19.3	0.1	—	1.8	1.9	18.0	21.5
11. Other	—	—	9.4	13.1	0.1	0.1	—	—	9.5	13.2
Total Order of Magnitude*	11.6	12.3	39.9	59.7	4.1	2.9	8.8	20.2	64.4	95.1

Source: Joint Economic Committee, U.S. Congress, *Federal Subsidy Programs* (Washington, D.C.: October 18, 1974), page 5.
* Individual items may not add to totals due to rounding error.

and 16.5 percent of all federal subsidies respectively in those years. Neither total includes welfare rent allowances, which were not defined as subsidies in this study. Their inclusion would raise the total for each year by at least $3.0 billion. Even without this inclusion, housing subsidies (as defined by this report) exceeded one percent of gross national product in both years.

d. Housing ranked second among major areas of activity in total size of federal subsidies provided in fiscal 1970, and third in fiscal 1975. General commerce received larger subsidies in both years, and health in fiscal 1975. A ranking of all types of subsidies (except "Other") is shown in Table 6-10 for both years (listed in order of their fiscal 1975 rankings).

e. Housing subsidies are now much larger than most people realize. They are usually calculated from annual budgetary expenditures only, which omit over 60 percent of the total.

THE ADMINISTRATIVE CENTRALIZATION ISSUE

1. Recent federal housing subsidy programs have been criticized because subsidized units are located not in accordance with a single overall plan, but in response to the separate initiatives of thousands of individual builders and sponsors. This does not result in a clearly rational and effective geographic pattern of subsidized housing placement in each metropolitan area, related to its specific needs.

Table 6-10   Ranking of Federal Subsidies by Area of Activity, Fiscal 1970 and 1975

1975 Rank Area of Activity	Approximate Total of Direct and Indirect Subsidies		Percentage of All Federal Subsidies		Ratio to Housing Subsidies	
	1970	*1975*	*1970*	*1975*	*1970*	*1975*
1. Commerce and Economic Development	18.0	21.5	27.9%	22.6%	1.54	1.37
2. Health	8.6	16.6	13.4%	17.5%	0.74	1.06
3. *HOUSING*	11.7	15.7	18.2%	16.5%	1.00	1.00
4. Education	3.2	6.5	5.0%	6.8%	0.27	0.41
5. Food	1.5	5.9	2.3%	6.2%	0.13	0.38
6. Natural Resources	2.1	4.4	3.3%	4.6%	0.18	0.28
7. Manpower	2.6	4.1	4.0%	4.3%	0.22	0.26
8. Agriculture	5.7	2.5	8.9%	2.6%	0.49	0.16
9. International	1.0	2.4	1.6%	2.5%	0.09	0.15
10. Transportation	0.5	2.3	0.8%	2.4%	0.04	0.15

Source: Joint Economic Committee, U.S. Congress, *Federal Subsidy Programs* (Washington, D.C.: October 18, 1974), page 5.

a. Consequently, some recent proposals call for transferring subsidy allocation power to a single housing agency with metropolitanwide jurisdiction in each metropolitan area, or a state agency with jurisdiction outside of metropolitan areas.

b. Theoretically, such centralized administration over subsidy allocations would allow development and implementation of a single, comprehensive pattern of placement much more effective than present practices in meeting each area's real needs.

2. To achieve this goal, such an areawide agency would have to meet six conditions simultaneously. It would have to be:

a. Able to place subsidized units within any local community in the area, regardless of whether or not the community's government or citizens approved, so long as those units met prevailing codes and zoning rules.

b. Free from political domination by those interests wanting to prevent widespread location of low- and moderate-income housing throughout the area. In most areas, these interests probably include a majority of all residents.

c. Run by leaders dedicated to the creation of a large amount of low- and moderate-income housing, and willing to take the initiative to see that it is built, regardless of how popular or unpopular taking that stand made them.

d. Not likely to be paralyzed by indecision resulting from conflicts of values or goals among different groups within the area.

e. Not likely to become bogged down in administrative delays.

f. Capable of developing comprehensive plans for meeting the housing needs of the entire area.

3. It is extremely unlikely that any areawide agency with even mildly effective political connections to existing local governments would be able to meet most of these conditions. Yet Congress is not likely to set up areawide agencies that are unrelated to existing local governments within each metropolitan area.

a. The main difficulty that areawide agencies would have is that most suburban governments and residents are opposed to placement of subsidized housing for low- and moderate-income households in their communities. Yet suburbanites constitute a majority in most metropolitan areas.

• Hence, the more politically responsive to the areas' constituents comprehensive agencies became, the less able they would be to place subsidized housing in their communities.

• Yet, in our opinion, a crucial ingredient in any effective areawide plan would be major dispersal of low- and moderate-income housing to nearly all parts of the area. The suburban majority would probably oppose such dispersal strongly, or at least attach to it so many restrictions as to make it ineffective.

4. The decentralized administration strategy of leaving the initiative to individual builders and sponsors actually meets five of the six conditions set forth above better than an areawide agency would. Its one deficiency is that it is incapable of developing a single comprehensive plan responsive to an area's needs.

a. The initiative of individual builders and sponsors is far less susceptible to being stopped by the political sentiments of a community than that of officials in an areawide agency controlling allocations, especially one that has political ties to existing governments.

b. HUD can impose a certain degree of comprehensiveness and rationality on the existing system by using standardized locational criteria, as it had begun to do before the 1973 moratorium. Since HUD area-office administrators are not directly elected or directly linked to local government officials, they are actually more likely to impose certain criteria upon reluctant communities than officials in an areawide agency would be, under most circumstances.

c. The effectiveness of the current system would be further improved by reductions in the ability of individual communities to exclude subsidized housing through manipulation of building codes and zoning ordinances. Hence, HUD should press for statewide codes and reasonable nonexclusionary zoning (as has been done in part through Operation Breakthrough).

If local communities could be "disarmed" in their ability to exclude directly subsidized housing, and HUD employed site selection criteria responsive to areawide needs and to the location of all other subsidized units, the current system could even approach development of an implicit comprehensive plan.

5. We believe that under present political conditions, the decentralized administrative strategy—augmented as described above by HUD policies—would probably result in more effective areawide placement of directly subsidized housing than the proposed centralized administrative strategy, at least in most areas.

However, sufficient uncertainty about this matter exists to warrant conducting several experiments or demonstrations involving areawide allocation agencies in specific metropolitan areas. We recommend initiation of five to ten such experiments as soon as possible. We believe this would be a far more sensible approach than immediately switching to such an untried mechanism nationwide.

THE FORM-OF-SUBSIDIES ISSUE

1.   In relation to overall housing strategy, which subsidy forms to use depends upon what characteristics are required to achieve the objectives of the basic strategy options chosen.

   a.   Regarding *spatial strategy* options:

   • *Dispersal strategies* require at least some new-construction-oriented subsidies that insert new units at low- and moderate-income levels. However, subsidies that allow more intensive use of the existing inventory could aid dispersal in older suburban and central-city peripheral areas with substantial vacancies.

   • *Nondispersal strategies* indicate greater emphasis upon a housing allowance or other subsidies calling for more intensive use of the existing inventory. However, they also require new-construction-oriented subsidies when vacancy rates in the older inventory are low in poor areas.

   • *Physical redevelopment strategies* that emphasize rebuilding inner-city decaying areas would require a mixture of both of the subsidy types discussed above.

   b.   Regarding *level of insertion strategy* options, the main alternatives are relatively self-explanatory in relation to subsidy forms. High-level insertion is aided by the income tax deductibility subsidy and accelerated depreciation. Low- and moderate-level insertions require direct subsidies that finance new construction of units for those income groups. The degree of emphasis upon a housing allowance is also part of the definition of each strategy option.

2.   It is not necessary to analyze the relationship between strategy options and the subsidy forms appropriate to each option in much more detail. The implications for subsidy forms of each strategy option can be rather easily developed once the options considered most desirable have been chosen.

PUTTING IT ALL TOGETHER

1.   It is apparent from the preceding analysis that choosing an overall housing strategy is an extraordinarily complicated task. We have attempted to approach that task by considering a number of strategic issues separately. The specific findings and conclusions derived from considering each issue can be applied to whatever choice is made among the many different options set forth concerning both the *spatial* and *level of insertion* aspects of an overall strategy.

2. However, in order to illuminate the real choices among those options further, we have combined the seven spatial strategy options and the seven level of insertion strategy options into one "grand strategy" matrix. This matrix is presented in Figure 6.1.

a. The purpose of this seemingly esoteric exercise is to narrow down the many theoretical possible combinations of these two types of options to a manageable number. Hopefully, the number will be small enough to provide a clearer insight into the types of choices that society really could make concerning its overall housing strategy. This, in turn, will allow clearer analysis of the possible consequences of each such choice, and provide useful guidance to those who must make that choice—or contribute to making it.

b. The Grand Strategy Matrix has Level of Insertion and Income Maintenance Options as columns, and Spatial Development Emphasis and Income Maintenance Options as rows. The result is forty-nine squares, each representing a logically possible combination of options.

c. However, not all forty-nine logically possible combinations represent practically consistent situations. In many cases, the characteristics of the Spatial Development Emphasis and Income Maintenance Option are incompatible with those of the Level of Insertion and Income Maintenance Option. The precise nature of these inconsistencies is spelled out in nine "Elimination Rules" shown at the right side of the figure. Each of the eliminated squares contains the numbers of the rules that describe its internal inconsistency.

- In fact, these rules eliminate thirty-six of the forty-nine logically possible combinations, leaving only thirteen that represent practically feasible combinations of these two different types of options.
- The thirteen feasible combinations are outlined heavily, and some have been given brief titles to indicate their nature.

3. The following significant conclusions can be drawn from an analysis of this Grand Strategy Matrix:

a. There is a strong linkage between major emphasis upon new housing construction inserted at all income levels and dispersal of low- and moderate-income households outside the areas where they are now concentrated. All feasible options containing the former also involve the latter. All but two of the nine such options containing the latter involve the former.

b. Dispersal is best accomplished through major multi-level insertion of new units because new units must be used to place low- and moderate-income households in new growth areas. This

Figure 6-1

Level of Insertion and Income Maintenance Strategy Options

Spatial Development Emphasis and Income Maintenance Options

		No Low- and Moderate-Level Insertion of New Housing		
		Trickle-Down Plus Minimal Anti-Poverty	Pure Anti-Poverty	Accelerated Trickle-Down
		A	B	C
Nondispersal Options	Contained Decay 1	Minimal Effort On All Fronts	4	4
	Noncapital Enrichment Only 2	6	Minimal Housing Subsidy	
	All-Out Enrichment Only 3	6 9 10	9 10	9 10
Dispersal Options	Decay Plus Dispersal 4	8	4 8	4 8
	Noncapital Enrichment Plus Dispersal 5	1 6	1	1
	Noncapital Enrichment, Dispersal and Delayed Redevelopment 6	1 6	1	1
	All-Out In All Areas 7	1 5 6	1 5	1 5

- Combination squares containing numbers are eliminated by the rules designated by those numbers.
- Possible combinations shaded—briefly titled where feasible.
- Starred option indicates RERC preference.

Major Low- and Moderate-Level Insertion of New Housing

Accelerated Trickle-Down Marginally Augmented	All-Out New Construction Plus Minimal Anti-Poverty	Mixed Options	All-Out New Construction and Anti-Poverty
D	**E**	**F**	**G**
4	2	2 4	2 4
//// Efforts ////	3 6	3	3
10	6 7 10	10	7 10
4	//// Maximum Pro Suburb Anti Central City Strategy ////	8	8
////	6		
////	6	//// * ////	
5	5 6	//// Near Maximum Effort On All Fronts ////	//// Maximum Effort On All Fronts ////

ELIMINATION RULES

1 Dispersal is not compatible with the absence of emphasis upon new construction. (Rules out 5-ABC, 6-ABC, and 7-ABC)

2 Contained Decay is not compatible with high volume new construction emphasis. (Rules out 1-EFG)

3 Noncapital Enrichment Only is not compatible with high volume new construction emphasis. (Rules out 2-EFG)

4 Decay is not compatible with large-scale income maintenance programs. (Rules out 1-BCDFG, 4-BCDFG)

5 All-Out in All Areas is not compatible with any forms of "Trickle-Down." (Rules out 7-ABCDE)

6 Minimal Anti-Poverty is not compatible with either Non-Capital or All-Out Enrichment. (Rules out 2-AE, 3-AE, 5-AE, 6-AE, 7-AE)

7 All-Out Enrichment Only is not compatible with large volume emphasis on new construction. (Rules out 3-EG)

8 Dispersal is not compatible with any version of "Trickle-Down" only. (Rules out 4-ABCFG)

9 All-Out Enrichment Only must have some low-level insertion. (Rules out 3-ABC)

10 All-Out Enrichment requires relocation outside of inner-city areas; hence, it requires at least some dispersal. (Rules out 3-ABCDEFG)

Source: Real Estate Research Corporation

can also be done to some extent by marginally augmenting a basic "trickle-down" strategy with some new building of low- and moderate-income housing on dispersed sites as in Options 5-D and 6-D.

c.   However, the reason why major multi-level insertion of new units requires dispersal is not obvious. The main reason is that *concentrating large-scale new construction of low- and moderate-income housing solely within inner-city decaying areas is not really feasible.* Most moderate-income households do not want to live in such areas, and investors hesitate to risk even limited equity capital there because of adverse environmental conditions. Public housing can be concentrated there. But most governments at all levels have concluded that large-scale public housing projects in such areas simply aggravate the problems of concentrated poverty.

  • At first glance, it might appear that large-scale multi-level insertion of new housing could be accommodated solely within inner-city decaying areas through All-Out Enrichment there. But experience shows that such major inner-city clearance and redevelopment would require relocation of many displaced low- and moderate-income households outside the areas where they are now concentrated. (Large-scale urban renewal had this effect in many cities; for example, St. Louis.) This requires a form of dispersal, even though it might mainly involve occupancy of existing older homes rather than new ones by the displaced households.

  • This implies that All-Out Enrichment Only really contains an internal inconsistency; it is not a practically feasible option because of this displacement effect. Hence, Options 3-ABCDEFG are all nonfeasible. Nevertheless, we have left this Spatial Emphasis Option in our matrix because its nonfeasibility is not obvious, and some people are seriously proposing this as a desirable national strategy (especially those who decry the "crisis of our cities").

d.   Counteracting existing physical decay in inner-city areas probably also requires at least some dispersal. Former HUD Secretary Romney and others have made some strong statements about the grim future of many of our large cities if the nation does not take effective steps to halt—and counteract—such decay.

  • Trying to counteract such decay without dispersal requires focusing remedial action upon pumping money into these areas through larger income maintenance and social service delivery. Then private markets would hopefully respond by improving the physical environment in response to the residents' expanded incomes.

• We are skeptical that much physical improvement would be forthcoming from such options. Private investors are not likely to sink risk capital into concentrated poverty areas without subsidies, especially since households who can afford nondirectly subsidized new housing will not move there.

• Perhaps large-scale rehabilitation would occur through private action in response to higher incomes among households in these areas. This is the assumption that underlies Options 2-B and 2-C. However, experience with large-scale rehabilitation programs indicates that they also displace occupants of the units being upgraded—almost as completely as clearance and new construction. Hence, it is by no means certain that large-scale rehabilitation could occur in inner-city areas without at least some dispersal required by the relocation of displaced households.

• Thus, the feasible nondispersal options that involve some anti-poverty efforts but only minimal direct emphasis upon physical redevelopment of inner-city decaying areas (Options 2-BCD) are not likely to generate much physical redevelopment —even rehabilitation. And if they do, they will become transformed into some other type of option involving some dispersal.

e. Dispersal of low- and moderate-income households outside of areas where they are now concentrated through deliberate use of direct housing subsidies is not a politically popular policy. In fact, President Nixon specifically stated his opposition to it, unless the communities concerned accepted such housing voluntarily (as very few have done). Yet this analysis indicates that such *dispersal can be avoided only at the price of failing to counteract effectively the spreading physical decay in large parts of our biggest cities.*

• The Grand Strategy Matrix thus illustrates the indissoluble linkage in the quality of life in most different portions of each metropolitan area. Those portions that have avoided the direct problems associated with poverty by deliberately excluding low- and moderate-income housing cannot continue to do so without condemning large parts of older central cities to continued— and worsening—physical decay. Thus, *an important part of the responsibility for the future quality of life in inner-city areas rests squarely upon the decisions and actions of those living in more affluent portions of each metropolitan area.* They cannot correctly argue that inner-city problems "are not their concern," because their refusal to stop excluding the relatively poor helps cause and sustain those problems.

• At the same time, it is important to remember that significant dispersal does not require locating low- and moderate-income households in every block throughout each metropolitan area, or even in every community. It only requires the entry of a large number of such households into portions of the metropolitan area where they are not now concentrated. However, such entry should be spread out among enough different places so that it does not lead to a renewed concentration of poverty in the newly entered areas sometime in the near future.

4.   Although our primary purpose in conducting this study was to provide others with an objective view of federal housing subsidies for their own decision-making, we were also asked to state our own policy preferences. We believe the best feasible choice from the Grand Strategy Matrix at this time is Option 6-F. It combines the "Noncapital Enrichment Plus Dispersal Plus Delayed Redevelopment" Option with the "Mixed Option" Strategy concerning levels of insertion of new units. We prefer this combination because:

a.   *It involves a significant degree of dispersal,* which we believe is essential to both the long-range and short-range amelioration of the most pressing inner-city problems in our society.

b.   *It initially emphasizes income maintenance and better social services delivery, rather than physical redevelopment, for inner-city areas.* We believe eventual physical redevelopment of these areas is appropriate, but it cannot produce effective results until dispersal is underway, and until the residents of these areas have higher incomes.

c.   *It makes use of a variety of housing subsidy approaches—*including direct and indirect, new-construction-oriented and existing-inventory-oriented ones—rather than emphasizing any one type or approach exclusively. We believe this Mixed Options Strategy is appropriate to the complex housing needs of our society, and allows better adaptation of program instruments to local needs in each area.

d.   *It contains major emphasis upon direct income maintenance.* The biggest single cause of housing problems in our society is poverty, and a crucial ingredient in combating poverty is giving more money to those who cannot earn their way out of poverty independently.

e.   *It does not call for placing an unrealistically high priority on housing in the allocation of national resources.* We believe that both "All-Out" Options (7 and G) are unrealistic because they assume that Americans want to make improvement of housing almost the top priority domestic policy objective. We do not think this is the case—although housing has a surprisingly high priority already, judging from the size of federal subsidies it receives.

f.   Naturally, our preference represents only one opinion among many. We believe the real contribution of our analysis consists of our presenting a method of approaching this incredibly complex subject that will help others arrive at better informed and more effective policy preferences of their own.

7

"New Cities": Are They Economically Feasible?

Although many regard new cities as an exciting way to escape the persistent ills of urban life, few new-community advocates have confronted certain unromantic but vital questions about economic feasibility. Will new cities pay for themselves, or must they be subsidized? If subsidies are required, who will pay for them, and who will reap the benefits? Would building new cities really help solve existing urban problems? Or would it merely divert leadership and other scarce resources from decaying older urban areas to glorified, high-income suburbs?

Before examining these questions, some definitions are required. In order to be considered a new city, a community must: (1) be initially developed under a single comprehensive plan; (2) contain multiple land uses—at least single-family and multi-family residential, commercial, office space, and recreational; and (3) be planned for a certain minimum population. I believe 15,000 people is a reasonable estimate for the smaller cities and 50,000 for the larger.

Several fundamentally different types of new cities must be distinguished on the basis of their geographic relation to existing settlements and size. Geographically, a new city can be *in-city* (within a heavily built-up area—such as the Welfare Island project in New York City), *peripheral* (on the edge of an existing metropolitan area, such as Foster City near San Francisco), *satellite* (outside of but within commuting distance of a metropolitan center, such as Columbia between

---

Revised version of "Private Investment and the Public Weal," *Saturday Review*, 15 May 1971, pp. 24–26 ff.

Washington and Baltimore), or *autonomous* (beyond commuting range of any existing metropolitan area such as Lake Havasu City in Arizona). For convenience I will use only two size categories. A *full city* contains a very broad spectrum of land uses, including industrial, and should provide nearly as many jobs within its boundaries as there are workers living there. A *mini-city* contains a much narrower spectrum of land uses, perhaps not including industrial, and relies mainly on surrounding communities to provide its residents with both jobs and key urban services and amenities.

From a strictly economic viewpoint, creating any new city is a special form of land development. The basic principle underlying all land development is to buy land cheaply, enhance its desirability, and sell it more expensively. The profit produced depends upon: (1) the spread between the buying and selling prices; (2) the costs incurred enhancing the land's desirability; and (3) the time required to complete the whole process.

The price spread is increased by making the buying prices as low and the selling prices as high as possible. Land prices generally decline with distance from already settled areas, so there is a strong pressure on developers of new cities to build satellite or autonomous projects. This pressure is especially powerful if they seek to create full cities, which require immense tracts of vacant land (6,000 acres or more). On the other hand, selling (or leasing) prices are maximized by the highest density uses, which are usually found near the centers of large cities. In all new (and existing) cities, the highest land prices are generated by high-rise office buildings, shopping centers, and high-rise apartments, and the lowest by single-family home sites. This is why many new-city developers rapidly sell single-family home sites to housing developers, but retain major commercial, retail, industrial, and high-rise apartment locations. High land values and rents generated by such sites have been the economic salvation of British new cities.

A crucial economic aspect of new cities is their attempt to internalize the economic "spillovers" that occur in all land development. Whenever someone builds a major regional shopping center or other commercial project, the value of all the land around it rises. If the shopping center developer does not own that nearby land, someone else captures the "spillover effects" of his investment. But a new-city developer initially controls enough land to capture almost all such spillovers within the community's boundaries. Furthermore, he deliberately plans all parts of the new city so their spillovers reinforce each other. This stimulates land values to rise even faster. For example, he designs local streets to maximize the convenience of his shopping center and then uses that convenience to convince both residents and retailers to move in. This ability to internalize and set up an "economic reverberation" among spillovers provides the greatest relative advantage of new-city development over traditional subdivision development. But this ability requires both a huge site and an excellent comprehensive plan, which add to development costs.

A new city's comprehensive plan offers environmental and esthetic qualities lacking in typical competitive subdivisions. Therefore, a well-planned new city is able to both offset its more distant location and speed up the process of marketing its land. Traditional land developers enhance land values by installing mains and sewers, creating streets and lakes, providing open space, donating school sites, building structures, or some combination of these. But new-city developers seek to create a completely new, almost self-contained environment through the careful positioning of many land uses under a single plan. In this respect, they are catering to a rising desire among Americans to purchase an entire environment along with their home. Thus, creation of an esthetically, socially, and environmentally attractive comprehensive plan is critical to any new city's success.

The most critical factor of all, however, is speed of development. New cities require huge "front-end" investments of cash to acquire big sites and to install enough facilities and improvements before anyone moves in to convince potential residents that they will actually receive the wonderful environment promised by the developer. If the developer has borrowed this money, it costs him staggering interest payments daily. (In the early stages of building Columbia, the Rouse Company was paying $5,000-a-day interest on money borrowed to buy the land, even before there was any real assurance that a new city could or would be built on it.) Tying up the developer's cash means sacrificing interest it could be earning elsewhere. Therefore, economic success requires speeding up development to shorten the period before sizable revenues start to flow back to the investors. Even if a new city eventually becomes completely occupied and a great human success, it can be an economic disaster for its developers if too much time elapses from start to finish. Locating as close as possible to an existing metropolitan area speeds up development by exposing the new city to a bigger potential market. But this drives up the initial purchase price of the land. Furthermore, creating an entire new city is an extremely complex process, involving three sources of delay not connected with traditional development: assembly of the entire site; development of a good comprehensive plan; and completion of intricate negotiations with a whole set of governmental bodies. These actions provide innumerable occasions for unforeseen delays.

Full-city-scale new cities are so large they would take from 12 to 20 years to complete even if everything occurred on schedule—which never happens. In fact, the longer the development period for any project, the more unforeseen delays are likely to crop up. Moreover, really large real estate projects like full-city-scale new cities are likely to span several business cycles in the general economy. This means they will encounter one or more periods of tight money when mortgage funds are difficult to obtain, or very costly, or both. These "credit crunches" inescapably slow down every new-city developer's ability to market housing units below the rate originally planned, and produce serious cash-flow problems. If rapid inflation of costs also occurs—as in the early 1970s—the carefully designed feasibility models on which these huge developments were originally based will prove terribly inaccurate. Consequently, the developers' cash requirements will sky-rocket. Precisely this combination of events has rendered almost all full-city-scale developments undertaken in the U.S. in recent years economically unfeasible. Either the original developers have gone bankrupt or they have had to be "rescued" by further infusions of money from public-spirited institutions. In almost every case, these projects have produced very low rates of return (or losses) on both equity capital and total capital invested.

Even in principle, therefore, creating new cities is an extraordinarily risky form of private investment—probably the riskiest of all. That is why the single most important ingredient in any new city is the principal developer himself. Only individuals with a rare combination of vision, persuasiveness, energy, financial acumen, inventiveness, promotional flair, and endless persistence have any chance of seeing a new-city investment through to profitable fruition. In light of these demanding conditions, who have tried to create new cities and how successful have they been? Our catalogue includes the following types of developers:

1. *Central governments* have created many new cities as a means of opening up underdeveloped areas, counteracting excessive urban centralization, or achieving other national objectives. Economic feasibility has been neither an objective for nor a constraint on such attempts, which include Washington, D.C., Canberra, Brasilia, Oak Ridge, Ciudid Guayana in Venezuela, and Chandrigar in India.

2. *Public corporations* have been created expressly to develop new cities in most nations that have adopted explicit new-city policies, such as Great Britain, France, and Sweden. These corporations have pursued economic feasibility, and in some cases have produced discounted rates of return on investment of around 8 percent. Although this is satisfactory for a public body, it would be unacceptably low for private capital.

3. *Owners of large land parcels* have sometimes chosen to create new cities rather than to sell or develop their land piecemeal. Such

developers have the tremendous advantage of not having to assemble or make a huge cash investment in a big site. Examples are most common in California, where remnants of Spanish land grants provided the basis for the giant Irvine project. The development of Miami Lakes (with a projected population of 50,000 residents), about ten miles northeast of Miami, by the Graham family is another illustration. Computing the initial land value is extremely difficult in such cases; hence no one really knows what rate of return on investment these new cities have produced.

4. *Developers who create sites through land-fills or clearance and drainage of swamps* also minimize land-assembly and initial-cost obstacles. Examples are Redwood Shore (municipally owned) and Foster City in the San Francisco Bay area, and many new communities in Florida.

5. *Combinations of individual entrepreneurs in partnership with large lenders or corporate investors*—with the former supplying the ideas, skill, and energy, and the latter putting up most of the money—as in Columbia, Maryland; Rancho, California; Reston, Virginia; and Clear Lake City, Texas. However, none of these projects have produced rates of return competitive with recent high interest rates. Several have had to be reorganized.

This list includes most new-city developers. It strongly implies that creating new cities is a task suitable only to very large organizations—whether public or private—possessing lots of cash and staying power. Most other new-city developers have enjoyed some hard-to-duplicate initial advantages, such as inheritance of a giant estate. Individual entrepreneurs operating on their own are notably scarce in this business. The few who try it have usually become partners with some source of big money, instead of following the mortgage route typical of other developments, in order to meet the large front-end cash requirement.

The size of this requirement is illustrated in part by land acquisition costs of $25 million at Columbia (an average of $1,700 per acre), $13.2 million at Reston ($1,780 per acre), $32 million at Westlake Village, California ($2,700 per acre), and $40 million at Park Forest South, Illinois ($5,000 per acre). Moreover, costs of infrastructure and buildings are much greater. In our recent preliminary analysis of a new community of 75,000 persons proposed for a suburban location near Detroit, we estimated total capital outlay requirements (public and private) would be $663 million over a twenty-year period (in constant dollars), of which only $7.2 million (1.1 percent) would be for land acquisition.

Another strong implication of this analysis is that mini-cities are far more likely to prove feasible for private investors than full cities. Mini-cities require smaller initial cash outlays for land and improvements, can be located closer to existing markets, need less complex plans and negotiations with governmental bodies, and take less time to carry out. Yet they can still be large enough (say, from 800 to 3,000 acres) to allow internalization of the most significant economic spillovers and creation of an unusually attractive environment through comprehensive planning. Chicago's privately owned Urban Investment and Development Company has proposed a series of suburban mini-cities, each to be built around a major regional shopping center—the key tenants of which are partners in the venture. Several of the projects proposed by New York's publicly owned Urban Development Corporation are new mini-cities either within or on the edges of existing metropolitan areas.

The 1970 Urban Growth and New Community Development Act sought to help both public and private new-city developers overcome some key obstacles. The most important forms of assistance it provided were:

1. Federal guarantees backing debt obligations issued by developers to pay for acquiring land, conducting initial development, and installing utilities. Such guarantees can be made up to $50 million for any one project for 100 percent of these costs for public developers and about 85 percent for private developers.

2. Federal loans to cover the interest payments on money borrowed by developers for financing the specific, front-end costs mentioned above, even when no federally guaranteed obligations are involved. No repayments on these federal loans need be made during the first few years of the project.

3. Public service grants to local government bodies to help them pay for essential public services required in a new city before it has an adequate tax base.

4. Planning grants to pay up to two-thirds of all planning costs for public developers, or two-thirds of special costs for private developers in excess of normal planning and feasibility studies.

5. Special supplements added on to thirteen existing federal programs (such as sewer and water aid) when they are used in approved new cities.

In theory, these programs could have provided major reductions in the front-end cash requirements of both public and private developers. But Congress did not appropriate funds for most of these programs, and budget restraints held down the amounts the Department of Housing and Urban Development requested. Hence most of the aids provided for in the 1970 act were never used, even though about 14 new communities did receive federal financing guarantees.

Using federal aid poses three added problems for new-city developers: more red tape; required inclusion of new low- and moderate-income housing (which is desirable socially but is a potential drain on profitability); and the need to tie up the site through purchase or options before applying for federal aid, without knowing whether funds will be provided. Consequently, I believe there are still formidable financial obstacles to the successful development of new cities, especially by private enterprise. In fact, I strongly doubt that creation of full-city-scale new cities represents an economically feasible private capital investment under any likely circumstances. Only public subsidies far larger and more extensive than any proposed up to now could overcome the hazards described above.[1]

Thus, if new cities are to represent much of the nation's future urban growth, creating them must be made still more profitable and less risky for private developers. However, Congress may be reluctant to adopt policies that would generate sufficient profits to attract large numbers of top-quality private developers into this field, or to lead to large-scale public development of new cities. Among such policies would have to be the following:

1.   Creation of state (or federal) public development corporations (like New York's Urban Development Corporation) with powers to condemn land, override local zoning and building codes, float their own financing, and actually build utilities and structures.

2.   Provision of special land-assembly powers usable by either public development corporations or private developers. The latter would first have to assemble some large fraction of a proposed new-city site, formulate an acceptable plan, and provide sound financial backing.

3.   Actual appropriation and expenditure of vastly greater funds for all the federal financial aids passed in the 1970 act. Congress and the administration usually allow far less spending than the amounts legally authorized. For example, HUD only requested new-city supplemental grants of $5 million in fiscal 1971, as compared to an authorization of $63.5 million.

4.   Priority allocation of existing federal planning, housing sub-

---

[1] This conclusion has been borne out by the economic failure of nearly all new communities formed under the Title VII program to provide reasonable returns on the investments made in them. Many will probably become insolvent.

sidy, sewer and water, and transportation program funds to proposed new cities meeting certain standards.

A possible alternative to large federal assistance might be provision of a powerful private financing mechanism such as the National Urban Development Bank recently proposed by David Rockefeller. It would make land-development loans to new-city builders with funds from special security issues or pooled bank loans.

The suggestions outlined above assume that both public and private efforts to build new cities should be encouraged simultaneously in order to maximize effective results. In addition, the following more experimental suggestions might be considered:

1. Designation of certain new-city zones by individual states, within which no new urban development could occur at less than mini-city scale. This would encourage landowners in such zones to aggregate their holdings.

2. Provision of highly accelerated depreciation write-offs for all private structures built in designated new cities.

3. Construction of one or two experimental new cities built around new federal installations, or existing installations in relatively remote locations, with special incentives for private firms to move there. Emphasis could be upon ecological-system innovation and improvement.

Unless many of these policies are forcefully carried out by key states and the federal government, there is little chance that any new cities will play a really important role in our future urban growth.

Under these circumstances, why should we worry about creating new cities? Why should we even consider spending taxpayer's money to encourage such developments through public subsidies?

Full-sized autonomous new cities offer our best chance to try out alternative urban forms that might reduce key problems (such as designing a city mainly for public transit to cut air pollution and traffic congestion). However, truly radical innovations would be extremely expensive as compared with continuing urban sprawl around existing urban areas. This is partly because new cities must contain *all* new structures, even though more than half the nation's households (and many firms) cannot afford to occupy new quarters without subsidies. Yet these people and activities are needed to make any city work economically. In existing areas, they can occupy older structures; but in autonomous new cities, they must be heavily subsidized because there are no older structures nearby. Moreover, radically designed new cities might be politically threatening to the chief beneficiaries of existing urban forms (such as the giant automobile industry). Therefore, I believe it highly improbable that we will build many such innovative autonomous new cities in the near future, though I support trying one or two.

Satellite and peripheral new cities—particularly mini-cities—could improve the neighborhood texture and quality of life in urban areas without generating enormous costs beyond those associated with normal urban development. They could also provide some planned economic-class mixture (if sufficient subsidies are granted to allow low- and moderate-income households to live in new units) and planned racial integration. In fact, unless both these elements are deliberately built into new cities by public policies, such settlements will become large-scale, well-planned, middle- and upper-income developments, thereby furthering existing spatial economic separation in our metropolitan areas.

But satellite and peripheral new cities would not reduce traffic congestion, air pollution, the solid waste problem, or other problems arising from the sheer size of metropolitan areas. Only a general urban growth policy that forbids or controls expansion of our largest areas could do that. This in turn would require stronger public controls over private land use.

No form of new city will significantly reduce the problems of older existing urban cores unless the "two urban frontiers" of core decay and suburban growth are explicitly linked together for their mutual benefit. This has recently been proposed in the "paired new city" concept of Detroit's Metropolitan Fund. Without some such linkage, there is a strong probability that society will concentrate most future resource investments in suburban areas and continue to let central cities decay physically and go bankrupt fiscally.

Thus, new cities are neither a panacea nor a Band-Aid for existing urban problems. Yet they offer definite opportunities for improving the quality of growth. But any policies supporting them should be part of a balanced program that also recognizes the need to improve older core areas and to upgrade traditional forms of urban growth which are still likely to dominate the future.

8

Stimulating Capital Investment in Downtown Areas and Inner-City Neighborhoods

INTRODUCTION

Many neighborhoods in U.S. central cities have recently been experiencing net physical disinvestment rather than investment. They are suffering from physical and social deterioration and decay, which seem to be spreading into more and more older areas. Even some downtown business districts have been affected. Many Americans believe continuation of these trends will gravely weaken the economies and the long-range viability of large parts of our central cities. That outcome would in turn adversely affect the quality of life in those cities and in outlying parts of surrounding metropolitan areas. Yet the obstacles to reversing such negative investment patterns seem overwhelming.

This paper seeks to describe those obstacles and to propose some tentative ideas about how they might be overcome. It suggests many admittedly untried and controversial ideas, policies, and programs. These suggestions are mainly focused upon what might be done in the relatively near future, without any massive federal funding. They are meant to be applicable *without* the type of reform that completely reshapes major portions of our existing institutional structure, even though such reform is clearly desirable in many areas.

Revised version of a paper written for an Urban Coalition Conference at Racine, Wisconsin, in early 1973.

KEY BACKGROUND FACTORS

Understanding this complex subject first requires knowledge of certain key background factors. In most cases, no attempt is made to present detailed empirical evidence corroborating my statements about these factors. This sketchy format has been chosen to conserve time for readers while still providing them with a common orientation concerning my approach to later sections.

Weakened Competitive Position of Central-City Downtown Areas

Downtown central business districts have largely lost their regional dominance and—with very few exceptions—are now just one of many large regional shopping/office/entertainment/hotel complexes in each metropolitan area. Huge suburban shopping centers offer very competitive clusters of modern shopping facilities, office buildings, hotels, theaters, restaurants, and other facilities formerly found only downtown. Moreover, these suburban complexes have three major advantages over downtowns: free and easily accessible parking, much greater personal and physical security (or at least greater freedom from feelings of insecurity), and close proximity to a large relatively affluent residential population that provides both customers and work force. On the other hand, most downtowns still have two advantages of their own: a bigger concentration of all types of facilities offering more variety than any one suburban center, and physically closer interrelationships among the many components of the complex (such as stores and hotels). Such components are separated by roads and seas of parking in most suburban complexes.

Racial Trends in Central Cities

Many bigger, older central cities have very large minority-group populations—especially blacks—living in mainly segregated residential areas. These populations have grown rapidly in the past 25 years, spreading out into more and more neighborhoods, usually almost completely displacing former white occupants. "White flight" from this spread of minority-group residency and from old and obsolete central-city housing has been the single biggest dynamic force in the suburban housing markets of the nation, just as minority-group growth has been the biggest dynamic force in many central-city housing markets.

Since minority groups patronize downtown stores disproportionately to their percentage of the total city population, many downtowns now have very high fractions of minority-group members among their consumer and work forces. This has caused significant white patronage withdrawal from some downtown areas (such as Detroit, Cleveland, and Newark). It has thereby adversely affected the economies of those central business districts. Because assessed values in downtowns are very high, central business districts provide a big share of the property tax base used to support many citywide services. Declines in downtown property values thus have serious implications beyond economic losses to downtown property owners. Minority-group dominance or near dominance of downtown areas has also caused many employers to locate facilities they might have placed downtown in outlying suburban areas. (The suburbs remain about 94 percent white nationwide, whereas all central cities combined are about 79 percent white, and some large cities are much less than that.) Furthermore, possibilities of retaining middle-income white residents in central cities, or attracting them back from the suburbs, are strongly affected by the prevailing white reluctance to enter neighborhoods that are now predominantly black, Chicano, or Puerto Rican, or seem likely to become so in the near future. Most white parents are also reluctant to send their children to public schools that are mainly black, Chicano, or Puerto Rican. Yet the public school systems in *most* of the nation's largest cities are now predominantly attended by minority-group children.

Poverty Trends in Central Cities and Suburbs

Contrary to widespread belief, the distribution of incomes in central cities is not lower than that in the nation as a whole, but almost exactly the same. Far worse poverty is found outside metropolitan areas than in central cities. Yet central cities are significantly poorer than suburbs on the average. In 1969, the percentage of families with incomes below $5,000 was 20.8 percent in central cities and 12.2 percent in suburbs. In contrast, the percentage with incomes above $15,000 was 18.9 percent in central cities and 26.6 percent in suburbs. About one out of seven central-city residents was poor in 1969, according to the official definition of poverty, as compared to about one out of fourteen suburbanites. Yet almost half of all white poor persons living in metropolitan areas live in the suburbs, not central cities.

Housing Abandonment

Since about 1965, certain large central cities have experienced increasing housing abandonment. This phenomenon has occurred mainly in all-black neighborhoods marked by high percentages of households on welfare, high crime rates, frequent vandalism, and many absentee landlords. The causes of abandonment are complex. They include such factors as difficulty of getting financing for repairs, poverty among housing occupants, "instant wreckage" of vacant units by organized vandals, and flight from neighborhoods by households with enough income to live elsewhere. I believe abandonment is essentially the ultimate stage of the "trickle-down" process. However, this stage appears only when there is a sufficient total surplus of housing in the overall housing market so that even the poorest households have some place to live other than the worst quality units. This situation has begun to appear only recently because of lower urban birth rates, slower in-migration of poor households to big cities, and massive numbers of new housing units started each year.

Diversity of Conditions Among Cities and Within Each City

Although the above paragraphs describe factors and trends found in many U.S. metropolitan areas, these generalizations must be qualified by the existence of four different kinds of diversity among and within such areas, as follows:

1. Large, older central cities with high fractions of minority-group populations vary sharply from most smaller central cities and many large, newer ones.

2. The single term "suburbs" refers to a tremendous variety of communities. Many older, close-in suburbs are more like the central cities next to them than like brand-new suburbs farther out from downtown.

3. Within large central cities, conditions differ sharply from one neighborhood to another. Some of the oldest, most deteriorated areas are experiencing falling population and rising abandonment. Other rather old but not yet deteriorated areas nearby are experiencing rapid increases in total population. They are either being "invaded" by households fleeing from abandonment areas or are experiencing transition from middle-income to lower-income occupancy. Still other old areas remain stable because they have retained their desirability as high-income residential neighborhoods. Finally, peripheral portions of many central cities are relatively new; they might even be considered "disguised suburbs."

4. Age changes in different neighborhoods increase diversity. Where child-oriented families are departing, the fraction of elderly may be rising. In neighborhoods being "invaded" by lower-income families with children, the school-age population is rising sharply.

The resulting diversity of conditions must be kept in mind in prescribing specific policies for improving investment in central cities. This diversity is often obscured by methods of gathering and analyzing data which treat all parts of a central city alike or do not deal separately with conditions in different neighborhoods. Much more intensive "micro-area" research on central-city conditions is required as a basis for accurate policies in many cases.

Difficulties of Relocation in Urban Renewal

For several years, most urban renewal projects involving large-scale clearance of existing housing have been stalemated by the difficulty of achieving relocation in a way satisfactory to all concerned. The type of "loose" housing market prevalent in the early 1970s is quite favorable for finding alternative accommodations for displaced households. Moreover, new legislation has helped finance relocation more adequately. However, either households object to moving away from their present neighborhoods, or households living in areas to which the displacees would move object to receiving them, especially if they would be housed in public housing or other directly subsidized units. Thus, the relocation problem encountered today is more political than economic. Political representatives of families likely to be displaced usually advocate creating new housing for those families in the same area in which they now live. But such a tactic would fail to reduce the existing concentration of poor households there. That, in turn, would make it hard to market new housing units in the proposed renewal projects to middle- and upper-income households, who do not want to live in areas where poverty is dominant. On the other hand, it appears politically difficult for a local government to displace many poor households from some site, and then use public subsidies (such as land write-downs) to create housing on that site mainly for middle- and upper-income households. This tactic seems perverse to the poor households being displaced. These conditions have confronted urban renewal agencies and city politicians with a dilemma they have been unable to resolve up to now.

Requirement for Greater Community Control
Over Investment Decisions

A high fraction of the residents in inner-city poverty areas are renters in buildings owned by absentee landlords. This form of tenure reduces the desire of each housing occupant to maintain the property well and increases the owners' willingness to let it deteriorate, since the owners do not have to suffer the consequences of living there. Thus, the absence of any effective proprietary attitude toward individual dwelling units in these areas is a key cause of their physical deterioration.

However, many of the residents have developed great concern for the quality of their neighborhoods, especially if they are among the few owner-occupants. In fact, their political consciousness has been developed to the point where they take a "proprietary attitude" toward developments in the neighborhood as a whole, not just toward their own property. This attitude can in the long run be a great asset for rebuilding such communities. However, it also implies that local residents will not be very sympathetic to having nonresident "outsiders" or "intruders" buy up land in their areas and place private or public investments there without any community inputs. Rather, they will want to have a significant voice in determining what any such investments will be like. This need for significant "community participation" or "community control" may require private developers to enter into joint developments with local development corporations or neighborhood groups in order to win sufficient local acceptance to make their projects feasible. This creates one more difficult obstacle for developers seeking to invest in such areas to hurdle.

The Nature of Risk in Central-City Investment

Most of the obstacles to private central-city investment can be summed up under the headings of *low-level incentives* and *high-level risks*. In many cases, the degree of incentive would be adequate to call forth significant investment if the degree of risk could be substantially reduced. The following observations are relevant to achieving effective risk-reduction.

1. The risks of such investment are perceived quite differently by different parties. Thus, certain outcomes would not be considered nearly as risky by a community development corporation as by a private absentee investor. Hence assessing risks depends upon whose viewpoint is involved, as well as the objective conditions concerned.

2. In many cases, the risks of investing in central city areas—or of living or working in those areas—are greatly exaggerated through the influence of myths, rumors, fears, and irrationalities. These errors can even affect investor attitudes towards things about which accurate information exists, such as loan repayment rates among employed households. This in turn can lead to behavior that has a self-fulfilling prophecy impact. For example, "red-lining" certain areas and refusing to make loans there speeds up local property deterioration, thereby "confirming" the lenders' judgments that the areas are "unsound."

3. Many types of risk reduction require public actions, rather than private ones, or in connection with private ones. Examples are improved police protection and patrolling in high-crime areas, improved effectiveness of the criminal justice system in general, improved drug addiction treatment facilities, and better schools in inner-city poverty areas.

4. Prevailing levels of riskiness connected with central-city investment in any given area may be related to the type of legal and organizational investment vehicle most appropriate. A possible set of such
relationships is shown by Table 8-1 (which considers *only risk,* although other factors are almost always also relevant).

Table 8-1 assumes that public development corporations should
sometimes act as "developers of last resort" when risks are high but the
social benefits to be gained from at least some investment are very
significant too.

The Fiscal Squeeze on Central-City Governments

Local governments in large cities are suffering from a "fiscal squeeze"
that has limited their ability to finance the local share of urban renewal.
On the revenue side, receipts are not growing rapidly because of stagnant property values in decaying areas, plus very strong resistance by
taxpayers to higher property taxes. On the expense side, costs continue to escalate rapidly, especially because of pressures for higher
wages from municipal employees, including policemen, firemen, and
teachers. Furthermore, as the proportion of *relatively* lower-income
households in central cities rises, the need for high-cost public services also rises. So do demands for better service from now-militant
poor areas wanting public service *outputs* equal to those enjoyed by
upper-income areas, even though that requires far more costly *inputs*
per household in the former. General revenue sharing has temporarily
"bailed out" local governments in many areas. But rising costs will
probably soak up that source of funds quickly and confront cities with
the same situation again in the near future.

The Importance of Public-Sector Action Capabilities

One of the most crucial factors determining the success of any private
central-city investment is the quality of the local government there,
especially the capabilities of its personnel in certain key positions.

Table 8-1   Risk in Central-City Investment

Degree of Investment Risk	*Appropriate Form of Investment Organization*
Very low	Purely private
Moderate	Combined private and public
High	Purely public
Very high	None—Too risky

Only effective local government can produce certain community conditions required to make most private investments a success in both the short-run and the long-run. These include rather broad conditions like personal and property security, provision of adequate garbage collection and street cleaning and maintenance, property transportation facilities and arteries, good schools and responsible fiscal management. In addition, large-scale central city investments often require developers to work closely with key city officials in arranging proper zoning changes, utility connections, street connections, and direct public services for the new development.

Unfortunately, the capabilities of many local government staffs are extremely limited. In some cities, local personnel have simply been unable to cope effectively with the bewildering variety of federally financed programs that have been created in the past decade. Nor have they been able to anticipate and cope with key social and economic changes occurring within their communities. Until improved skills are available in these roles, the limitations of those performing them will remain a significant obstacle to private investment success.

This deficiency is made even more significant by the shift of federal funding toward greater emphasis upon revenue sharing. More revenue sharing means greater discretion by local government officials, with fewer checks and guidelines from federal authorities.

Another factor accentuating the importance of local government competence is the need to use public development corporations as "actors of last resort" in some very high risk investment situations.

Continuing Private Investment in Downtown Office Space and High Quality Residential Areas Within Central Cities

In spite of all the negative factors cited above, private investors have been sinking large amounts of capital into certain types of projects in some central cities. The main target has been creation of downtown office space and national headquarters cities (New York, Chicago, and Washington) and regional gateway cities (Boston, Atlanta, Miami, Houston, Dallas, Denver, Los Angeles, San Francisco, Minneapolis-St. Paul, and Seattle). Most other large downtowns have received some investment, but not as much as the key centers where demands for office space are unusually high. However, much of this downtown investment has come from institutional firms that are "locked in" to downtown locations (such as large banks creating office monuments for themselves), rather than from entrepreneurs trying to achieve competitive rates of return on invested equity. As a result, there is now a short-term surplus of downtown (*and* suburban) office space in most major cities. In housing markets, until 1974, private investors motivated by desires for tax shelter have been building new housing—especially high-rise apartments—in high quality neighborhoods within many large central cities, especially where those areas are distant from concentrations of the poor. There was even a large burst of investment in subsidized housing for low- and moderate-income housing under Section 235 and 236 programs from 1968 through 1973. These housing investments were encouraged by an unprecedented flow of money into real estate-oriented lending institutions from 1971 to mid-1973, especially savings and loan associations and real estate investment trusts. However, there is still a dearth of all types of investment in older, deteriorating residential areas. In fact, failure of owners to maintain and repair property in such areas has created positive disinvestment there, especially in neighborhoods marked by abandonment.

SPECIFIC OBSTACLES IMPEDING PRIVATE CENTRAL-CITY INVESTMENT

From the preceding background factors and other sources, we have derived a list of specific obstacles impeding private central-city investment. We have also related those obstacles to particular types of investment in particular areas of central cities to see which obstacles are most important in each. This classification is a prerequisite to discussing possible means of overcoming these key obstacles.

Types of Central-City Areas Considered

For purposes of this analysis, we have divided the central city into the following spatial zones:

    1. The central business district and its immediate "frame" area containing ancillary (mainly nonresidential) land uses. We call this the *downtown area.*

    2. Inner-city neighborhoods suffering from serious abandonment and/or high concentrations of very poor households, including many on welfare. We call these *inner-city poverty areas.*

    3. Older central-city neighborhoods near inner-city poverty areas, but not yet suffering from major abandonment or advanced deterioration. We refer to these as *gray areas.*

    4. Newer neighborhoods at the periphery of central cities or in the suburbs, occupied mainly by middle-income and upper-income households. We call these *high-quality peripheral areas.*

    5. Older central-city neighborhoods that have maintained high property values and mainly middle-income and upper-income occu-

pancy, even though they are near the heart of the city, because of proximity to some outstanding amenities, such as a lakefront or riverfront, a university, or park. We call these *high-quality in-city areas.*

The discussion and recommendations in this paper concentrate on what could be done to increase private investment in *downtown areas, inner-city poverty areas,* and *gray areas.*

Types of Investment Considered

This paper analyzes *residential* investment and *commercial* investment separately. Attention is focused upon investment in housing for low- and moderate-income households, although we also consider all types of residential investment in the areas being analyzed.

Types of Obstacles to Private Investment

The myriad obstacles to private residential and commercial investment in the areas described above could be classified in many different ways. For convenience only, we have separated them into three groups, while recognizing that many other divisions might be equally plausible. These groups are described below, with the specific obstacles in each listed and with the terms used to refer to each obstacle in italics.

1. Neighborhood conditions: Obstacles consisting of local environmental conditions that inhibit private investment, including those that reduce the marketability of any new facilities created and those that generate high construction or maintenance costs. These obstacles are as follows:
    a.   High *crime rates* and the feelings of insecurity they generate.
    b.   *Vandalism.*
    c.   Relatively *poor-quality public schools* (as judged by existing and potential residents).
    d.   Serious *traffic congestion.*
    e.   Relatively *poor-quality public services*—such as street cleaning, building code enforcement, garbage removal, street repair and maintenance, and fire prevention. It should be emphasized that the poor quality of these services is here evaluated in terms of the *quality of their results,* not their *input costs* or the *quality of inputs* in terms of salary costs, skills, years of service, etc.
    f.   Presence of *abandoned buildings* not yet demolished.
    g.   *Poor* property *maintenance* and upkeep by private owners.
    h.   High concentrations of households on welfare (referred to as *concentrated poverty*).
    i.   Generally *"messy" neighborhood appearance* caused by the

presence of papers in the streets, abandoned cars, and general debris in many streets, vacant lots, and backyards.

j. *Non-child-oriented environment* that lacks open space suitable for playgrounds, has high-rise dwellings that make watching over children difficult, and is generally more oriented to adult activities than those of children.

2. Market conditions: Obstacles consisting of market conditions or behavior patterns adverse to successful investment in commercial or residential properties. These are as follows:

a. *White withdrawal* from and refusal to enter residential areas that are primarily black, Puerto Rican, or other minority-group occupied, or are perceived by the white housing market as likely to become primarily so occupied in the near future.

b. A downward shift in average incomes that occurs when a neighborhood undergoes "massive transition" from middle-income to low-income occupancy. This sometimes coincides with racial transition from white to black occupancy, though not always. We will refer to this as the *income shift.*

c. *Fragmented ownership* of land parcels and properties that makes both assembly of large sites and enforcement of codes and maintenance very difficult.

d. An *excess supply of housing* in the metropolitan area housing market in relation to market demand for it without direct subsidies, not necessarily in relation to "needs" for it.

e. The *need to use subsidized housing* to accommodate low- and moderate-income households who must be included in central-city projects for social and political reasons, even though this reduces project profitability and adds greatly to red tape and potential time delays.

f. Adverse market effects of newer, better located, and generally *superior suburban competition* from similar facilities appealing to the same markets.

3. Cost-increasing conditions: Obstacles consisting of conditions or factors (other than neighborhood conditions) that tend to increase the costs of investment or development, thereby reducing profitability. These are as follows:

a. *High land costs.*

b. *High construction costs* resulting from need for union labor, need to use high-rise construction, congested streets, and other factors.

c. *High property taxes,* especially on new or rehabilitated properties.

d. *High insurance costs* resulting from high risks of vandalism and fire or riot.

e. *High security costs* resulting from the need for 24-hour guarding of building sites to prevent theft and vandalism, for patrolling and guarding completed housing far more intensively than competitive suburban units, and for paying extra to induce workmen to work in high crime areas.

f. *Government delays* in granting permissions and approving plans. The more government aids that are provided, the greater the delays, other things being equal.

g. *High borrowing costs and unavailability of financing* because of greater risks and lender refusal to invest without federal guarantees.

h. *High land assembly costs* because of fragmented ownership, political resistance to consolidating parcels, needs to demolish old buildings, and legal complexities of clearing title when abandonment has occurred and tax and other obligations exist.

i. *Excessive uncertainty* about what rules and characteristics public authorities and citizen groups will impose upon a development, often changing these requirements in the midst of the development process.

It certainly would be possible to add other factors to these three lists, or to classify those presented here differently. However, we believe this classification is adequate for the purposes of this paper.

THE RELATIVE IMPORTANCE OF SPECIFIC OBSTACLES FOR PARTICULAR TYPES OF INVESTMENT

The 25 specific obstacles listed above have widely varying degrees of importance in relation to particular types of private investment in particular parts of central cities. Some obstacles may be crucial hindrances to one type of investment in a certain kind of area, but may be wholly irrelevant to another type in another kind of area. To show which obstacles are most important for each type of investment in each kind of area, we have developed the *significance chart* (Figure 8-1). This chart is a matrix with specific obstacles forming the rows and combinations of investment types and areas forming the columns. Each box at the intersection of a row and a column has been used to show the *relative* significance of the specific obstacle concerned in hindering private investment (either residential or commercial) in the particular kind of area concerned. Symbols have been placed in these boxes to indicate varying degrees of relative significance in hindering private investment. Three qualifications must be made concerning Figure 8-1. First, the ratings shown are based upon our subjective judgments. Others with greater experience concerning some of these investments can undoubtedly improve the chart by altering some of these ratings. Second, many obstacles have overlapping effects; hence, the influence of some may be duplicated. For example, high security costs are caused by high crime rates and vandalism. Third, no one-at-a-time rating of specific obstacles can adequately convey the overall situation faced by private investors in these areas. Therefore, in the following paragraphs, we present a capsule narrative summary of the chief impediments to investment in each area. It is based upon the significance chart, but it seeks to provide a more subtle overview and weighting of individual obstacles than can be shown on such a table.

Residential Investment

1. *Downtown Areas.* The biggest obstacles to downtown residential development are very high land and land assembly costs, plus difficulties in marketing apartments or condominiums right downtown because of fears of personal insecurity. However, insecurity can be overcome by creating a "vertical walled enclave" that has controlled access and contains many different facilities inside the enclave (housing, theater, restaurants, laundry, and some convenience shopping). Thus, the really crucial problem is very high land costs. Land values right in the central business district are established by the high prices paid for office building sites, so they all but preclude residential development. Nearby land is also so costly only luxury units can be built on it. Construction costs are high because high-rise buildings are the only kind that are feasible with these land costs. The resulting high densities also make traffic congestion and parking serious problems. Government delays and uncertainty can become serious in large-scale "new town in-town" projects, but they need not be troublesome in smaller projects that do not require planned unit development zoning.

2. *Inner-City Poverty Areas.* As the chart shows, residential development in these areas is plagued by almost every possible type of problem. At the outset, it is extremely difficult to generate any market demand for housing in these areas from people with enough money to pay for it, since they also enjoy choices of alternative locations. Their reluctance to live in these areas is caused by white withdrawal, high crime rates, vandalism, and the other adverse neighborhood conditions starred on the chart. Vandalism leads to high insurance, construction, and security costs. It also causes high borrowing costs and unavailability of financing. Since any housing in these areas must contain at least some subsidized units to accommodate low- and moderate-income households, it is subject to government delays and uncertainty.

In our opinion, the fundamental difficulty is the heavy concentration

Figure 8-1

Figure 8-1   Relative Significance of Specific Obstacles in Hindering Private Investment in Different Parts of Central Cities

Type of Obstacle		High crime rates and insecurity	Vandalism	Poor quality public schools	Traffic congestion	Poor quality of other public services	Abandoned buildings	Poor property maintenance	Concentrated poverty	Messy neighborhood appearance	Non-child-oriented environment
Gray Area Investment	Comm.	•	•	•	*	•	—	•	*	•	—
Gray Area Investment	Resid.	*	•	*	—	•	—	*	—	•	—
Inner-City Poverty Area Investment	Comm.	*	*	•	•	•	•	*	*	•	—
Inner-City Poverty Area Investment	Resid.	*	*	*	—	•	*	*	*	•	•
Downtown Area Investment	Comm.	•	—	•	•	—	—	—	•	—	—
Downtown Area Investment	Resid.	*	—	—	*	•	—	—	•	—	•

Key
* Crucially important
• Significant, but usually not crucial
— Of minor or negligible importance

	Market Conditions					Cost-Increasing Conditions								
*	*	|	|	|	*	•	•	•		•	|	|	|	*
*	*	*	*	|	*	•	•	•	|	•	|	*	|	*
*	*	|	|	|	|	•	•	•	*	*	•	*	|	*
*	*	*	•	*	|	•	•	•	*	*	*	*	|	*
*	•	|	|		*	*	•	•	|	•	•	|	•	|
•	|	*	•	•	•	*	*	•	|	•	*	|	•	*
White withdrawal	Downward income shift—low demand	Fragmented land ownership	Excess supply of housing	Need for subsidized housing	Superior suburban competition	High land costs	High construction costs	High property taxes	High insurance costs	High security costs	Government delays	High borrowing costs and unavailability of financing	High land assembly costs	Excessive uncertainty

Prepared by Real Estate Research Corporation.

of very poor households in such areas. This results in a total level of demand inadequate to support good quality housing, and generates many adverse neighborhood conditions, thereby causing households affluent enough to support good housing to stay out of inner-city poverty areas.

3. *Gray Areas.* Gray areas have residents with high enough incomes to sustain adequate property maintenance, if all owners are compelled to do so. Yet many of these areas are "threatened" by possible future transition to lower-income occupancy. Hence, private investors are fearful of committing funds on any long-term basis, as is required for *new* housing. Moreover, it is often hard to persuade all owners to keep up their properties, especially absentee owners of large apartment buildings. They are reluctant to spend large sums upgrading their obsolete buildings because of the same uncertainty about the area's future. Thus, the population dynamics of each central city are crucially important in determining the economic feasibility of residential investment in its gray areas. More effective planning to control future population dynamics is probably unlikely. If so, then shortening the capital recovery period on private investment may be the only way to cope with existing uncertainty, other than a complete cessation of new investment. Yet shorter recovery periods cannot be accomplished through higher rents, since the housing in these areas competes with newer units in peripheral neighborhoods. That is why government housing programs have turned to tax shelters as a way of inducing private investment in such areas (as in the Section 236 program).

Commercial Investment

1. *Downtown Areas.* The biggest obstacles to downtown commercial development are high land costs, the longer-term threat of white withdrawal from downtown patronage in some big cities (as in St. Louis), and a vast expansion of high quality suburban competition in retail, office space, hotel, and entertainment markets. Nevertheless, many cities have experienced big downtown increases in new office space and some rises in hotel space, even enough to produce temporary market surpluses. Commercial investment in downtown areas still has the greatest feasibility of any of the six basic types of investment covered by this analysis.

2. *Inner-City Poverty Areas.* The two main obstacles shutting off most such investment are lack of demand because of relatively low incomes in surrounding neighborhoods, and high operating costs resulting from crime, vandalism, and the need for far greater security measures than in suburban areas. As noted in relation to residential devel-

opment, lack of demand is in turn aggravated by insecurity, since the latter keeps people with money from entering these areas.

Also, low-quality schools turn out too many young people inadequately trained to enter the labor force in terms of either their technical skills or their attitudes and acceptance of work discipline. (This affects commercial investment in all three kinds of areas.)

3. *Gray Areas.* Uncertainty about the long-term future of these areas makes investors reluctant to put new or upgraded facilities in them, even though present demand is strong enough to sustain such facilities. Actually many new commercial facilities have been built in gray areas, especially by national or regional chain operators who can afford to take relatively high risks on a few of their many units. As with residential investment in these areas, some way of reducing future uncertainty about which ones will undergo "massive" downward income shifts—or of eliminating such shifts by dispersing future increases in the low-income population—would greatly improve investment prospects in those areas likely to retain their economic viability. Even now it is easier to generate commercial investment in such areas than residential investment. Many large-scale commercial operators have strong credit ratings they can use to obtain financing; whereas residential investment is financed mainly through the credit generated by each property itself, which in turn comes from its occupants.

ENCOURAGING CENTRAL-CITY INVESTMENT BY INCREASING ITS PROFITABILITY

Both developers and investors are motivated mainly by the desire to make profits, so obstacles to central-city investment can be viewed as factors that reduce its profitability. One basic strategy for encouraging more such investment is improving its profitability, either by reducing the obstacles described earlier or in other ways. This section of the paper explores some implications of such a strategy. It starts with a statement of certain assumptions underlying the tactics to be suggested and then discusses those tactics.

Assumptions Shaping Profit-Improving Tactics

1. *Development—as distinct from investment—is a vitally important economic function that requires great skill and perseverance and can be generated only by adequate economic rewards.* We define a *developer* as one who initiates a construction or other urban environment-enhancing project and manages it through to its conclusion. His

major functions are: (1) conceiving of and defining the project; (2) identifying and organizing all the specific "actors" and resources necessary to carry it out; (3) providing those "actors" with incentives that motivate them to act; (4) providing the constant inputs of energy necessary to keep all these "actors" moving toward project completion; and (5) overcoming all the anticipated and unforeseen obstacles that arise in connection with any project. It takes great skill, energy, imagination, and perseverance to perform these functions. Supplying these ingredients is an act different from, and usually independent of, *investment,* which we define as putting up the money required to finance a project. Developers deserve to earn significant profits in return for supplying these nonfinancial ingredients. Moreover, if they are not offered the prospect of earning such profits, they will not supply the ingredients, and no central-city development will occur. These points may seem obvious, but they are constantly contested by people who object to the "exorbitant" profits developers supposedly receive from urban renewal and other central-city investment. It seems clear to us that the profits from central-city investment are nowhere near high enough, or else there would be a lot more of it going on.

2. *In general, private developers are far more effective in creating housing and commercial facilities than public agencies acting as developers.* We believe this is true for the following reasons:

a. Private developers are more willing to take risks than public officials, and most development in central cities is a high-risk business.

b. The potential rewards of private development, especially long-term capital gains and tax shelter for other income, can be much larger than any rewards that public agencies can offer their members. Hence, private development attracts people with much higher levels of entrepreneurial skill than can normally be employed by public agencies.

c. Private developers do not have to please as broad a constituency as public officials and, therefore, can define their goals more narrowly, even though they are still subject to the influence of numerous citizens' groups.

d. Private developers have strong incentives to complete a project as rapidly as possible, since failing to do so can be very costly to them personally. Public officials have no such incentives. On the contrary, they are motivated to delay whenever further action is likely to stir up controversy. This is true because the rewards of private development depend upon positive results; whereas those of public officialdom depend mainly upon survival through avoidance of negative reactions.

3. In light of the above, *the best strategy for coping with the present inadequate profitability of central-city development is somehow to increase its profitability so as to attract private developers, rather than to turn it over to public agencies.* The development function described above must be performed if significant improvements are to be built in central cities, especially in inner-city poverty areas and gray areas. If central-city development does not provide sufficient rewards to motivate private developers, it is a delusion to think that turning responsibility for it over to public agencies will somehow generate performance of that function. The real alternative to motivating private developers is having no one motivated to perform the functions described earlier, since public officials normally cannot be motivated to do so effectively.

This conclusion does not mean there should be no role whatever for public agencies as developers. Some facilities, such as certain kinds of public housing, should definitely be owned and operated by public agencies. In other cases, public agencies should act as "developers of last resort," as discussed in Section VII of this paper. Nevertheless, this strategy implies the desirability of using private developers wherever that is both possible and compatible with the basic objectives and functions concerned.

Specific Tactics for Improving Development Profitability

1. *Participation in high-risk developments or financing serving relatively low-income areas could be linked to participation in low-risk developments or financing projects elsewhere that offer excellent potential profits.* Private developers and investors would then be motivated to assume the burdens of the former in order to reap the rewards of the latter. For example, awarding contracts for the construction of "routine" city facilities such as police garages, street construction and repair, school buildings, etc., could be made contingent upon simultaneous participation by the contractor in the creation of subsidized housing in inner-city poverty areas. This can be viewed either as "rewarding" those developers courageous enough to carry out the latter, or "raising the ante" for those who normally perform only the former.

It should be recognized that such "packaging" of several contracts for developments of widely varying types would require a degree of cooperation, advanced planning, and coordination among city government departments that is now rarely achieved. Moreover, it would probably result in somewhat higher average construction or financing costs for low-risk projects. Private developers or lenders would have to include a larger average risk allowance on a package combining several projects of varying risks than they would on a single low-risk project.

Nevertheless, this is a way to increase the attractiveness of presently unattractive types of central-city developments without tapping any major new sources of funds.

As noted above, this technique could be applied to financing as well as to construction. The profitable privilege of handling city bonds or tax warrants might be linked to the riskier provision of interim financing or "front money" on inner-city projects or participation in long-term mortgages for them.

Such linkage of diverse projects into "pooled contracts" can be done only by relatively large development firms. Unfortunately, nearly all indigenous inner-city development firms are rather small and could not therefore undertake such projects except as subcontractors to larger developers. However, experience indicates that many of these relatively new inner-city developers need added resources and administrative assistance from more established firms anyway; hence such joint or subcontractor relationships could still help them develop and expand their capabilities.

In some places, such linkage of different construction projects in a single contract might be considered illegal. Present bidding laws may require awarding contracts for each job to the lowest bidder. However, it might be possible to modify such laws or devise contractual arrangements for "pooled projects" which did not violate them.

2. *City governments could set up special centralized "expediter" offices to help developers negotiate various governmental and other permissions.* This would reduce both the time cost and uncertainties of central-city development. New York City has created such "expediters" as part of its subarea city planning efforts (as in Lower Manhattan and Midtown Manhattan). However, an "expediter" would not have to directly be engaged in physical planning to be effective. If the "expediter" were part of the mayor's office, and had access to all relevant departments with some of the influence of the mayor, he could act as an "inside advocate" for the developer. Some cities have used this approach in economic development efforts to keep large employers in the city or attract new ones. True, the "expediter" would not have unlimited authority and would still encounter delay and bureaucracy in individual departments. But he would have continual business with each department, and therefore could develop much easier and faster informal communications channels than an individual entrepreneur working one project. This tactic may not seem impressive, but we believe the tremendous uncertainties attached to central-city development comprise one of the biggest obstacles keeping developers out of such activity. A developer never knows how long a proposed project will take, or just what audiences he must please to get it approved, or what changes in rules will occur after his project is well underway. If this

type of uncertainty could be drastically reduced by a centralized "expediter," the time cost of development—a crucial one—could be greatly reduced and stabilized.

3. *Existing real estate assessment practices could be modified to provide stronger incentives for new development.* In particular, the full burden of real estate assessment related to a new property's market value could be placed on the property gradually over some initial incentive period, rather than all at once. For example, if a new office building had a market value of $25 million, and the assessor's typical assessment ratio was 50 percent of market value, the "proper" assessed value would be $12.5 million as soon as the building was completed. However, the assessor might use only 20 percent of the $12.5 million as the assessed value in the first year, 40 percent the second year, 60 percent the third year, 80 percent the fourth year, and 100 percent thereafter. This kind of policy should be based upon explicit local council approval or should at least be openly described by the assessor and applied uniformly to new income properties—not at his discretion in a variable manner.

Similarly, individual home rehabilitation and repairs could be gradually phased into assessment revisions, instead of a full and immediate upward reassessment occurring upon completion of rehabilitation. Such "gradualism" is better than either an immediate upward assessment for the full amount or just ignoring the increase in value. The latter eventually causes the entire assessment system to lose any uniform relationship to market value and therefore to become highly inequitable and unfair.

4. *Public agencies could be empowered to use eminent domain procedures to assist private developers in assembling key sites.* This could be done whenever (1) the private developer had a publicly approved plan serving the public interest, and (2) the private developer had assembled some majority percentage of the proposed site without public assistance (say, 75 percent). This arrangement would undoubtedly require new city or state legislation, but it has a strong precedent in urban renewal legislation. The big differences would be eliminating blight as a requirement for acquisition and using the power of eminent domain on behalf of a private organization directly instead of through the two-stage process in urban renewal. Such procedures would help reduce "hold-out" costs without costing the public any major funding.

5. *New real estate appraisal techniques should be developed for land in downtown areas so that the speculative element now "artificially" inflating land prices there can be removed to encourage residential development.* At present, the prevailing price for downtown parcels potentially suitable for high-density office use is set by the possible income from a very tall office building erected on the site. However, the

number of big office buildings the market can absorb in the near future is much smaller than the number of potential sites for them. Consequently, owners of such sites make mutually inconsistent forecasts of the future uses of their sites. Many more believe they will "capture" big office buildings than can possibly do so in fact. As a result, each owner is led by uncertainty to hold out for a price much higher than the *average* price that would prevail if all the land downtown were evaluated as though it were all owned by one person. This "fallacy of composition" is masked by the practice of appraising property one parcel at a time, each time assuming *that* parcel will enjoy a better-than-average "capture" of the future market. An alternative to present appraisal methods would be collectively appraising the entire downtown area at once, then using an average price derived from such an appraisal, adjusted by particular site traits, to establish a value for each site. This method is used in new-town developments where large multi-use parcels like downtowns are in fact owned by one party. We believe a similar approach could be worked out for downtown areas and might drastically reduce the prices which public authorities would have to pay to acquire downtown sites for residential uses right in the midst of present office areas.

6. *City governments could develop two-quality-level housing codes that differentiated between minimum requirements in poverty areas and higher quality standards in nonpoverty areas.* The minimum requirements in poverty areas would be those physiologically necessary for safety and health but not necessarily up to the prevailing aesthetic and size standards of the middle class. This frank recognition of prevailing dual quality standards would perhaps allow authorities to enforce the minimum quality standard rigorously in even the poorest neighborhoods. They cannot do so now without imposing such high repair costs upon owners that they abandon the housing rather than sink that much money into it. Yet it would also allow authorities to enforce much higher-quality standards in nonpoor areas where the residents can really afford to pay for maintenance of a much better environment. (We have doubts about the practicality of this tactic, because even meeting minimum quality requirements may still be so expensive for owners in poverty areas that they will prefer abandonment.)

7. *FHA might develop a property value insurance program for residences located within some set distance of any publicly subsidized housing built for low- and moderate-income occupancy.* This insurance should guarantee the owners that their property would not decline in value (if they maintained it) as compared with its value when the subsidized housing was built. This program might reduce some prevailing fears that the presence of subsidized units will depress property values in central-city areas.

8. *The federal government could grant tax credits to business firms creating net additional jobs in certain designated inner-city high unemployment areas.* Although efforts to create new employment in inner-city areas through public incentives have not proven very effective to date, no incentives nearly as powerful as tax credits have been tried. It might be worthwhile at least experimenting with them, if they were awarded only for creation of new jobs in areas where very few are now being created (so we would not be paying firms to do something they were going to do anyway, as most tax credit programs do).

9. *Present Title VII ("New Community") financial aids could be extended to smaller planned-unit-developments in central cities, especially in inner-city poverty areas.* Such aids include federal guarantees for bond issues used for land purchases and installation of infrastructures, plus expanded grants for certain types of development-furthering activities (such as installation of sewer and water treatment facilities). These aids could be expanded in scope—especially to cover initial planning—and extended to inner-city investments at the planned-unit-development scale, rather than just the larger "new city in city" scale, as at present.

HELPING DEVELOPERS CREATE VIABLE RESIDENTIAL ENVIRONMENTS

The most crucial obstacle to all types of central-city investment is the absence of a viable and desirable neighborhood environment. If any given area has a safe, clean, attractive neighborhood environment well provided with adequate-quality public services, and people believe it will remain that way in the future, then households with money are willing to live, work, or play there. Their willingness constitutes a financial resource upon which private investment can be built and sustained. But many parts of central cities lack such an environment for the many reasons cited earlier. In our opinion, no strategy for encouraging central-city investment can possibly succeed unless it contains effective tactics for markedly improving the neighborhood environments now dominant there. This section of the paper explores some assumptions underlying such tactics and then suggests some tactics.

Assumptions Shaping Neighborhood-Environment-Improving Tactics

1. *Households with sufficient incomes to support decent-quality housing without direct subsidies want to live in neighborhoods where other such middle- and upper-income households are dominant,* both

residentially and in local schools and public facilities. They seek such dominance because they believe it is conducive to orderly and safe movement on the streets, to value-reinforcing experiences for their children in and around schools, to adequate and physically attractive property maintenance and street cleanliness, and to the absence of vandalism, burglary, drug addiction, and other conditions they (along with most people) regard as undesirable. *This situation creates a need for both private developers and city authorities to cooperate in establishing areas of stable middle-class dominance within central cities if they really want to encourage development and investment.* This conclusion is quite controversial, since it implies that neighborhoods occupied mainly by low- and moderate-income households cannot successfully attract much new investment aimed at nonsubsidized residents.

2. *Personal and property security are absolutely essential ingredients in creating the type of neighborhood environment that will attract private investment.* Moreover, except in very small areas, adequate security cannot be achieved solely through the efforts of public police forces, as by adding more and more patrols. Rather, it also requires one or more of the following ingredients:

a. Controlled access to "enclaves" within which high intensity surveillance and/or patrol are maintained.

b. Physical design which facilitates security, as described in Oscar Newman's book *Defensible Space* (New York, Macmillan: 1972).

c. Active community participation in surveillance and reporting of strangers or illegitimate incidents or suspicious behavior.

Creating these conditions requires a willingness of public authorities to set up "enclaves" with highly limited access, even within all-publicly-owned establishments such as public housing projects. This is a departure from libertarian concepts that everyone ought to have access to any space that is publicly supported. Yet without such willingness, it will be extremely hard to generate the conditions of security required to promote private investment.

3. *The desired neighborhood environment must be created at a certain minimum-sized neighborhood scale in order to be effective and believable.* As noted above, this high-security environment must be differentiated from surrounding lower-level security areas. Moreover, the area included within the high-security zone must be large enough for households to conduct most of the normal actions associated with those parts of their daily lives related to their dwelling units. To attract child-oriented households with school-aged children, this scale must be at least large enough for the support of an elementary public school in which children from this high-security environment are dominant.

For adult-oriented populations, the scale can be smaller, even down to a single high-rise building if it has direct access to transportation out of surrounding low-security environs. But even for such populations, the preferable minimum scale is large enough so that residents can share certain community-oriented facilities, such as a store, tennis courts, a swimming pool, etc., solely with other members of this "enclave."

4. *Creating the type of neighborhood environment required to attract investment requires a cooperative effort of local government authorities and private developers.* Public authorities must provide certain public services with adequate quality, or at least a basic level of such services which can be coordinated with additional inputs from private developers. These services and feasible mixtures of public and private inputs for them include the following:

Table 8-2   Neighborhood Services Needed to Attract Investments

Service	Type of Mixture of Public and Private Inputs Which Is Feasible	
	In Middle- and Upper-Income Developments	In Developments Also Serving Some Low- and Moderate-Income Households
Personal and property security	Mainly private on the site	Public base, limited private access control and resident surveillance
Schools	Mainly public, some private	Almost entirely public
Street and public space cleaning	Mainly private	Partly public, partly private
Fire protection	Entirely public	Entirely public
Enforcement of property maintenance	Private with public as latent threat	Private with public threat also

5. *In cities where the total low-income population is expanding significantly (or the total minority-group population is expanding significantly), it is impossible to "stabilize" the population of every neighborhood (that is, to prevent "massive transition" from present occupancy by one group to future occupancy by another) unless at least some members of the expanding group enter many neighborhoods distant from the edges of the areas where they now predominate (so-called "ghettos").* This in turn requires some type of "dispersal" strategy concerning at least much of the growth of the expanding group (though not necessarily concerning its present population). Such "dispersal" can involve either integrated or segregated scattering of the

households concerned. However, exploring this aspect of overall urban development strategy is beyond the scope of this paper.

Specific Tactics for Improving Neighborhood Environments to Attract Investment

1. To facilitate assembly of large enough sites to achieve the necessary scale of redevelopment, the following tactics could be used:

a. Employment of eminent domain powers to assist private developers, as explained in the preceding section of this paper.

b. Focus of major redevelopment efforts on sites now largely nonresidential in use, such as old railroad yards, navy yards, and obsolete industrial districts. This avoids the needs for household relocation which make it politically difficult to use large sites which are presently residential.

2. *Public authorities should be willing to create "walled enclaves" within cities* with controlled access to them as a means of raising the level of average security there. I recognize that this tactic is repugnant to many liberals. Nevertheless it is a realistic response to our inability to halt rising urban crime rates.

3. *The physical designs of all residential structures in central cities, especially all those using public funds, should conform to principles of security-enhancement like those described by Oscar Newman in "Defensible Space."* For that purpose, the city should create a board of security design review staffed by architects familiar with— and sympathetic to—those principles. It should use that board as a mandatory part of the planning review and building permit process for high-crime areas.

4. *Experiments should be carried out testing neighborhood security surveillance organizations, staffed by local residents (perhaps voluntary, perhaps paid small amounts).* These residents should be given specific surveillance and reporting assignments, plus adequate reporting equipment, so as to supplement normal police patrol activities in high-crime areas. The function of these organizations should not be law enforcement, but crime prevention through surveillance which is well known to exist within the community.

5. *Experiments should also be carried out with new legal and organizational mechanisms for neighborhood management of all the residential property in a designated area.* The purpose would be to treat the entire area as though it were a single entity. This is in recognition of the externalities among individual parcels which create immense interdependencies among them. Thus, all property would be maintained up to a single quality standard. Either the individual owners would keep it at that standard or the neighborhood management organization would have the power to repair and improve it and charge

the owners for the costs of doing so. The neighborhood management organization would also be empowered to take immediate control over any individual units in the area that became vacant, so as to stop vandals from wrecking them. Furthermore, it would be desirable to have this same organization control the occupancy of *all* rental units in the area so as to keep the area from becoming heavily populated by very poor families through many individually uncoordinated decisions by separate landlords. In essence, the management organization could when necessary exercise almost all the powers of ownership, but without actually buying the properties concerned. This is a critically necessary step in upgrading the environment in inner-city poverty areas. It is needed to prevent abandonment of one structure from having "contagion" effects that lead to the abandonment of many other basically sound structures nearby. Clearly, new legislative action would be required to create such organizations and give them the powers described above. The idea is not to usurp any powers of owners who are responsibly managing their own property; they should be left to run it. But society must develop some mechanisms that recognize the interdependence of the fragmented parts of those poverty areas and also recognize that private behavior patterns that are effective in middle-class areas simply do not work here. The organizational vehicle could be a community development corporation, or a semi-public corporation, or something else. Such mechanisms will be essential to allow continuation of the strategy of "flooding the housing market" with new units, thereby depressing the values of old ones. We need a way of achieving an "orderly withdrawal" from those old units that ought to be destroyed without dragging down whole neighborhoods.

IMPROVING LOCAL GOVERNMENT CAPABILITIES

As noted earlier, the capabilities of local government play crucial roles in making private—or public—investment profitable. Therefore, a basic strategy for encouraging more private investment in central cities is upgrading local government skills, powers, and organization in ways directly related to the needs of private investors—or to compensate for investors' inabilities or even their absence. This section sets forth some assumptions underlying such a strategy and some tactics for accomplishing it.

Assumptions Underlying Improvements in Local Government Capabilities

1. *Local government's main functions relevant to central-city investment are as follows:*

a. Providing the basic background services that comprise much of a desirable neighborhood environment.

b. Helping private developers obtain required local and other public approvals, meet desired standards, and overcome obstacles to investment.

c. Serving as "developers of last resort" where private investment is not economically feasible but some action is needed.

d. Making use of needed public investments to stimulate desirable private and public economic development within central cities.

2. *Public development corporations normally are confined to one or a relatively small number of projects each. They cannot usually generate large-scale investment like that which many private developers can create in the aggregate.* In this respect, each public development agency is like a single moderate-sized private developer. But dozens or hundreds of private developers can be stimulated into action very rapidly by an effective incentive scheme, such as the Section 236 program for rental housing. It is much harder—perhaps impossible—to obtain similar large-scale results anywhere near as fast from public developers.

3. *State governments play a crucial role in influencing the feasibility of investments in central cities and could do much more to improve that feasibility.* They do this by setting the basic rules controlling local government powers over building codes, zoning, property taxation, etc. How they might increase feasibility is described below.

Specific Tactics for Improving Local Government Capabilities

1. *State governments could create public development corporations that can enter joint ventures with private firms and act as developers of last resort.* Examples are the housing development agencies created by many states (such as Illinois and New Jersey) and the New York Urban Development Corporation. The former mainly act as means of providing financing for subsidized housing; whereas the latter acts as the direct planner and developer of specific projects.

2. *States should empower cities to create their own public development corporations and major cities should do so.* The operations of such corporations could be financed in part by revenue bonds, or general obligation bonds in some cases. Such corporations could then exercise powers of eminent domain for land assembly and could borrow money at lower rates than private developers because of the tax-exempt status of their securities.

Municipal development corporations could also create neighborhood-oriented subsidiaries to provide local community participation in inner-city poverty area projects. Municipal development corporations are almost necessary to allow adequate-sized land assembly for "new towns in town" and to insure that the land-use pattern adopted will meet community needs rather than be designed solely to maximize profits (which would generate mainly high-density, high-income uses).

3. *State governments should require local governments receiving revenue sharing through state agencies to devote certain proportions of the funds so obtained to both personnel training and progress evaluation.* The federal government should also place such requirements on federal funds sent directly to local governments.

4. *States should adopt uniform building codes for all communities within their boundaries, precluding the deliberate raising of building costs as a means of excluding low- and moderate-income housing.* Stimulated by Operation Breakthrough, over twenty states have adopted uniform codes for modular housing. This movement should be extended to all building and housing codes. Obsolete cost-raising requirements should be eliminated from the codes operative in central cities.

5. *State governments should put pressure upon each metropolitan area to develop areawide plans controlling future urban growth and create incentives for the development of institutions capable of such planning.* Most metropolitan areas already have some type of regional planning agency, but it has little power to get its plans implemented. States could make receipt of many federal funding aids coming through state government agencies dependent upon development of a single comprehensive plan for the future growth of the entire area and creation of regulations binding local governments in the area to that plan. This would probably require some type of metropolitan-area council similar to that in the Twin Cities region.

6. *Under some circumstances, state governments might guarantee certain aspects of private investments to encourage private capital to take on high-risk ventures.* Such guarantees might cover a certain return on capital invested over an initial five- to ten-year period—the very period when most real estate investments yield low returns because of high "front-end" costs.

7. *State governments might also pay local property taxes on certain types of investments during an initial five- to ten-year period.* This would be better than tax abatement, since local governments cannot afford to cut their incomes from properties to which they must furnish adequate services. Yet property taxes represent the single largest operating expense in most real estate projects—from 15 to 25 percent of gross income. Hence state payment of this significant amount would make private investment far more likely to be profitable.

CONCLUSION

This chapter is designed to provide background perspective for discussions concerning how to improve the prospects for central-city development and investment and to suggest a few specific tactics for achieving that goal. The tactics described in the paper are certainly not all-inclusive; many others could be devised. Moreover, many tactics suggested are tentative and exploratory and might prove undesirable upon further analysis. Hopefully, the background factors set forth and the tactics listed will stimulate identification of many more tactics and the improvement of those suggested herein.

9

The Law of Peak-Hour
Expressway Congestion

Recent experience on expressways in large U.S. cities suggests that traffic congestion is here forever. Apparently, no matter how many new superroads are built connecting outlying areas with the downtown business district, auto-driving commuters still move at a crawl during the morning and evening rush hours.

To many a frustrated commuter, this result indicates abysmally bad foresight by highway planners. However, the real cause of peak-hour congestion is not poor planning, but the operation of traffic equilibrium. In fact, its results are so automatic we can even put them in the form of Downs's Law of Peak-Hour Traffic Congestion, or Parkinson's Second Law adapted to traffic: *On urban commuter expressways, peak-hour traffic congestion rises to meet maximum capacity.*[1]

Behind this law lies a complex set of forces which we can best

Reprinted from *Traffic Quarterly* 16, no. 3 (July 1962): 393–409, by permission of the Eno Foundation for Transportation, Inc. Some data have been updated for this edition.

[1] C. Northcote Parkinson, *The Law and the Profits* (Boston: Houghton Mifflin, 1960). It should be noted that this article deals exclusively with expressways which do not require their users to pay any direct tolls in order to drive upon them. The possibility of limiting congestion on such roads by introducing high tolls has been extensively discussed in the literature of economics and highway planning. However, most of the commuter expressways currently being built do not levy any direct tolls on their users. Therefore, the analysis presented in this chapter is relevant to the majority of cities in which commuter expressways exist, are under construction, or are being planned. For a discussion of the toll problem, see James Buchanan, "Private Ownership and Common Usage: The Road Case Re-Examined," *Southern Economic Journal* 22, no. 3 (January 1956): 305–316.

analyze by constructing a model of commuter decision-making based on the following assumptions:

1. Every commuter seeks to minimize the total amount of time he spends en route to and from work, within four major constraints:

a. *Income.* This constraint limits the means of transportation available to the commuter. Helicopters are now the technically fastest means of movement available to most commuters, but only one in a million can afford them. Thus time-minimization means seeking the shortest time that is economically feasible.

b. *Money costs of transportation.* A marked change in these costs (such as doubling of the subway fare) may shift a commuter from one means of transit to another. For purposes of our analysis, however, we will assume that no changes occur in the money costs of various forms of transportation unless specifically mentioned.

c. *Place of residence.* Some residential areas are not served by public transportation. Others have very restricted parking for automobiles. Hence, each person's choice of where to live influences to some extent what means of transportation will be selected in commuting. We will take everyone's place of residence as given for purposes of our analysis, even though the level of congestion may have definite feedbacks influencing long-run choices concerning job and residence location.

d. *Personal comfort.* Some auto-driving commuters could make faster time on public transportation, but the desire to avoid crowding and to be independent of time-scheduled trips undoubtedly makes comfort a factor in commuter patterns.

2. Most commuters follow the law of inertia. That is, once a commuter has selected a means of transportation and a specific route, he continues to follow it until some alteration in his environment pushes him across his route-decision threshold.

3. Route-changing alteration in a commuter's environment consists of some event which convinces the commuter that he could reduce his travel time by shifting his route (or his means of transportation).

4. For convenience, we can classify all commuters into two basic categories: those with low thresholds (explorers) and those with high thresholds (sheep).

a. *Explorers* are imaginative, high-strung, aggressive drivers who constantly search for some new route that will same them one or two minutes of driving time.

b. *Sheep* are more placid, patient, and resigned than explorers. They tend to follow the leader and to travel the same route unless some significant change in their environment occurs.

Every weekday morning, thousands of commuters set out from their homes for work. Within the constraints described and through a process of trial and error, they choose means of transportation and specific routes calculated to minimize their time en route. Assume that there are two routes for auto-driving commuters from Natick, Massachusetts, to downtown Boston. Both routes carry commuters over roads also traversed by many more motorists driving to Boston from other suburbs, and by other motorists driving across the down-town-bound flow of traffic. Thus the congestion experienced by commuters from Natick is a result of the decisions made by residents of a great many other parts of the metropolitan area besides Natick. Out of these myriad individual decisions comes a "typical" time consumed going downtown from Natick on Route A and another "typical" time consumed by going on Route B.

TRAFFIC EQUILIBRIUM

If these two times are about equal, then a balance is established for auto-driving Natick commuters. If they are not equal, imbalance exists. Explorers shifting from one route to the other, because of ephemeral obstacles on their usual path, will soon discover that one (say, Route A) takes less time; hence they will make Route A their normal path. Gradually word will filter around Natick and more driving commuters will shift from B to A. Similarly, commuters who live in other towns but also use routes A and B will be reacting in the same way. As the level of congestion on Route A rises and that on Route B falls, the total time required on Route A increases and that on Route B decreases. When the two travel times become equal, equilibrium has been established.

Normally, each such equilibrium is relatively stable because of the sheep, whose inertia keeps them grooved in the same route unless they receive decisive knowledge that another route is consistently faster. Since sheep outnumber explorers, the main streams of traffic on each major route remain the same day in and day out. On the margin, the explorers are ranging afield, testing other possibilities. If conditions change and they discover a faster route, they all vanish from the slower ones and gradually some of the sheep follow. Ultimately, a new equilibrium is established.

In order to analyze the effect of a new expressway upon commuter congestion, let us assume that traffic equilibrium has been reached prior to the creation of the expressway. Then a new superhighway is opened connecting the downtown business district with outlying suburban areas. This road is a nonstop limited-access highway with multiple lanes in each direction. It has been cut through the city in such a way that its linear length is less than the length of any alternative combinations of existing streets. As a result, the no-traffic, nonstop driving time between the residential areas served by the new road and downtown is much less than on previously existing routes at any given automobile speed.

What happens to commuter congestion when such a new highway opens? To some extent, the answer depends upon what forms of public transportation are operating in the city concerned. Therefore we will consider three separate cases. We will also assume for the moment that both the total number of commuters and automobile ownership among them remain the same before and after the new expressway is opened.

CASE A: A CITY WITH AUTO-DRIVING COMMUTERS ONLY

Where all commuters travel by automobile, the opening of a new expressway reduces peak-hour traffic congestion on many previously existing streets, because large numbers of commuters shift onto the new expressway. At first, they are able to make much better time on the expressway. However, word of this time disequilibrium soon spreads, and even more commuters shift from other routes onto the expressway. Gradually the time required for commuting on the expressway rises as peak-hour congestion increases; whereas the time required on alternate routes falls as traffic on them decreases. When these two times become identical, equilibrium is restored.

At the new equilibrium point, the rush-hour level of congestion on previously existing routes paralleling the expressway is considerably lower than it was earlier. Commuting on these routes therefore requires less time than before.

However, the rush-hour level of congestion on the expressway almost always exceeds its designed optimal capacity. For example, assume that the new road is designed to move 6,000 cars per hour past a given point at a speed of 50 miles per hour. When traffic volume at the peak-hour has risen to 6,000 cars per hour, these cars will still be moving at 50 miles per hour. Since this speed is probably faster than the speed attainable on previously existing city routes marked by cross streets and stoplights, equilibrium will not have been reached. More cars will move onto the expressway from other routes until the speeds on all routes are identical. However, even at this point, equilibrium will not have been reached. The expressway is shorter than the other routes; hence motorists traveling at the same average speeds over all routes will still arrive at their destinations faster on the expressway. Therefore route-shifting onto the expressway will continue until the average speed on the expressway is reduced to *below* the average speed on alternate routes. Clearly, the expressway was designed to handle traffic at *higher* speeds than previously existing roadways; yet, at equilibrium, traffic on the expressway is moving *more slowly* than traffic on the older routes. Therefore we can say that *congestion on the expressway has risen to surpass its optimal capacity.* This result is a necessary outcome of the forces of traffic equilibrium.

It should be pointed out that the maximum capacity of an expressway is not attained at the relatively high speed at which the designers of the expressway intended it to carry traffic. As the average speed of traffic along a major road increases, the average interval between cars rises, because drivers tend to allow themselves more room for braking. This reduces the total number of cars passing a given point in any period of time. In lower ranges of speed, such increases in interval are more than offset by the fact that more cars can pass a given point during one hour because the cars are moving faster. But above 35 to 40 miles per hour, the effect of larger average intervals between cars outweighs the effect of increased speed, so the total number of cars that can pass a given point in an hour declines. Therefore, as the number of cars entering an expressway per hour rises, a point is eventually reached at which all cars must slow down to accommodate the heavier traffic going by a given point in one hour.[2]

Since most modern expressways are designed to carry traffic at 50 miles per hour or faster, the number of vehicles they can carry past a given point per hour at this optimal speed is smaller than the maximum number which they can carry by this point in an hour. Therefore, when traffic volume rises markedly, the commuters' average speed is forced below this optimal speed, and congestion surpasses the optimal capacity of the expressway. As we pointed out above, this is exactly what happens in our theoretical model of commuter behavior.

The only way in which such heavy congestion could be avoided is through creation of a single expressway or system of expressways with such an enormous capacity that all the commuters formerly driving on parallel conventional streets could use the new facilities and still maintain optimal speeds. Furthermore, such facilities would have to be wide enough to carry most of these commuters *simultaneously.*

---

[2] For a discussion of relation between speed and hourly capacity, see Theodore M. Watson, Wilbur S. Smith, and Frederick W. Hurd, *Traffic Engineering* (New York: McGraw-Hill, 1955), p. 382. The table on the indicated page shows the following specific relationship for highways of four or more lanes:

Vehicles per lane per hour (maximum)	Speed
1,500	35–40 mph.
1,250	40–45 mph.
1,000	45–50 mph.

Some auto-driving commuters attempt to avoid peak-hour congestion by leaving earlier or later than the period of greatest crowding. However, even if a new expressway were wide enough to carry *all* the peak-period traffic formerly moving on conventional streets, a telescoping of this "spreading out" over time would probably occur after the expressway opened. Drivers who previously left earlier or later than the peak moment to avoid maximum crowding would soon discover that they could depart closer to the peak moment, since the new expressway would reduce congestion at that moment. Therefore, more and more commuters would tend to leave right at or around the moment of maximum convenience (assuming most government offices and businesses continued to open and let out at about the same time). This would tend to push the level of crowding at that moment back to where it was before the expressway was opened, although it would also make the total peak period of shorter duration. Thus convergences in commuters' *time schedules* as well as their *route schedules* tend to force the level of congestion on an expressway during peak hours upwards to the maximum capacity of the expressway. In pure theory, only a road or system of roads wide enough to carry every commuter simultaneously at an optimal speed would be sufficient to eliminate all peak-hour congestion. It is obvious that no such roads are practical unless we convert our metropolitan areas into giant cement slabs. Therefore, Downs's Law still holds: congestion at the peak hour will rise until the commuters' average speed is forced below the optimal speed for which the expressway was designed.

In summary, a new expressway serving the downtown district of a city in which all commuters travel by car will have the following effects:

1. It will reduce traffic on existing streets, thereby decreasing the average journey time on those streets for the commuters who still use them.

2. It will carry very heavy traffic loads during rush hours, heavier than its optimal capacity; hence, serious congestion will be created. Nevertheless, commuters using the expressway will have faster commuting trips than they did before it was opened.[3]

3. It will shorten the duration of the period of peak traffic congestion.

Whether the total time savings experienced in a city after a new expressway is opened—plus other benefits, such as greater safety— are sufficient to balance the cost of constructing the road depends

---

[3] For some evidence verifying this conclusion, see Paul T. McElhiney, "Evaluating Freeway Performance in Los Angeles," *Traffic Quarterly* 14, no. 3 (July 1960): 296–312.

upon the particular factors involved in each city; hence, we cannot reach any conclusion about it here.

CASE B: A CITY WITH BOTH AUTO-DRIVING AND BUS-RIDING COMMUTERS

A great many U.S. cities have extensive bus networks (some including fixed-rail streetcars) which carry thousands of commuters to work each day. How will the effects of a new suburbs-to-downtown express-way in such a city differ from its effects in a city with only auto-driving commuters?

Right after the expressway is introduced, congestion on all exist-ing streets falls, as described in the first case above. This enables buses as well as cars to move faster at peak hours, thus providing better service to bus riders. However, in relative terms, bus service does not speed up as fast as commuting by automobile. Buses must stop and start to pick up and discharge passengers. Such delays take about the same time no matter how much traffic exists on the streets. The total amount of time thus consumed is a "fixed cost" of each bus route. For express buses which load in a few stops in outlying areas and run nonstop downtown (vice versa in the evening), this fixed cost constitutes a relatively small proportion of total trip time. But for local buses which stop every few blocks throughout their route, this fixed cost may consume a considerable portion of total trip time.

Therefore, even though the time cost of both bus and automobile commuting falls when the expressway opens, the time costs of bus commuting falls considerably less than that of automobile commuting. As a result, some commuters shift from buses to driving their own cars. This causes a rise in congestion that partially offsets the initial improvement in travel speed effected by the opening of the express-way.

The extent to which this feedback tends to return traffic conges-tion on city streets to its pre-expressway level depends upon such factors as (1) the percentage of commuters who traveled by bus on routes paralleling the expressway before the latter was opened; (2) the percentage of such bus commuters who used local as opposed to express bus service; (3) the incomes of bus commuters; and (4) the availability and cost of terminal parking facilities in the downtown area.

If any large number of commuters abandon buses and start driving to work, a second feedback occurs: the cost of bus travel per person rises. As passenger revenues fall, bus lines find themselves under increasing pressure to reduce service or to raise fares. Either move has the effect of driving more bus commuters to using their automobiles, thus worsening the bus revenue situation.

This second feedback has two possible outcomes. In the most drastic case, each attempt by the bus line to adjust to lower passenger revenues by raising fares or cutting service causes so many more passengers to switch to automobiles that another adjustment is required, which causes more passengers to quit riding, thus requiring another adjustment, etc., until the bus line goes bankrupt and ceases operation.[4] However, it is unlikely that construction of any one expressway in a city will cause its bus lines to go bankrupt. Each expressway serves only a part of the entire metropolitan area; whereas its bus routes usually serve a much larger portion of the area. Therefore a very slight fare increase over the whole bus system would probably compensate for a very large withdrawal of customers in the section competing with the expressway. For this reason, the shifts in modes of transportation caused by the opening of one new expressway are likely to bring about a new equilibrium at a point where most of the bus service extant before the expressway appeared is still in effect.

But completion of a whole series of new expressways in one city may produce a very serious cumulative effect upon the city's bus system. If all of these expressways together serve almost the entire area also served by the bus system, the total withdrawal of commuting bus passengers into private automobile commuting may be very large indeed. Hence the downward spiral into bankruptcy described above may actually occur. Of course, insofar as any revenue losses induced by new expressways are made up through subsidies to the bus lines, no spiral effect such as that described above will occur.

Assuming that some bus lines are still operating after a new equilibrium point is established, this equilibrium will have the following characteristics in relation to the pre-expressway situation:

1. Commuting time will be less than before the expressway opened for all commuters.
2. A smaller proportion of all commuters will ride buses to and from work and a larger proportion will use automobiles.

---

[4] The ultimate equilibrium point (even if it occurs only when the bus operator becomes bankrupt) is essentially determined by the immediate shift in the demand for bus service caused by the opening of the new expressway. If the demand for bus service shifts completely to the left of the average total cost curve of the bus company, bankruptcy will inevitably result eventually. If not, equilibrium will eventually be established with some buses still running. The spiral of repeated fare increases and passenger losses which I have described is simply the process by which the bus company discovers the new equilibrium point (which may be bankruptcy). The spiral thus does not *cause* such an equilibrium to come into being. I am indebted to Donald Bear for pointing out this relationship.

3. Either the per person, per mile cost of providing bus service will have risen because of fewer passengers, or total bus service will have been curtailed, or both.

4. Because more automobiles will be used in commuting than formerly, a smaller improvement in traffic congestion (and hence a smaller reduction in commuting time) will have occurred than would have been the case if the same number of commuters used automobiles as before the expressway was opened.

CASE C: A CITY WITH SEGREGATED TRACK PUBLIC TRANSIT AND AUTO-DRIVING COMMUTERS

The third major type of commuter transportation (besides autos and buses) employed in the United States is transit with segregated tracks. That is, its rails or roadways are separated from other land uses and other forms of transportation (including streets) by elevation, depression, or fencing. Such transit includes subway trains, elevated trains, and steam and diesel-electric railroad trains. These forms of transportation all have one crucial characteristic in common: since their rights-of-way are completely separated from automobile traffic, the level of automobile congestion has no direct effect upon their speed or efficiency.

In a city served by such segregated track transit facilities, the effects of the opening of a new expressway are initially the same as those described in the two preceding sections. Traffic congestion falls on all city streets, and the expressway experiences heavy peak-hour congestion, but all street-using commuters (including those on buses and streetcars) spend less time en route than they did before the expressway opened. However, because the fall in traffic congestion on city streets has no effect whatsoever on the speed of vehicles using segregated tracks, commuters riding such vehicles experience no reduction in commuting time. *Thus there is a sharp change in the relative desirability of automobiles versus segregated track transit—a change favoring automobiles.* Consequently, many commuters who formerly used segregated track transit shift to automobiles.

Furthermore, the expressway cuts even more deeply into the segregated track system's noncommuter traffic. During rush hours, the expressway becomes extremely crowded, as indicated in previous sections of this analysis. But between rush periods, the expressway provides a relatively congestion-free, high-speed means for shoppers and other noncommuting travelers to move to and from the downtown area; hence it constitutes a dramatic improvement over preexisting streets or other means of transit. This improvement creates a sharp disequilibrium in the previous distribution of noncommuting passengers among means of transportation—one proportionally much greater than the corresponding disequilibrium concerning commuters. Therefore a great many non-peak-hour travelers shift from fixed-rail transit to automobiles. As a result, the total passenger load of the fixed-rail, segregated track system becomes more and more concentrated in rush hours.

The New York subway system provides a striking illustration of this tendency. In the period from 1948 to 1956, the number of subway passengers entering the Manhattan business district on a typical business day during the morning rush hours (from 7:00 A.M. to 10:00 A.M.) fell 11.7 percent. But during the other 21 hours of the day, inbound passenger loads dropped 20.8 percent. These figures reflect both impacts of increased automobile usage upon segregated track transit: a decline in overall traffic and a much heavier concentration of the remaining traffic in a few peak hours.[5]

These two impacts reduce both the total revenue accruing to the system and its efficiency in terms of cost per passenger per mile. As revenues fall and costs rise, the system finds itself in a perilous "squeeze." Its usual reactions are increases in fares and reductions in service or both. As with bus travel, these adjustments often cause further withdrawals of passengers from the system.

A dramatic example is provided by the Chicago and Northwestern Railway. Often cited in recent years as a model of commuter service modernization, the Chicago and Northwestern was making a small profit on its suburban passenger business before two new expressways opened in late 1960. Each of these superroads paralleled a set of existing Chicago and Northwestern tracks connecting downtown Chicago with outlying areas. Within three months after these two expressways opened, the railroad's suburban passenger traffic declined 9.6 percent. Furthermore, this fall in traffic shifted the results of overall suburban passenger operations from a profit to a loss.[6]

In any city where the number of nonautomobile commuters is relatively large, the shift from other means of commuting to automobiles may become extremely significant, especially if a whole network of

---

[5] Edgar M. Hoover and Raymond Vernon, *Anatomy of a Metropolis* (Cambridge, Mass.: Harvard University Press, 1959), p. 218.

[6] Figures taken from a statement made by Mr. Larry S. Provo, then Vice-President and Comptroller, at a hearing before the Interstate Commerce Commission concerning the future of the Chicago and North Shore Railroad. Mr. Provo emphasized that the loss of passengers indicated was not a result of the general economic recession of 1960–1961, since the number of suburban passengers on the Chicago and Northwestern Railway had been rising in the recession months before the expressways opened, and also rose during the previous recessions of 1953–1954 and 1957–1958.

expressways is built converging on the downtown areas. Some of our larger metropolises still have sizable pools of such potential "shifters" riding segregated track transit. In Chicago, about 37 percent of all persons entering the central business district on a typical day in 1973 used such transit.[7] In New York, 62 percent of all persons entering the Manhattan business district on a typical business day in 1971 traveled on segregated track facilities.[8] However, the number of persons using this type of transit is steadily declining as the automobile gains in popularity. Thus the percentage of persons entering Manhattan's central business district by auto and taxi rose from 15.7 in 1948 to 26.6 in 1971; whereas the percentage using segregated track transit fell from 72.4 to 61.9 during the same period.[9]

As more and more commuters start using their automobiles to reach work, the level of traffic congestion begins to return to the level existing before the expressway improved traffic conditions. Theoretically, such shifting could continue until the original automobile commuting time was re-established in spite of the added capacity introduced by the expressway.

Since the time required for commuting by rail is not changed by the introduction of the expressway, it would seem that the original equilibrium would reappear when the initial automobile commuting time was again required. But the original situation can never return. The new expressway has absorbed a great many former riders of segregated track transit, thereby permanently lowering the number of passengers using such transit. Therefore, even if congestion on the expressway rises so high that the original automobile commuting time is restored, the number of passengers riding segregated track transit at that point is much lower than it was before the expressway opened. Because of the high fixed costs in transit operations, such a fall in total traffic almost always raises the average cost per passenger. Thus when total passenger traffic falls, and that which remains becomes more concentrated during peak hours, segregated track transit firms are forced to raise fares or reduce service or both, as noted before. These changes diminish the attractiveness of their service compared to automobile transportation.

If a very large number of persons shift from segregated track transit to automobiles, the cost of such transit per passenger may rise so high that its attractiveness is drastically reduced. In such a case,

---

[7] *Cordon Count 1973, Central Business District of Chicago,* Department of Streets and Sanitation, City of Chicago, 1973, Table 2.

[8] Tri-State Regional Planning Commission, *Hub-Bount Travel 1971,* Interim Technical Report 4296-1205 & 1206, New York, July 1972.

[9] Ibid.

congestion on the highways may have to become slightly worse than it was before the expressway was opened before automobile travel becomes just as undesirable as segregated track transit travel. But only the marginal equality of these two undesirabilities can establish a new equilibrium. We thus arrive at the paradoxical conclusion that the opening of an expressway could conceivably cause traffic congestion to become worse instead of better, and automobile commuting times to rise instead of fall!

In fact, this result is almost a certainty if the segregated track transit firms are caught in the kind of downward spiral into bankruptcy described in connection with buses. For if these firms actually go bankrupt and are forced to withdraw their services from the market altogether, all commuters formerly riding them will have to use automobiles or buses, and congestion on the streets will rise to record levels. The bankruptcy of the New York, New Haven and Hartford Railroad shows that this analysis is by no means purely theoretical. Of course, if government agencies or public receivers take over the bankrupt transit facilities and run them at a loss, this drastic outcome would be prevented.

However, it is probably likely that a new equilibrium will be established before highway traffic congestion has reached its pre-expressway level. But even in such cases, the expressway will be extremely crowded during peak hours—almost certainly loaded beyond its optimal capacity. Therefore the basic "Law" propounded at the beginning of this article—congestion rises to meet maximum capacity—will still hold true.

When a new equilibrium is finally established, it will have the following characteristics in relation to the pre-expressway situation:

1.   A larger proportion of all commuters will use automobiles, and a significantly smaller proportion will use segregated track transit.

2.   Passenger loads on segregated track transit will not only be smaller; they will also be more heavily concentrated during peak travel hours.

3.   The aforementioned load changes will raise the per person, per mile cost of providing segregated track transit.

4.   Segregated track transit facilities will have made a stable adjustment to their higher costs and lower revenues in one of the following ways:

    a.   By raising fares.

    b.   By reducing service.

    c.   By accepting lower profits (or greater losses), whether or not compensated by more subsidies.

    d.   By some combination of the above.

    e.   By going out of business.

5. Peak-hour congestion and average commuting time per trip on city streets other than the expressway may be less than, equal to, or greater than it was before the expressway opened, depending upon the shift of commuters from nonautomobile to automobile commuting.

6. Peak-hour congestion on the new expressway will surpass its optimal capacity; hence the average *speed* of commuters using it will probably be lower than the average speed of those using alternative routes on older city streets (although the total commuting *time* for both will be the same), even if the average commuting *time* for all auto-driving commuters has fallen.

MORE PEOPLE AND MORE CARS

Throughout the preceding analysis, we have assumed that both the number of commuters and automobile ownership among them were the same before and after the expressway was opened. Removal of these two assumptions raises still further the probability that a new expressway will be overcongested during rush hours.

In spite of the rapid population growth in most U.S. metropolitan areas during the past twenty years, the number of persons in each major city commuting daily between outlying areas and the central business district has not always risen. In Chicago, for example, the total number of persons entering the central business district during a typical day in May declined from 1947 to 1973 by about 18 percent. However, the number of persons using automobiles to enter the same area during the same periods has risen about 18 percent.[10] Figures for New York City show similar trends.[11]

The primary causes of the shift to automobiles shown by these statistics are (1) higher automobile ownership and use and (2) the isolation of new areas of population growth from nonautomobile transit. From 1947 to 1973, automobile registration in the City of Chicago rose by 575,000 vehicles, or 96 percent; whereas total population declined by over 250,000, or 7 percent.[12] For the nation as a whole, motor vehicle registration rose from 1945 to 1973 by 93.8 million, or 306 percent, but population increased by 69.9 million, or 50 percent.[13]

Thus, throughout the nation, the tremendous increase in ownership of automobiles during the postwar period has markedly raised the inclination of commuters to drive to work. Furthermore, low-density

---

[10] *Cordon Count 1973,* loc. cit.

[11] Tri-State Regional Planning Commission, op. cit.

[12] *Cordon Count 1973,* op. cit., Figure 2.

[13] U.S. Bureau of the Census, *Statistical Abstract of the United States, 1974,* 95th ed. (Washington, D.C.: U.S. Government Printing Office, 1974), p. 556

suburban housing has spread across the landscape into many areas quite distant from the nearest nonautomobile transportation. In such places, use of automobiles for getting at least part way to and from work is absolutely essential.

If we introduce into our model of commuting behavior analogous changes in (1) automobile ownership, (2) total population, and (3) population distribution, our conclusions regarding peak-hour over-crowding on expressways are strongly reinforced. Furthermore, auto-mobile ownership is expected to continue rising rapidly, especially if real incomes continue to increase. The conclusion is inescapable that peak-hour traffic congestion on commuter expressways is likely to in-crease throughout the foreseeable future.

All of the preceding analysis is based upon the axioms concerning commuter behavior stated early in this article. If those axioms accu-rately describe the way commuters behave in the real world, our analysis leads to the following major conclusions:

1. Peak-hour traffic congestion on any expressway linking a cen-tral business district and outlying areas will almost always rise to sur-pass the optimal capacity of the expressway.

2. Therefore, in relatively large metropolitan areas, it is impossi-ble to build expressways wide enough to carry rush-hour traffic at the speed and congestion levels normally considered optimal for such roads. The forces of traffic equilibrium will inevitably produce enough overcrowding to drive the actual average speed during peak hours to a level below the optimal speed.

3. Commuters driving on expressways should resign themselves to encountering heavy traffic congestion every day, even though they may spend less time commuting than they did before using express-ways.

4. Since urban expressways cannot be designed large enough to eliminate rush-hour traffic congestion, other design goals must be employed to decide how large a capacity each such expressway should have. The only goal regarding commuting which is feasible is reduction of the average amount of time spent by commuters per trip. Low congestion and optimal speeds during nonpeak hours probably constitute much more practical goals for the design of urban express-ways than any goal connected with rush-hour traffic movements.

5. Under certain conditions, the opening of an expressway may make rush-hour traffic congestion worse than before the expressway was built. This outcome can occur only in cities in which a high pro-portion of commuter traffic is carried by segregated track transporta-tion facilities before the expressway is opened.

6. Thus any program of expressway planning and construction

must be integrated with similar programs concerning other forms of transit in the area if it is not to cause unforeseen and possible deleterious effects upon the level of automobile traffic congestion therein. In particular, marked improvement of roads without any improvement in segregated track transit may cause automobile traffic congestion to get worse instead of better. Since the U.S. has already launched a massive road improvement program, which includes construction of many urban expressways, continued failure to undertake an analogous program for other forms of urban commuter transit may result in a generally higher level of rush-hour automobile traffic congestion in those cities which now have extensive segregated track transit facilities serving commuters. Therefore such possibilities as the charging of direct tolls on expressways and the expenditure of auto toll collections or gasoline tax revenues on segregated track transit should be thoroughly explored as a means of developing a *balanced* urban transportation system.

10

A Realistic Look at the
Final Payoffs from
Urban Data Systems

The glamorous capabilities of computerized "urban information systems" appear so dazzling that no major city planning proposal is considered respectable unless it contains at least one section on EDP, ADP, or an urban data bank. Nevertheless, automated data systems are still regarded with uncertainty and uneasiness by many key urban decision-makers. How can anyone, even a trained data technician, judge whether these systems are really worth the huge costs involved? Even more significant, how will these systems affect the relative power and influence of various individual decision-makers?

Ultimately, the answers to these questions depend upon assessing the final payoffs from urban data systems. *Final payoffs* are actual *improvements in government or private action,* as distinguished from *improvements in the information* on which such action is based.

Up to now, most of the concern with urban data systems has not been focused upon final payoffs for three reasons. First, the technical design of these systems has seemed more exciting, more novel—and more amenable to analysis. Second, most detailed analyses of the decision process have been performed by members of computer hardware firms. Naturally, they have concentrated upon describing the impressive improvements in information they can undoubtedly deliver. Third, it appears obvious that better data in urban decision-making

Reprinted from *Public Administration Review* 27, no. 3 (September 1967), by permission of the American Society for Public Administration.

would have huge final payoffs, because it has hardly been doubted that better information would reduce both the frequency and the magnitude of planning mistakes.

This intuitively plausible but actually misleading assumption has caused us to deemphasize final payoffs. Therefore, this article will concentrate upon analyzing them.

All final payoffs from urban data systems consist of improvements in the effectiveness of decision-making. *Technical payoffs* are at least potentially beneficial to all participants in the decision-making process. They result from technical improvements in data inputs, processing, and outputs. Examples are greater speed of processing, greater consistency among outputs, and wider distribution of information. *Power payoffs* are gains in one person's decision-making effectiveness made at the expense of another person's. They are *redistributions* of the benefits of decision-making.

In reality, every change in urban data-reporting or data-processing systems has both technical and power repercussions. Hence, anyone analyzing the impact of automated data systems upon urban decision-making or forecasting the attitudes of government officials toward such systems must take both types of impacts into account. Yet in almost all studies of urban data systems, power payoffs are considered too political and too controversial to discuss. As a result, we get one-dimensional dialogues about problems which in reality have two or more dimensions.

It is time we faced this reality by taking a hard look at power payoffs. But first it is necessary to examine technical payoffs in more detail.

TECHNICAL PAYOFFS

A careful analysis shows that the technical payoffs from urban data systems are smaller than intuition would lead us to suppose. Also, they have certain characteristics which will strongly influence the forms of future urban data systems.

Technical Improvements in Data Caused by Urban Data Systems

Computerized data systems could improve the data underlying current urban decisions by providing the following:

1. Lower operating costs of data processing.
2. Faster availability of information.

3. Wider distribution of information.

4. Generation of new information never before observed, record-ed, or reported.

5. Greater consistency in reporting data.

6. Reduced distortion of data reported to top levels.

7. Eventual development of a giant data inventory. This could ultimately be used to formulate, test, and modify theories about causal relationships in the urban environment which we can now only guess at.

8. Greater freedom from routine recordkeeping.

On the other hand, the following technical costs are required to gain the above improvements:

1. Increased capital costs, including both hardware and software.

2. Demands for much more highly skilled personnel.

3. A tendency toward greater reliance upon quantifiable and measurable variables.

4. Increased narrowness of comprehension, particularly concern-ing incipient changes in the environment. Machine systems can re-spond only to stimuli they have been programmed to perceive, and in ways they have been programmed to react. Hence they are not sensi-tive to new types of data or to nuances in information that may signal changes in the entire situation.

5. Reduced sensitivity to the opinions and self-interest of inter-mediate-level officials in operating organizations. Information sent "straight through" from events to top-level administrators by automatic systems does not contain the interpretations of middle-level officials which often help place it in context, even though such interpretations always embody some biases.

These costs are often vastly outweighed by the improvements described above. Nevertheless, a balanced and impartial view of urban data systems must consider both.

Estimates of Technical Payoffs from Technical Improvements

The increased capabilities described above can greatly improve the data available to urban decision-makers. However, three factors make it hard to prove that these better data will lead to more effective decisions.

First, it is extremely difficult to measure the effectiveness of many decisions vital to urban affairs.[1] The errors of such measurement are

---

[1] Some of these difficulties are discussed in Robert Dorfman, ed., *Measuring Bene-fits of Government Investments* (Washington: The Brookings Institution, 1963).

often likely to exceed by a wide margin even the most generous estimates of possible increases in effectiveness caused by better data.

Second, even when the effects of decisions can be readily measured, variances in those effects may be due to factors other than data inputs. Whenever the same kind of decision is made over and over, it may be possible to test one set of decisions based upon "old fashioned" data vs. another set based upon all the same inputs except data from an automated system. However, it is difficult to do this before installing the automated system when such knowledge is critical to deciding whether the system is worth its cost. Moreover, it is impossible to set up adequate controls concerning unique or irreversible decisions to measure the degree of improvement in their effectiveness created by better data.

Third, many persons with different goals are affected by every decision. Whether given payoffs should be considered positive or negative —and to what extent—depends upon whose values are used in making the calculation.

All these major obstacles to measuring the technical payoffs of urban data systems become more severe the broader the decisions involved. For truly "sweeping" choices: (1) the relative effectiveness of alternative decisions is harder to estimate; (2) the number of factors considered other than quantitative information is much larger; (3) the decision is more likely to be unique and irrevocable; and (4) there is a higher probability that more groups with conflicting values will be affected. Consequently, *it is much easier to prove that urban data systems will provide positive technical payoffs concerning narrow operational decisions than concerning broad policy or operating choices.*

Technical Payoffs and the Type of System Most Likely to Be Used

Much of the academic and intellectual support for urban data systems has resulted from the seemingly enormous technical payoffs to be gained from truly comprehensive systems.[2] Such systems (1) service *all* government departments from a central data processing complex; (2) link these departments in a single information and report-printing network; (3) provide a single massive memory based upon a uniform coding system; and (4) allow instantaneous random access to this "joint memory" from remote stations in each department. In theory, such a comprehensive system should be able to bring together and analyze masses of data from all the various departments affected by even the broadest municipal government decisions.

---

[2] A summary of some of these benefits can be found in Edward F. R. Hearle and Raymond J. Mason, *A Data Processing System for State and Local Governments* (Englewood Cliffs, N.J.: Prentice-Hall, Inc., 1963), pp. 92–100.

But in reality, even if such huge systems existed, it would be tremendously difficult to *prove conclusively* that they provided significant technical payoffs concerning broad decisions. This is true for the reasons set forth previously. Yet comprehensive systems are immensely expensive. Much narrower data systems often provide the greatest *demonstrable technical payoffs* in decision-making, at least in relation to their costs, which are much lower. This implies that, in the near future, many urban politicians will buy narrowly designed data systems (such as those serving individual city departments) rather than comprehensive, "all-department" systems.[3]

In the long run, the biggest technical payoffs from improved urban data will probably arise from better knowledge of underlying causal relationships in the urban environment now shrouded by ignorance.[4] But developing theories about these causal relationships and then testing those theories requires an enormous stockpile of data about how each factor varies under a wide diversity of conditions. Hence this important technical payoff may not become available for something like a decade after massive urban data systems are installed and working.[5] This situation will further discourage many urban governments from initially purchasing comprehensive urban data systems.

The large extra costs of a comprehensive system must be borne immediately, or soon; whereas the extra payoffs it generates will not accrue for years. Even then, their appearance is by no means certain. Moreover, human judgment can never be eliminated from the application of results derived from even the most sophisticated computer analysis. But when urban decision-makers realize that no data system, however comprehensive, will ever "give them all the answers," many will be reluctant to pay huge additional costs for what will probably seem like only marginal gains in final payoffs. After all, the bigger the role of judgment in the final decision, the greater the probability that a wise man will make the right choice without the help of a comprehensive computerized system.

For all these reasons connected with purely *technical* payoffs, it seems likely that many—though not all—cities will avoid early commitment to costly comprehensive data systems. As we shall see, consideration of *power* payoffs further strengthens this conclusion.

---

[3] This same tendency, but in relation to the use of computers in business organizations, is discussed in George P. Shultz and Thomas L. Whisler, eds., *Management Organization and the Computer* (Glencoe: The Free Press, 1960), Chapter 1.

[4] See Melvin M. Webber, "The Roles of Intelligence Systems in Urban-Systems Planning," *Journal of the American Institute of Planners,* November 1965, p. 294.

[5] To some extent, this waiting period can be reduced by collecting comparable data simultaneously in a number of different places.

Updating and Its Impact Upon the Type of System Chosen

Most of the technical payoffs promised by promoters of urban data systems require continuous data acquisition after the systems are installed. Such updating creates a major cost in any data system—in the long run, often the single largest cost, even exceeding the cost of hardware.[6] This huge on-going burden is tolerable only if the system itself is associated with an operating department which continuously procures the necessary data anyway as part of its normal behavior. This is another reason why many urban data systems are likely to start out as narrow departmental tools rather than as broad comprehensive ones.

POWER PAYOFFS

Because of the uncertainties connected with the technical payoffs from urban data systems, power payoffs loom large in the minds of those who must decide whether such systems will actually be built and installed.[7]

How Power Payoffs Arise

Power payoffs arise because every change in organization, techniques, or decision processes shifts the relative power of at least some of the individuals involved. Invariably, these individuals place heavy weight upon such shifts in judging the desirability of proposed changes. True, in public they rarely if ever speak of these power shifts. Instead they usually refer only to the technical impacts of the changes being considered. But this does not fool anyone who really knows what is happening.

The power payoffs from urban data systems spring from four technical impacts of such systems. First, automated systems tend to transmit many data directly from events themselves to top-level officials, or at least to reduce the number of intermediate steps separating these two extremes. As a result, lower- and intermediate-level officials often have little or no opportunity of "filtering" important data before they reach top-level officials. "Filtering" can mean either distorting information by altering or leaving out parts of it, or adding personal interpretations to it, or both.[8]

---

[6] Webber, op. cit.

[7] Most analysts of urban data systems have ignored power payoffs. Exceptions are Webber, op. cit., and Shultz and Whisler, op. cit.

[8] Shultz and Whisler, op. cit., p. 13.

Second, urban data systems inevitably shift some emphasis in decision-making toward more easily quantifiable factors and away from immeasurable ones. Third, such systems free lower-level officials from many routine reporting and recording chores. Fourth, they provide those officials capable of understanding and using them with much better information about certain aspects of urban affairs than those persons who do not use them.

The technical impacts of urban data systems described above tend to produce seven specific power shifts among the various "actors" in the urban decision-making process. The net power gainers from such shifts regard the data system causing them as having positive power payoffs; whereas the net power losers regard its power payoffs as negative. Any given person may gain from one power shift and lose from another. In fact, a single system might provide him with far more power regarding certain decisions or actions, and far less regarding others. Nevertheless, most well-informed people affected by a given data system will have definite opinions about whether it improves or worsens their overall power.

The Power Shifts Caused by Automated Data Systems

Automated data systems cause the following seven power shifts in urban decision-making or in decision-making at state and federal levels when introduced there:

1. *Lower- and intermediate-level officials tend to lose power to higher-level officials and politicians.* The reduction in "filtering" of data at lower and intermediate levels of city hierarchies deprives officials there of some of their former influence, since machine systems often bypass them entirely.

2. *High-level staff officials gain power.* Since lower-level officials no longer condense data as it moves upward, an enormous amount of information flows directly to the "top of the heap." The politicians and line executives located there simply cannot cope with all this information unaided. So they rely on expanded staffs, or ever-more overworked staffs, to provide the interpretation and filtering formerly done by lower-level officials.

Since the politicians and top-level executives concerned receive "filtered" information both before and after urban data systems are installed, it might seem that they are not net power gainers. However, this conclusion is false for three reasons. First, automated data systems often provide certain types of highly useful information never available before, or now available much faster. Second, staff advisors are likely to be more directly loyal to their top-level bosses than lower-level line operators, who have strong loyalties to their departments. Third, expanding one's staff creates additional channels of information which can be used to check up on the activities of operating departments. As every public and private executive knows, development of such seemingly redundant channels of information is crucial to keeping oneself well-informed about "what is really going on down there."

3. *City and state legislators tend to lose power to administrators and operating officials.* The latter are generally more sophisticated, have more technical training, are equipped with larger staffs, devote more time to their city jobs, can focus more intensively upon narrow specialties, are in a better position to control the design and operation of urban data systems, and are more likely to receive continuous reports from those systems by virtue of their positions.

4. *The government bureaucracy as a whole gains power at the expense of the general electorate and nongovernmental groups.* Government officials have continuous "inside access" to the data generated by automated systems, and they also control which data are built into those systems. No matter how idealistic they are, they will vigorously resist universal accessibility to these data. This occurs because accurate and detailed reporting of the behavior of any large organization—private or public—will inevitably reveal operating deficiencies that would be embarrassing if widely known. Moreover, the general electorate and most nongovernmental groups are not technically sophisticated when it comes to understanding and interpreting complex data.

5. *Well-organized and sophisticated groups of all kinds, including some government bureaus, gain power at the expense of less well-organized and less sophisticated groups.* The former are much better equipped than the latter to collect, analyze, understand, and react to the data outputs of automated systems. However, organization alone is not enough to counteract potential power shifts caused by urban data systems. Even well-organized groups may lose some power if their members are not technically sophisticated.

6. *Within city governments, those who actually control automated data systems gain in power at the expense of those who do not.* Most city officials are acutely aware of this potential power shift. Each operating department naturally wants to retain as much power as possible over its own behavior and its traditional sphere of activity. Its members are especially anxious to prevent "outsiders" from having detailed knowledge about every aspect of the department's operations. Hence nearly every department with operations susceptible to computerized management will at least initially fight for its own computer and data system controlled by its own members.

At the other extreme, city planners and budgetary officials will both eventually espouse centralized data systems. They will view such systems at least in part as means of gaining control over the information channels vital to all operating departments—and thereby capturing some of the latter's power. Therefore, *much of the controversy which is sure to arise concerning the proper design and operation of urban data systems will reflect a power struggle for control of those systems.*

7. *Technically educated officials within city governments gain power at the expense of old-style political advisors.* The latter are the "wise old (or young) men" found clustered around the head of every local, state, and national government. Their function has always been to provide good judgment in the face of uncertainty. But urban data systems tend to substitute new types of uncertainty (such as that concerning statistical reliability) for old (such as that concerning the accuracy of individual insights). Well-educated data technicians will seem much more capable of coping with these new uncertainties than will the traditional "wise men."

However, politicians will soon discover that data technicians cannot really deliver on their promises to make accurate predictions of crucial variables. Our ignorance is still too profound for such accuracy. Hence a new advisory role will appear for men who possess *both* technical sophistication and wisdom. Although many men can learn sophisticated techniques, true wisdom is extremely scarce; so such advisors will acquire increasing power.

How Power Payoffs Influence Types of Urban Data Systems Used

The power shifts described above will markedly affect the attitudes of specific groups and individuals toward the use of automated data systems. However, not all power losers will oppose the system, and not all power gainers will support it. In the first place, most people who will be affected by a new system will be uncertain about whether they will gain or lose when it is introduced. Hence, their attitudes will be ambivalent, unless they oppose it out of sheer inertia. Second, some power losers may accept the system because of its large technical payoffs, and some gainers may oppose it because its costs outweigh the technical payoffs they perceive. Third, some people who realize in advance how a new data system will affect their power will not attempt to influence the decision about whether to use it. Either they feel they cannot affect that decision, or they believe its impact will be slight. Therefore, only a minority of the persons whose power will in fact be affected by a new urban data system are likely to support or oppose it in advance because of their beliefs about its power impacts upon them.

Nevertheless, this minority will exert very significant influence for two reasons. First, a minority with strong opinions about highly technical matters almost always has great influence in our democratic society concerning those matters. The majority of persons are too ignorant or apathetic to express any technical views at all. Second, the only people likely to be in this particular minority are those who hold powerful positions in the urban decision-making structure, especially within the city government.

The officials in this minority will consist of two groups. On the one hand, city planners, administrative assistants to mayors and city managers, and other high-ranking staff members, plus some top politicians, will press for early introduction and widespread use of fairly comprehensive data systems. On the other hand, many officials in specific operating departments will drag their feet about introducing automated systems, restrict the use of such systems sharply, and insist upon allowing each department to set up and operate its own system.

In the long run, the former group will prevail. The higher technical payoffs of comprehensive systems will eventually become clear to everyone. But in the short run—which may last for a decade or even longer—the latter group will be more powerful in many cities in spite of its lower rank. In most city governments, the people who run the everyday affairs of each operating department invariably exert much greater influence over how those affairs are carried out than central staff members or even top-level elected officials. Introducing any automated data system into an ongoing department requires great changes in day-to-day procedures. Therefore, it necessitates overcoming the department's inherent inertia.

Few mayors or city managers, however powerful, are strong enough to fight such inertia in all departments simultaneously. Yet that is precisely what they would have to do in order to install a single comprehensive system covering all city operations, unless individual department heads become convinced that such a system would greatly aid their own shops. Furthermore, resistance to automated data systems within each department will be greatly reduced if its top-level officials have a strong incentive to use them. They would if those systems were designed specifically for their benefit and operated by them. Therefore, *perception of power payoffs by departmental officials is likely to cause many cities to adopt a highly piecemeal approach to the adoption and use of automated urban data systems.* Thus both piecemeal and comprehensive approaches will be followed by different cities in the next few years.[9]

---

[9] To a certain extent, this tendency of cities to adopt both approaches is corroborated in Don Rose, ed., *Automated Data Processing in Municipal Governments: Status, Problems and Prospects* (Chicago: Public Administration Service, 1966).

It is quite likely that the total costs of eventually arriving at a single integrated data system in any city will be much greater via the piecemeal route than they would via initial adoption of a comprehensive system. The former approach will require gradually developing links between disparate individual systems not initially designed to function as a unit. The cost of such development will probably exceed that of providing such links right from the start in one integrated system. Moreover, some of the data necessary for development of basic theories about causal relationships in the urban scene can emerge only from an integrated system. But it will take much longer to create an integrated system through piecemeal construction. Hence technical payoffs based on knowledge of these causal relationships may be delayed for years. Similarly, under the piecemeal approach, those parts of government which receive automated systems last will not enjoy the technical payoffs thereof until much later.

In spite of these drawbacks, it is at least arguable that the piecemeal approach has sizable advantages for technical reasons as well as power payoff reasons. If cities refrained from installing any automated data systems until adequate research for fully comprehensive systems were completed, they would have to pass up sizable technical payoffs which can be achieved immediately in certain departments. Moreover, any attempt to install a comprehensive system in a large city might wind up as a piecemeal approach anyway. By the time the last "integrated" units were installed, technical changes might have made the first units obsolete.

CONCLUSIONS

It can hardly be doubted that automated data systems will soon have profound effects upon government and private decision-making in urban areas—and at state and federal levels too. Nor is it debatable that these revolutionary impacts will spring from the immense technical improvements in data which such systems make possible. Nevertheless, the future form and use of automated data systems will not depend solely upon improvements in data. Rather they will depend upon the ways in which data improvements increase the effectiveness of actions and change the power positions of the actors involved. These two outcomes constitute the *final payoffs* from using automated data systems.

Therefore, in order to forecast how automated data systems are likely to be designed and used in government, we must shift our attention from the dazzling technical capabilities of computer systems to the ways in which men apply those systems in the real world.

Three major conclusions emerge. First, significant technical pay-offs from automated data systems are much more ambiguous and difficult to demonstrate than technical improvements in data. Second, the ways in which public (and private) officials use automated data systems will be determined just as much by their perceptions of the resulting shifts in personal power as by their desire to reap technical benefits for the public interest.

Third, the nature of both technical and power payoffs implies that many city governments—as well as state and national governments—will develop automated data systems in a piecemeal, department-by-department fashion. Hence the glamorous comprehensive urban systems we hear about from "computerphiles" are likely to be a long time in coming in many areas.

One final observation is warranted. Experts who set up urban and other automated data systems should pay more attention to power payoffs in designing those systems. Every data system serves real flesh-and-blood people. These people sorely need the help obtainable from automated data systems. But they will not accept or effectively use such help unless it is offered to them in a way that takes their own interests into account.

11

New Directions for
Urban Research

THREE WAYS TO DEFINE AN URBAN RESEARCH AGENDA

Defining an urban research agenda is a challenging task which requires a great deal of subjective judgment. The first step is choosing one or more of the three basic approaches to formulating any research agenda. The approach most often used in universities is to have no formal rules for selecting subjects, but simply to let a group of capable people study whatever they find interesting. This *pure research* approach dominates urban research in the United States today, because so much of it is done in universities. In essence, this approach shifts the problem from defining the most important subjects to selecting the group of people whose interests are to be relied upon. However, since I am not a university expert capable of picking the best researchers, I must avoid this method.

The second possible approach is *goal-oriented.* It typifies the form of decision-making usually called "planning," in which one starts by defining objectives and then figures out how to achieve those objectives most efficiently. Unfortunately, in our society it is not easy to define social objectives in a widely acceptable way. This is true whether we look at short-run social issues, where conflicts of interest make definition of nearly unanimous objectives almost impossible, or

Revised version of an article appearing in *Technology Review* © 1971 by **Alumni Association of the Massachusetts Institute of Technology,** reprinted by permission of the Alumni Association of M.I.T.

long-run issues, where defining objectives would amount to specifying some ultimately desirable social order. I can hardly seek to resolve the major conflicts of interest relevant to urban problems in this short paper. Moreover, I do not believe any perfect society can ever be created on this earth; so I cannot define the traits of such a society and use them as goals. Therefore, I am also incapable of using this approach to selecting the most important topics for research.

The third approach to defining a research agenda emerges from attempting to cope with what seem to be our most pressing problems at the moment. This fits the form of decision-making often referred to as "disjointed incrementalism."[1] It is *disjointed* because thousands of individuals make decisions without much attempt in advance to take account of what others are doing. It is *incremental* because they make those decisions in response to their immediate problems, rather than striving to attain long-range goals. I will follow this approach in developing a suggested agenda for urban research.

Before beginning, however, it is necessary to confront exactly what is meant by the word *urban* in "urban research." In our highly urbanized society I believe *urban* research for all practical purposes encompasses *all* socially oriented research relevant to the majority of our population. Therefore, I will make no attempt to limit the scope of what I consider urban research to subjects that are explicitly identified with cities, suburbs, or metropolitan areas. The only area I will rule out consists of research exclusively devoted to rural or nonmetropolitan activities or problems such as those concerning farming or forest conservation.

WHAT ARE THE HIGHEST-PRIORITY URBAN PROBLEMS ABOUT WHICH RESEARCH SHOULD BE UNDERTAKEN?

The most common method of delineating high-priority urban problems is to go down a list of basic subject areas related to urban affairs and identify the most critical issues in each area in the opinion of whoever is making the selection. These subject areas include health, pollution, housing, crime, transportation, poverty, hunger, unemployment, job training, education, and aesthetics. However, I will take a somewhat different approach by defining three basic issues which cut across all these specific subject categories. I believe these three issues encompass our most serious problems, but do not receive sufficient attention

---

[1] This term was coined by Charles E. Lindblom and is explained at length in Charles E. Lindblom and David Braybrooke, *A Strategy of Decision* (New York: The Free Press of Glencoe, 1963).

precisely because we usually approach urban research in the manner I have just described.

The first major issue concerns the well-known gap between the rate of speed at which technological change occurs in our society and the rates at which social, legal, political, and administrative institutions change. I will refer to this issue as the *need for institutional change.*

The second major issue concerns the nature and development of *individual and social values.* How are these values formed and stimulated? How diverse are they becoming? How much value-diversity can our society stand without generating excessive conflict?

The third basic issue concerns *the persistence of serious inequalities* in our society (and in all other societies, for that matter). I refer to economic, social, political, and even physical inequalities. What are the origins of these inequalities? To what extent are they desirable and to what extent undesirable? How can we ameliorate those which are undesirable?

In the remainder of this paper, I will discuss each of these three key issues in turn, and suggest some directions for urban research derived from each.

RESEARCH RELATED TO THE NEED FOR INSTITUTIONAL CHANGE

In his State of the Union speech in January 1970, President Nixon pointed out that moving towards a solution of the major social and economic problems of our nation will require significant institutional changes in a variety of different fields. Marginally changing the functioning of existing institutions can indeed create some important improvements regarding key problems. But really launching an effective attack upon most of them will require a fundamental restructuring of many existing institutions. The Family Assistance Program recommended by the first Nixon administration provides an example of such restructuring in the field of welfare activities.

In my opinion, at least three major areas of research are suggested by this need for significant institutional change in society. The first consists of *providing much better evaluations of the performance of many existing institutions or possible future ones.* Our past successes in evaluating huge areas of our own public actions and our capabilities for analyzing the potential effectiveness of future actions are incredibly poor. This ineffectiveness has not arisen because officials are stupid or analysts incompetent. Rather it occurs for two other reasons: the extraordinary difficulties of performing worthwhile and accurate eval-

uations of social programs and the inherent reluctance of public officials—like all other human beings—to expose their own shortcomings
to public view. In order to tackle these deficiencies, we need to devote
far more research attention to the following subjects:

1. *Methods of coping with the multiple values and objectives involved in most public programs.* Evaluation involves measuring the
actual performance of some activity in attaining a specified set of
goals. But there are a great many different and often conflicting goals
involved in every major public program. Hence, it is extremely difficult
to decide against which ones performance should be measured or
how to measure it against all of them simultaneously.

2. *Methods of measuring, or at least estimating, the intangible
benefits of many programs.* Almost all cost/benefit analyses of public
programs break down because a significant proportion of key benefits
cannot be measured with the usual empirical tools and concepts. Until
we develop some new methods of taking these benefits into account
and weighing them quantitatively, we will be unable to evaluate the
effectiveness of most important social programs.

3. *Creation of a standardized means of incorporating income distribution questions into evaluation analysis.* In most real situations, it
is patently false to assume that redistribution questions can be ignored
because the costs are borne and benefits received by the same set of
people. On the contrary, the way most public programs take resources
from some people and provide benefits for others is a critical factor
that must be taken into account in assessing the value of those programs. Hence, it is almost never sufficient to simply add up the total
costs and benefits of a program (assuming they could all be quantified) to determine which is larger on a net basis. In addition, its redis-
tributional aspects—that is, who gains and who loses—must be taken
into account in a way that can be employed from one case to another,
and will be widely accepted as just and accurate by key decision
makers.

I believe these objectives can best be attained only by actually
trying to evaluate many particular social programs. This will certainly
not be easy. In fact, the tremendous difficulties involved are one of the
key reasons we have failed to perform evaluations effectively in the
past. Yet our approach to evaluating each particular program must be
carried out with full recognition of the many purposes it serves, the
intangible costs and benefits it involves, and the welfare distribution
questions it raises. For example, I have recently been doing some
work on analyzing the effectiveness of various devices for carrying out
racial desegregation in the public schools. This analysis clearly shows

that school desegregation is not entirely, or even primarily, an educational process. Rather, in most communities where it occurs, school desegregation represents a fundamental social change or is a symbol of such change. Hence it creates repercussions throughout the local community above and beyond those which occur within the schools. Viewing school desegregation either solely as an educational event without regard to its social consequences or solely as a social event without regard to its educational consequences can lead to tremendous errors in understanding and evaluating this process.

A second basic area of research suggested by the need for fundamental institutional change in society is an *exploration of how basic social changes really take place.* Is it true that human values must be altered before major behavior patterns can be changed? Or can actions which first change behavior patterns then generate repercussions that alter values? Or are both of these relationships valid under various circumstances? If so, under what conditions would it be most effective to change behavior first, and under what conditions should values be altered first? In my opinion, it is not always necessary to change human values before altering behavior patterns related to those values. For example, many white southerners vowed they would never provide equal treatment in public accommodations for black citizens because their values forbade it. But the Civil Rights Act of 1964 called for provision of such treatment, and forced everyone to comply with it. As a result, not only has southern white behavior regarding public accommodations altered dramatically in many cases, but also southern white attitudes and values have swung markedly towards greater acceptance of racial equality. I believe this change in values, which Dr. George Gallup has called the most dramatic in the history of his polls, results directly from the prior alteration of long-entrenched behavior patterns through the force of law. On the other hand, it is certainly true that not all values can be changed by legally altered behavior patterns.

Certain causal aspects of institutional change also deserve further research. For instance, how are major institutional changes started? Who starts them? What are the processes by which support and opinions are mobilized behind, or in resistance to, such changes? Are there certain well-defined sets of factors involved in these processes, or is there no recurrent pattern? Many of these questions have been researched for a long time, particularly in regard to other cultures. In fact, a great deal of theory exists concerning them. But how well does that theory hold up under the conditions of modern mass society, particularly where mass media have such tremendous (though unknown) effects?

Another related question concerns the difficulty of mustering majority support for public programs which essentially benefit minority-sized groups. Most urban problems involve deprivation or the bearing of serious costs by *relatively* small groups in society, while the majority is reasonably well off concerning that problem. For example, in 1973, 11 percent of the population of the United States lived in poverty by the official definition. That percentage encompassed nearly 23 million people. Yet over 88 percent of the population did *not* live in poverty. Moreover, nearly one-half of all poor persons cannot earn their way out of poverty. They cannot work because they are either too old, too young, disabled, or mothers of young children. These people can escape poverty only if the majority which is not poor provides resources for them. Thus, any social program aimed at significantly reducing poverty must involve persuading the nonpoor majority to aid the relatively small (though absolutely large) minority.

Most of our severely pressing urban problems are quite similar in structure. These include the prevalence of hunger, inadequate medical care, direct suffering from crime and drug addiction, poor housing, mental illness, unemployment, and racism. How can majority support —which is necessary for large-scale public action in our majority-oriented political structure—be created for minority-serving programs aimed at attacking these problems? How is the creation of such support related to the ability of relatively wealthy minority groups (such as newspaper publishers or giant oil production firms) to garner support for public policies (like newspaper anti-trust exemptions and oil import quotas) which clearly aid even smaller minorities?

A further field relevant to institutional change which needs a combination of greater research and more profound analysis is *attempting to define alternative future institutional forms that represent possible improvements on existing ones.* Real Estate Research Corporation has recently been working on one such problem in the field of transportation planning. We attempted to design alternative institutional arrangements to improve the present means of planning and building major transportation arteries in urban areas, including highways and rapid transit. This task is staggeringly complex. For example, after formulating a number of possible institutional formats at the state, metropolitan-area, and local levels, I calculated that over 800 million possible combinations of institutional structures could conceivably be used for transportation planning. Our fee for this assignment was reasonable, but it was hardly enough to evaluate 800 million possibilities in depth! So I rather arbitrarily narrowed the choice down to under 100. This example illustrates the inescapable need for subjective judgment—indeed, wisdom—in performing such institutional simulations, for that is what they really are. Yet I believe there is a tremendous shortage of new ideas about feasible institutional forms. Anyone with half a brain can effectively criticize many of our existing institutions. But we tend to take their structure so much for granted that it is hard to visualize and formulate practical alternatives that might work anywhere near as well! The basic economic concept of "opportunity cost" should train economists—and social scientists generally—to compare any particular policy or arrangement with alternatives that are realistically possible, rather than with unreal perfection that can exist only in pure theory. This form of thinking also has the great advantage of imposing a critical self-discipline upon the mind, because it rules out "fairy-tale" solutions to real problems. In my judgment, we need a great deal more of this combination of the *imagination* to visualize significantly different alternatives plus the *intellectual discipline* to confine oneself to those which are really possible.

RESEARCH CONCERNING INDIVIDUAL AND SOCIAL VALUES

The second major issue which I believe should be a key focal point for urban research concerns the nature, formation, and operation of individual and social values in our modern world. Admittedly, this is an extremely difficult subject to study. Moreover, it is by definition "value-laden," so no one can be wholly objective and scientific about it. For that reason, most social scientists have shied away from dealing with values. Yet I believe no subject is more critical to the survival of freedom and growth in our society.

The first topic that I would suggest for research under this basic heading concerns the impact of modern communications media, especially television, upon our values. Television is the most effective communications medium in the history of the world in terms of its degree of penetration of a large society. Over 95 percent of all the households in the United States, including those at the lowest income levels, contain television sets. Those sets are on between 25 and 35 percent of the time that anyone in those households is awake. In fact, some experts have estimated that the average child growing up today spends more time by the age of 18 watching television than attending school. Clearly, considering the millions of dollars that advertisers are willing to spend upon this pervasive medium to influence people, its commercials must have significant effects upon us; so I presume the rest of its contents also affect us.

But what are these effects? Is it true that television programs and commercials, and the commercials from other media, stimulate the poor to want more than they can afford, and to be less patient with poverty than ever before in history?[2] Is it true that the tendency of television news and other programs to focus on the extreme, the marginal, and the unusual because of their entertainment value creates an exaggerated picture of extremism that frightens the middle class in our society? Is it true, therefore, that television helps polarize the conservative middle class and those in society seeking institutional change? How do all these things affect our national life? Frankly, I do not know with any certainty, but I am convinced that the answers are extremely important to all of us.

Some of the issues involved in television's effect upon values can be illustrated by a story which Marshall McLuhan tells about television newscasters. He sets forth three contrasting views on how newscasters are related to the content of the news they report. These views are stated in the form of an analogy to three baseball umpires describing how they make decisions in a ball game. The first umpire says, "I call them the way they are." In McLuhan's opinion, this is the view which former Vice President Spiro Agnew believed TV newscasters ought to have: they ought to accurately reflect reality without bias. The second umpire says, "I call them as I see them." According to McLuhan, this represents the view which the vice president opposed in television newscasters, whom he accused of imparting their own biases to the reporting of news. The third umpire says, "Until I call them, they ain't!" This reflects McLuhan's own view that television news broadcasts cannot possibly mirror reality in any meaningful way. After all, there are 3.5 billion people in the world, and each undertakes at least ten acts every day. Yet the average television newscast reports somewhere between 15 and 35 different events (excluding weather and sports reporting). It is totally impossible for any selection of such a tiny fraction of all events to accurately represent reality, even if each event involves the activities of several thousand people on the average. Therefore, argues McLuhan, newscasters do not and cannot select items in order to reflect reality faithfully. On the contrary, since they want to attract high audience ratings, they select those items which they believe the audience itself wants to see. So the audience, in effect, "manages the news" in a circular chain of causation, which is only partly influenced by the values of newscasters themselves. The main point is that the concept of "pure" reporting of reality simply makes no sense under these circumstances. This creates a tremen-

---

[2] The impact of modern communications media upon aspirations is likely to become even more dramatic on a world-wide scale in the next few decades, according to a fascinating analysis in Zbigniew Brzeżinski, *Between Two Ages* (New York: Viking Press, 1970), especially pp. 35–51.

dous dilemma about how media *ought* to behave, considering their impact upon our perceptions of reality and upon our values. My own admittedly immense inadequacy in grappling with this subject illustrates the infantile nature of our general thinking about this crucially important area. It cries out for further research and for profound analysis based upon more than the hunches of socially responsible observers.

A second vital research topic related to values concerns the role of expectations and feelings of satisfaction and dissatisfaction in influencing social and individual behavior. It sometimes seems that we live in a society where millions demand instant gratification of every sensual and other desire. As novelist Saul Bellow puts it in his book *Mr. Sammler's Planet:*

> What it amounted to was limitless demand—insatiability, refusal of the doomed creature (death being sure and final) to go away from this earth unsatisfied. A full bill of demand and complaint was therefore presented by each individual. Nonnegotiable. Recognizing no scarcity of supply in any human department. Enlightenment? Marvelous! But out of hand, wasn't it?[3]

These demands are usually made without any regard for the cost of producing the social outputs necessary to satisfy them. Yet I believe a good case can be made for the conclusion that our higher levels of social tension do not result from lower production or poorer performance by the social system as a whole. On the contrary, in many respects, it is more successful at producing valued outputs and ameliorating serious problems than it has ever been. What is at fault is the immense escalation of our expectations and demands. But we need research to determine whether this conclusion is true. And if it is, what causes aspirations to outrun performance? How can socially responsible leaders reduce the gap between aspirations and performance?

A related question concerns the impact of widespread *impressions of victimization* which have been created in many groups in our society. I worked on the Kerner Commission Report, which I believe accurately described the way whites have victimized blacks through racism in the last 400 years in America. But did the commission's enunciating this truth so clearly cause blacks to feel even more intensely like victims? Did this contribute to a "victimization syndrome" that weakened their efforts at self-improvement and instead channeled their energies into righteous indignation and socially destructive protests? A striking example of current efforts to create feelings of victim-

---

[3] Saul Bellow, *Mr. Sammler's Planet* (New York: Viking Press, 1970), p. 34.

ization in people who do not now think of themselves in this way is the women's liberation movement. The avowed purpose of many relatively moderate leaders of this movement is to greatly *escalate discontent* among American women, many of whom do not now feel much need to be liberated. Their present feelings of relative satisfaction in society (polls show that most American women feel they have easier lives than most men) constitute a horrible error, according to women's liberation leaders. This error must be rectified by producing far more intensive unhappiness with their present state among millions more women in order to create social and institutional change. Here is an explicit strategy of deliberately multiplying discontent, escalating aspirations to probably unrealistic levels, and thereby increasing tensions and anxieties in at least *half* of the population! Will it work? If so, how and why? And how is this deliberate creation of dissatisfaction related to unconscious stimulation of unrealistic aspirations by advertising, criticisms of society by comparing it with perfection, and media exposures of social injustices and corruption at all social levels?

Related questions concern the impact on values of our entire educational system, with its heavy stress upon empirical inquiry rather than the acceptance of authority. Is such stress undermining the acceptance of even the minimally necessary degree of authority in society? To what extent are conservatives correct about effects of permissiveness, not only in child rearing, but among intellectuals concerning socially destructive actions by young people? That is, does such permissiveness weaken the minimally necessary adherence to a core of social values shared by everyone (and thus liable to be considered "conformist" by some)? Heretical as it may seem to academicians, I do not believe these are foolish or irresponsible questions. On the contrary, attempting to answer them in a rational way, making maximum use of empirical findings, seems to me an extremely important step towards discovering how to preserve the necessary cohesiveness of values at the heart of any society. Only such a core keeps the society from either falling apart or reacting violently to impending anarchy by accepting repression and dictatorship.

The third value-oriented research topic I believe should be investigated involves the *diversity of values* in our society. How diverse are the major values held by our population? In particular, how varied are our standards of public behavior? Who is teaching what values to whom and by what means? What values are children learning from their parents, their peers, television, schools, churches, or other influences? I believe any society can tolerate only a certain degree of diversity about core values and still retain an important element of individual freedom. Are we teetering on the brink of this tolerance plateau? Or can we sustain far more diversity without serious difficulty? I don't know. But I believe we should seek to find out much more about this subject than we know now, and as soon as possible.

RESEARCH CONCERNING SOCIAL INEQUALITY

My third suggestion of a basic topic for urban research is *the great degree of inequality in our society,* as measured by almost every known indicator of either condition, trait, benefit-receipt, or output. This topic already occupies a central place on the agenda of many social scientists and urban specialists. Therefore, a great deal of excellent work on it has already been done. Moreover, by nominating it as needing further research, I am not contending that all—or even most—existing inequalities are undesirable. Some are quite desirable; some are highly undesirable; some may be unimportant. In fact, identifying which are which is in itself an important topic for analysis.

The first aspect of this subject which I believe needs much more research concerns who is really getting the benefits of various public programs and who is paying the costs. Admittedly, this is extraordinarily difficult to determine in many cases. But it is very worth investigating, in part because some of the answers are so surprising. For example, the proponents of spending more money on highway construction extol what they call the "user benefit principle" as a means of tying motor fuel tax money into the building of roads. Since motorists pay these taxes, such proponents argue, the money ought to be solely devoted to building roads on which those motorists can drive. Otherwise society would "violate" the user benefit principle *modally* by using the money for something else. But closer analysis reveals that the road builders themselves "violate" this principle *geographically.* They use money collected from big-city motorists to build a disproportionate amount of roads serving rural areas. But they do not discuss this "violation" of the user benefit principle, or even recognize it. In my opinion, the same basic principle could be invoked to demand that all the money generated by motorists in a given metropolitan area be retained in that geographic area, but spent on either roads or mass transit as the area's needs dictated. This combination of "geographic purity" and "modal violation" of the user benefit principle would be just as consistent—and inconsistent—an application of that principle as the present combination of "modal purity" plus "geographic violation." In addition, it would provide far more benefits to the lower-income groups who must use public transportation.

Another question of who gets the benefits and who pays involves the recently-popular concept of the "forgotten middle-class Americans." Is there such a "forgotten" group, or is it a mythical creation of constant repetition of an idea by public officials, politicians, and major media? I am a board member of a major hospital, and I believe there indeed is a "forgotten middle-class" concerning medical care. Patients on welfare and those who are wealthy enough to buy insurance get better medical care at less cost themselves than those just above the welfare line. But in housing, the major subsidy of deducting mortgage interest and property taxes from federally taxable income goes to the middle-class and the wealthy, not the poor. What is the true *overall* picture regarding the sizable group of Americans in the middle of the income distribution?

If we wish to overcome such inequalities as we detect through better research and analysis, what basic delivery strategies can be devised to accomplish this? What new institutional structures do we need to carry out these delivery strategies—concerning food, housing, medical care, and schools, for example? How can political support be aligned to achieve these changes? Clearly, these topics need more research and thought.

In the back of my mind lurks a feeling, as yet empirically unproven, that our society may not be able to effectively attack many key inequalities without physically, geographically, and socially mixing different economic and social classes in schools, in neighborhoods, at work, and perhaps even genetically. Is this feeling accurate? Or is Professor Edward Banfield correct in asserting that there is a "lower-class" group in society that cannot be elevated but can only resolve its problems by dying out?[4] What implications do these two conflicting ideas of mixing classes or isolating one of them have for geographic dispersal of the poor in suburban growth areas? And if it seems desirable to increase dispersion of low-income households in middle-income suburban and other neighborhoods, how can political support for this be developed in a middle-class-dominated electorate?

One issue concerning inequality of particular interest to the academic community involves the future role of universities in society. I believe we now suffer badly from lack of any socially prestigious or acceptable path to maturity for young people other than getting a college education. Yet many young people are neither intellectually, emotionally, or vocationally suited to college and university training as it has been traditionally carried out. Can we devise some other path to maturity which will give these people self-respect, social esteem, and decent incomes without a college degree? Or must we follow another path to greater equality—already being tried in some institutions—by opening up the gates of college to everyone? If we indeed universal-

---

[4] Edward Banfield, *The Unheavenly City* (Boston: Little, Brown and Company, 1970).

ize our colleges and universities to give the trappings of educational equality to everyone, those institutions will have to be radically altered, because everyone cannot fit the traditional concept of a university. Which of these two fundamentally opposed means of broadening our presently too-narrow paths to maturity should society adopt? And how is this subject related to the high level of teen-age unemployment among noncollege ghetto residents? Some people believe much of that unemployment is a voluntary manifestation of the same withdrawal from the labor force that higher-income young people carry out by attending college. These and dozens of other vital questions require a new mode of approach which can take into account social values, use simulation of alternative institutional structures, and employ wisdom as well as observational skill and analytic excellence.

THE CHARACTER AND ORGANIZATION OF THE TYPES OF RESEARCH REQUIRED FOR INVESTIGATING THESE ISSUES

The key issues described above can be effectively researched and analyzed only through the use of certain methods and techniques which I believe are now "underemployed" in urban affairs. *Such research must first of all be highly policy-oriented.* Policy orientation in turn implies a great deal of simulation of possible alternatives, explicit grappling with questions of human and social values, and a willingness to deal with highly controversial subjects.

Second, *research on these topics must be multidisciplined.* The real world pays no attention to the intellectual straitjackets of academic departmentalization. Frankly, I have long been a nonbeliever concerning the ability of universities to perform team-oriented, multidisciplinary research. The intellectual atmosphere of universities has in the past attracted mainly individualists, as perhaps it should. Hence, most academic researchers do not like to merge themselves into larger research teams. One reason for this is that academic professions do not reward people for research-team participation nearly as much as for individual brilliance, however useless it may be in relation to the major social problems of the day. If academic teams will not work, then within the academic community, and perhaps generally, individual researchers must themselves become more multidisciplined in their knowledge and capabilities. Moreover, a high proportion of the most meaningful research on the issues I have described will have to take place outside of universities in organizations where research is a full-time profession, and team disciplines can be sustained. That may sound like a commercial for my own type of enterprise, but it reflects my honest opinion.

A third characteristic of research on the topics I have described is that *much of it must be conducted at a very large scale of fact-gathering and analysis.* Many of these topics can be studied only by surveying ideas, values, media impact, and other phenomena in relatively large sample populations. This means a great deal of money must be spent in order to study these topics. Yet, contrary to the opinions of many who do not really know much about urban research, very little money is spent on it in the United States in spite of the tremendous attention which urban and other social issues get in the media. The United States will spend about $20 billion on research and development this year, but only a tiny fraction will go into the kinds of "software" analysis I have described. For example, the Department of Housing and Urban Development spends less than $80 million on research each year. Moreover, the most influential officials in the Congress and the present administration, with a few notable exceptions, have by and large not yet realized that it is the *institutional* side of our urban problems, rather than the *hardware or technological* side, that now needs the most research. They have also not yet learned that such research can be quite expensive.

The final characteristic of the research topics I have described is that *they are inherently controversial in nature.* They involve the most essential and profound elements of our lives. So whatever we find out about them, the results will undoubtedly disturb millions of people and bring the white hot heat of politics to bear upon the researchers. That situation makes life much tougher, more morally ambiguous, and even more intellectually threatening than ever for researchers and universities. But these are precisely the prices of becoming "relevant" in the true sense of that word. And I believe that many of us in the social sciences must seek to become more relevant. We must become more concerned with both truly understanding and responsibly analyzing the central issues of our society, rather than pursuing methodological trivia or exploring curious byways. Otherwise, it is all too easy for many elements in society—including academicians—to engage in heated but erroneous rhetoric or to display irresponsible intellectual pyrotechnics like those which some ecologists are now using to pollute our mental atmosphere. These tactics betray the commitment to truth which lies at the heart of any great university, and of any decent human being, whether engaged in research or not.

Unfortunately, one net effect of the four research characteristics described above is a strong tendency to discourage possible sources of research funds from investing in efforts to study these most vital subjects.[5] Congress naturally tends to shy away from research projects

---

[5] I am indebted to William Gorham, President of the Urban Institute, for pointing out this conclusion.

which are expensive, controversial, and deal with fundamental value questions, particularly when it is hard to demonstrate any immediate practical results emanating from such research. Foundations have become politically skittish about policy-oriented research on controversial topics for the same reasons, especially because of recent legislation. They, too, are shifting towards more immediate-action orientation; whereas some of the subjects I have described can only be investigated through what amounts to "basic" or "pure" research. Thus, ironically, the kinds of research we most desperately need to help solve our most severe urban problems are precisely the kinds we are least willing to finance. In fact, the same thing can be said of the kinds of policies and programs we most need to solve those problems. I do not know of any easy way to resolve this dilemma. My own contribution in this paper is to try to illuminate its nature and thereby minutely shift prevailing opinions among funding sources toward a greater willingness to recognize and finance these types of research.

CONCLUSION

In the long run, we in the social sciences should be willing to steel ourselves to be objective and truthful in the heat of these controversial topics and to devote our resources and intellectual energies to pursuing them in spite of personal disadvantages and pressures. Otherwise we will condemn ourselves to either of two unsatisfactory alternatives. One is retreating to the secure social obscurity of counting trivial angels on the heads of methodological pins. The other is gaining the fleeting fame of flaunting sensational but erroneous rhetoric about our problems—while failing to organize the hard-won resources or display the patient persistence needed to cope with those problems effectively. Thus, as we examine the difficulties of actually performing the kinds of research concerning urban problems which we most need, we finally confront our own ambiguities and weaknesses as researchers. So it is really up to us in the urban research profession to decide what to do about urban research, and do it effectively.

12

Separating the Planning and Procurement of Public Services from Their Production and Delivery

The fastest growing part of the American economy since 1950 has been the public sector, especially state and local governments. Employment by all governments now exceeds 18 percent of all civilian nonagricultural employment—the highest level in American history. Even more striking, from 1950 through 1970, around 33 percent of all *net additions* to total civilian employment consisted of new government jobs. From 1970 to October 1974, state and local government employment rose by 1,775,000—22.5 percent of the total national gain in civilian employment, and 26 percent of that in civilian nonagricultural employment.

These facts emphasize the vital importance of improving human resource productivity in the public sector as a means of increasing the economy's total output. Yet productivity gains in the public sector have historically lagged far behind those in the private sector. At least that appears to be the case, based upon the highly imperfect available measures of human resource productivity in both sectors. This article examines some major deficiencies in the current use of human resources in the public sector. It then proposes a new approach to remedying those deficiencies by altering the institutional structure of many

Revised version of a speech presented to a Conference on Problems of Growth and Development in the Great Lakes Region (Chicago, October 18, 1972) and to the Annual Meeting of the Council of State Planning Agencies (San Francisco, February 15, 1973).

agencies now responsible for producing public services. Public education in big cities is used as an example of how this approach might be applied.

THREE MAJOR DEFICIENCIES IN PRESENT PUBLIC SECTOR USE OF HUMAN RESOURCES

Inadequate Incentives for Improving Individual Productivity

The public sector provides extremely ineffective incentives for either workers or managers to improve the amount of useful output per unit of input. The most striking examples of this deficiency is the constant pressure from public employees for higher wages without any offsetting increases in productivity, or at least none that are visible. Local citizens are paying teachers, policemen, firemen, and other "public servants" more and more money to do no more work—and in some cases, to do less work. This is an economically untenable situation in the long run. After all, society cannot increase the *total per-member compensation* of all its members unless their *total per-member productivity* rises. This is obvious when we consider society as a whole. But whenever any one group in society gets higher pay with no higher productivity, the members of that group are redistributing incomes to themselves at the expense of others. In the last decade, municipal employees have been redistributing incomes to themselves from other municipal taxpayers. Because of the regressive nature of most city tax structures, this means middle-class teachers and other city workers have been enriching themselves at the expense of the urban poor, without providing much added service to the poor in return.

Admittedly, it is very difficult to measure productivity in most public sector jobs. Their outputs are partly intangible, and we have failed to define those outputs very carefully. Therefore, public workers may have been improving their productivity somewhat in hard-to-measure ways. Nevertheless, it seems clear to me that we have greatly increased salary payments to educators in recent years without a commensurate rise in output.

For example, per-pupil spending in Chicago's public schools rose 48 percent from 1967 to 1971, and the vast majority of that increase consisted of higher teachers' salaries. During those four years, the consumer price index rose 21 percent. Judging from parental complaints about the schools, it is questionable whether per-pupil educational outputs rose at all. They certainly did not increase 48 percent, or even 20 percent. So Chicago and other Illinois taxpayers are paying a lot more per pupil and getting very little more—if anything—in return.

The blame for this undesirable outcome rests with public sector *managers* as well as public sector employees. The prevailing incentives for government managers do not reward more effective use of human resources as much as they reward certain other activities. These include building staff empires, pleasing constituents who want expanded services, and avoiding political controversy. Hence, managerial incentives aggravate the cost-expanding tendency of employee incentives, instead of counteracting them as in the private sector.

Why are public sector incentives for efficiency so weak? I believe the main reason is the relative *monopoly of supply* enjoyed by producers of most public services. Unlike the consumers of private goods that are available from any of several competitive suppliers, the consumers of federal, state, and local government services cannot easily influence their suppliers by threatening to take their patronage elsewhere. True, consumers of public services provided by any government can theoretically express dissatisfaction by moving into the territory of some other government. Yet such inter-governmental competition provides almost no check on the monopolistic position of the federal government, not much check on that of state governments, and only a limited check on that of even local governments. For one thing, moving is difficult and expensive; so public services must become highly undesirable before a household shifts its location just to improve them. Moreover, most households are geographically linked to employment in some way; hence, they can choose only among those localities within commuting range of the jobs involved. Even more important, many low-income households living in older central-city neighborhoods cannot afford any of the housing and private transportation in surrounding suburbs. Consequently, the poor are a "captive market" for the agencies providing public services in the central cities concerned.

Producer Dominance in Determining What Services Are Provided

A second major deficiency in the present provision of most public services is that the producers themselves largely determine what consumers will receive. Neither the consumers nor those who pay for such services—taxpayers in general—have much to say about what is to be produced or how it is to be delivered. The producers defend this arrangement by claiming the services involved are too technically complex for "mere laymen" to understand. But thousands of commercially produced products, such as television sets, computers, and automobiles, are equally complex, yet consumers exercise a great deal of influence upon what they receive by choosing from among many different products offered by competing suppliers.

In competitive markets, consumers "vote with their dollars," thereby raising total demand for products they like and lowering it for those they dislike. Producers rapidly respond by increasing the output of much-demanded items (such as small cars) and reducing that of little-demanded items (such as the Edsel). Thus, the technical complexity of products need not eliminate consumer influence over output, as long as there is significant competition among sources of supply. It is the *monopoly of supply sources* that deprives consumers and tax-payers of meaningful participation in determining output.

Unfortunately, whenever the *members* of any production organization become more influential in determining what it produces than its consumers, those members invariably shape their decisions primarily to promote their own survival and convenience. They make decisions about what is produced, how much it costs, and how it is delivered so as to serve their own interests first and the interests of consumers last. Of course, this producer-serving bias is obscured by a fog of public relations rhetoric that claims just the opposite.

Yet one of the major conclusions in my book, *Inside Bureaucracy,*[1] is that large bureaucracies almost *never* carry out major changes in their behavior as a result of purely internal developments, including internal decisions that services ought to be improved. Rather, major changes nearly always occur because of intensive pressure from outside the organizations themselves. That pressure can take any one of three basic forms: *increased competition* (other sources of supply who say they can do it better); *starvation* (major slashes in budgets that require big changes in behavior); or *flooding with new resources and new demands* (as NASA was flooded when the U.S. decided to put men on the moon). In my opinion, applying these external pressures is the only way to make providers of public services more responsive to consumer needs and desires than they are now.

Where these external pressures are lacking, provision of public services becomes dominated by rules and decisions that sacrifice the interests of consumers to the benefit of producers. For example, in big-city public schools, increased funds are used far more for higher administrator and teacher salaries than for broadened services, improved equipment and books, or more parent counseling. Teachers unions impose one rule that allows the most experienced teachers to choose where they will be located and another rule prohibiting payment of differential salaries for locating them in the lowest-income schools where they are most needed. Both unions and administrators oppose even experimenting with widespread use of performance measurement or merit pay to give the highest rewards to the most effective teachers. I realize there are plausible arguments in favor of these

---

[1] Anthony Downs, *Inside Bureaucracy* (Boston: Little, Brown, 1967), pp. 191–210.

decisions. Yet the net impression one gets from studying big-city bureaucracies is that most of their administrative decisions and arrangements are designed to benefit their own members, often at the expense of improved consumer convenience or higher output.

Lack of a Powerful Consumer-Oriented Intermediary in the Service Production Process

In theory, elected politicians represent the citizenry in general in dealing with agencies that supply public services. Governors, mayors, legislators, and other elected officials are supposed to influence public bureaucracies so the latter provide what the citizens want. But this "consumer advocacy" role of elected officials has been tremendously weakened. As a result of the three factors discussed below, no powerful, persistent consumer-oriented force strongly influences the production of most public services.

The first weakening factor is the "removal from politics" of certain service-producing bureaucracies that have succeeded in "professionalizing" themselves. Examples are most school systems and many police departments. This shift from former political control of service production to civil service or professionalism occurred in response to past corruption and undesirable patronage practices. Hence, this change achieved certain very desirable results. But the price has been to render these agencies far less responsive to consumer demands than they would be if they were more politically sensitive. In fact, in many areas, rigid civil service rules make it almost impossible even to discharge grossly incompetent workers, let alone change well-entrenched policies. I believe the pendulum of change has now swung too far away from political sensitivity.

The "consumer advocacy" role of many elected officials is also weakened by their identification as *heads of service production* in their own minds and in those of the public. Governors and mayors in particular are considered the chief administrators of public agencies providing many services. As such, they are held responsible for what those agencies do. Consequently, they often adopt a defensive stance towards agency behavior rather than an aggressive "consumer ombudsman" stance. This weakens both their ability and their willingness to impose consumer desires on those agencies whenever doing so either reduces the convenience of agency members or implies that present agency actions are ineffective.

The third factor weakening the "consumer-advocacy" of elected officials is their lack of capabilities for evaluating the outputs of public service agencies. Few governors, mayors, or legislators have large enough personal staffs to effectively analyze the activities of the many huge bureaucracies theoretically under their jurisdiction. In order to conduct such analyses, they must rely heavily upon data and even studies produced by members of the agencies being evaluated. This procedure does not lead to the most objective or penetrating results, for obvious reasons. Moreover, most elected officials are strongly oriented towards relatively short-run concerns keyed to the date of the next election. Hence, they tend to allocate their limited analytic resources to "fighting fires" caused by immediate "crises" rather than to conducting longer range studies of agency performance or consumer desires. Furthermore, chief executives must expend much of their energy trying to achieve a workable balance of resources among many different agencies rather than becoming familiar in detail with the workings or inadequacies of any of them.

As a result of these three factors, the effectiveness of most elected officials in acting as "consumer advocates" against public service agencies has been seriously reduced. This is one reason why so many "consumer advocate" groups are dissatisfied with the claims of state and local government officials that the present processes of representative government adequately protect consumer interests. Such ineffectiveness is also a cause of the recent demand for more direct "citizen participation" in public decisions, such as the location of new highways and the construction of power generation facilities. Yet no really satisfactory institutions have yet been devised for achieving effective consumer representation in the process of producing most public services. What we need is a powerful consumer-oriented actor who is much closer to the service-production process than the chief executive can possibly be. In fact, this probably requires a strong consumer advocate concerning each major type of public service, whose role is strategically structured in the midst of the process of producing that service.

SOME CRITERIA FOR INSTITUTIONAL STRUCTURES THAT WOULD IMPROVE FUTURE USE OF HUMAN RESOURCES IN THE PUBLIC SECTOR

Clearly, it would be desirable to devise institutional structures that would help remedy the above-described deficiencies in public-sector use of human resources. The first step toward doing so is to formulate some specific characteristics—or criteria of desirability—that any such structure should possess. Four such criteria derived from the above analysis are as follows:

   1. *Each such institutional arrangement should emphasize defining specific service outputs, measuring the effectiveness of producers in creating those outputs, and making the results known to consumers.*

Although participants in, and observers of, the public sector have been talking about doing this for a long time, not much real progress has been made. The main reason is that only the service-producing agencies themselves possess the resources and information required to define and measure outputs. Yet they have strong incentives not to do so, because no organization—or person—likes being objectively evaluated. Those agencies or other parties with strong incentives to perform such evaluations have not had the information or resources required. We need to combine both the capabilities and the incentives in a single organization that is closely related to the service production process.

2. *Each such institutional arrangement should shift more choices about what services will be produced and how they will be delivered directly to consumers themselves.* Consumers can then play a stronger role in setting goals *and* allocating resources through their choices. But consumers can exercise meaningful choices only if they can select among differing services or means of delivery offered by alternative sources of supply. So *creating greater consumer choice requires creating competition of some type within each presently monolithic supply source, or among different sources of supply,* perhaps including private sources. There is no other way.

3. *The compensation of the managers and employees in each such institution should be closely linked to their performances in producing the desired outputs.* This means that salaries and incentive payments would be significantly tied to production and efficiency, not primarily to longevity, educational qualifications, seniority, union bargaining power, or other strictly input characteristics. Conforming to this criterion may require adopting some compensation schemes that seem almost revolutionary for the public sector. Admittedly, this will not be easy to achieve in the face of bitter opposition from the service-producing agencies themselves. Nevertheless, I believe we must begin confronting the need to create public sector institutions that provide effective incentives for improved performance rather than mainly rewarding mere survival or avoidance of controversy.

4. *Each such institutional structure should act as a consumer-oriented counterforce to producer domination of the public service production and delivery process.* To do this, the new structure must be located very close to the production process for the specific service or type of service concerned and must be fully informed about what goes on in that process. Yet it must not be responsible for service production or delivery.

Undoubtedly, additional criteria of desirability for such institutions could be formulated. But these four—all derived from the preceding analysis—already pose a difficult enough challenge for the remainder of this article.

SEPARATING THE PLANNING AND PROCUREMENT OF PUBLIC SERVICES FROM THEIR PRODUCTION AND DELIVERY

At first glance, it may seem impossible to design any institutional structure capable of meeting the above criteria. However, the Citizens League of the Twin Cities Area has suggested an approach that I believe has an excellent chance of working quite well. This approach is described at length in their outstanding report, *Why Not Buy Public Services?* I have borrowed many ideas from that report, and the remainder of this paper represents my expanded and somewhat modified version of the basic concept suggested by the Citizens League.

The essence of this concept is separating the *planning and procurement* of public services from their *production and delivery.* This could be done institutionally by altering the functions of the present leadership in each major public service agency from *producing outputs* to *procuring services produced by others.* The leadership would have to stop thinking of itself as in charge of creating services and start thinking of itself as solely a procurement agent serving consumers.

A striking example of such an orientation in modern bureaucracies is provided by Robert McNamara. When he became Secretary of Defense, he deliberately separated himself from the three armed services, who are the *producers* of national defense. He rapidly built up his own staff of analytic experts entirely different in character, abilities, and background from the staffs of the armed services. He created this large "counterstaff" so he could develop his own studies and recommendations independently from those provided to him by the producer-dominated staffs of the armed services. In essence, he viewed himself as a procurer of defense services, not a producer thereof. Although some of his major decisions later proved mistaken, I believe his basic conception of the secretary's role was sound. Unfortunately, the defense bureaucracy is so large that trying to control it in this manner tends to exemplify one of Downs's Laws of Bureaucracy: Any attempt to control one large bureaucracy begets another. Nevertheless, creation of a sizable "counterstaff" in the office of the chief executive (who should really be seen as the chief *service purchaser*) is probably a necessary price for meeting the criteria set forth above.

In the case of local or state government, we could divorce the present head of each major service-production agency from responsibility for service production, and instead conceive of him or her as responsible for the planning and procurement of certain services desired by the public. At first, the vast majority of those services would probably be procured directly from the public agency that now produces them. But separating planning and procurement from production and delivery would immediately produce some favorable results. For one thing, since the agency head would no longer be responsible for service production, he or she would be far more willing to try objectively to define desired outputs and measure the effectiveness of the production agency in creating them. Second, this official would no longer have a vested interest in maintaining the present organizational arrangement of the service-production agency. Hence, the official would be more willing to act as an *external force* pressuring that agency to change so as to serve consumer needs and desires more effectively, even when doing so required changes inconvenient or threatening to the existing production bureaucracy. If we defined the official's role in terms of maintaining such an advocacy posture, we could expect a marked shift in the behavior of agency heads.

However, in the long run, these officials could put really effective pressure on service-production agencies to change only if they had the ability to select alternative sources of supply. Presumably, they would do so only when the agencies failed to produce what the officials thought would best serve consumers. But how can true competition be created for a large monopolistic service-production agency like a local school system?

I do not believe this can be done immediately concerning all aspects of the services produced by such an agency, except through radical and disruptive institutional changes that are not very likely to be adopted. However, a significant *marginal* increase in competition could be created without unduly disrupting existing institutions if the scope and variety of the services to be procured by a single "consumer advocate" were broadened so that more than one *existing* production agency was involved. These agencies would all produce services that are seen as essentially different *from the producers' viewpoint* but are seen as closely related or overlapping *from the consumers' viewpoint.* If several such agencies were placed under a single *consumer service procurement agent,* that agent could put pressure on each agency to change by proposing to shift a marginal amount of its existing resources to one of the other agencies that served some relevant consumer need better. This process is often used within the Defense Department concerning activities that serve the same *output function* (for example, destroying enemy targets with nuclear weapons) but use very different *processes of production* (for example, jet bombers vs. submarine-based ballistic missiles).

Such marginal-change pressure can be created only when different service-production agencies produce outputs that perform somewhat overlapping or closely related functions in the lives of their users. Yet this is a far more common occurrence than most people realize, particularly when both *private* and *public* service producers are taken into account simultaneously. Moreover, "threats" of marginal reallocations among already existing agencies could create immediate competitive pressure on all those concerned *without* requiring generation of whole new production agencies. This is far *less* threatening to existing bureaucracies—and less costly—than trying to create a whole new organization to compete across-the-board with each existing agency.

A public service planning and procurement agency could also pressure public service-production agencies to change their behavior by developing alternative sources of supplies within the private sector. True, where any large, presently monopolistic public bureau is concerned, it would be impossible to seek private suppliers for all or even most of the services provided by that bureau, at least not in any relatively short time period. The public school system in a large city could not feasibly be suddenly displaced by one or even many private suppliers of education. Nevertheless, a separate planning and procurement agency could effectively influence at least some of the public school system's behavior by proposing to move marginal amounts of its activities into the private sector. The mere solicitation of proposals for such a shift from private producers might stimulate considerable innovation or at least flexibility within that part of the public agency likely to be cut back. Furthermore, if even small amounts of the public bureau's existing activities were successfully transferred to private suppliers, that would act as a demonstration of what might be done elsewhere in the bureau. Thus, it could have a far-reaching impact upon the entire bureau, causing much more sensitivity to both costs and consumer desires than now exists.

In my opinion, creation of at least the *possibility* of procuring some presently publicly supplied services from the private sector is a key reason for separating the planning and procurement of public services from their production and delivery, as proposed above. In fact, this has already been accomplished concerning higher education in some states. In Illinois, for example, a single Board of Higher Education is responsible for planning major educational strategy for all publicly financed institutions of higher education, but not for administering any production of educational services. Since public scholarship funds can be used in either private or public colleges and universities, the board must take both into account in looking at future educational needs in the state. This arrangement not only separates some of the planning of public services from their production, but also gives consumers them selves a major role in deciding how public funds will be allocated among competing producers in both the public and private sectors.

AN EXAMPLE: PUBLIC EDUCATION IN LARGE CITIES

Some Major Deficiencies in Present Big-City Schools

To illustrate the above-described approach, let us examine how it might be applied to public secondary school education in large cities. I have chosen this example partly because provision of this service is widely considered to be inadequate, ineffective, and unresponsive to true consumer needs and desires. However, I wish to emphasize that my comments are preliminary, tentative, and incomplete. They are meant to suggest an approach that requires a great deal more thought and exploration before it can be put into practice.

In many big cities, our most inadequate public schools are part of our general failure to cope with urban poverty. I conceive of poverty in America as primarily a *relative* phenomenon, following the theories of Lee Rainwater. Poverty-related behavior patterns arise because people feel *left out* of society. They are unable to participate in what Rainwater calls *validating activities*—uses of their time that are regarded as meaningful and rewarding by themselves and others. One of the most important types of validating activities is employment in a steady and rewarding job.

Our big cities now fail to provide many young people with work opportunities that are linked closely enough to public schools to make what happens in those schools seem significant to the students. For example, the schools are not successful in teaching many young people such vital basic work disciplines as daily attendance, reasonable punctuality, and willingness to follow simple instructions. Presumably, one reason why young people are not interested in absorbing these disciplines from their education is that there seems to be no relationship between what happens in school and access to good jobs.

Jobs are controlled for the most part by private firms and schools are controlled by a public bureaucracy. No one agent or actor with control or even influence over both has the function of trying to end unemployment among young people by closely tying their schooling to job opportunities. Presumably, if students were convinced that learning well what was taught in school would *guarantee* them a job, and failing to learn would prevent their employment, they would be far more strongly motivated to apply themselves in school. But that implies a much closer and stronger link between schools and jobs than now exists. It would require very significant changes in the behavior of both private employers and public schools and perhaps extension of the recent public jobs program. Yet lack of constructive employment opportunities for young people is probably a major cause of such key urban ills as high crime rates, drug addiction, broken families, and juvenile delinquency. Consequently, effective remedial action is certainly worth pursuing.

Creating a "Board of Maturation"

Why not seek to remedy this situation by having state and local governments view secondary education, vocational education, job training, job creation, and even youth employment as diverse parts of a single process—the maturation of young people? If this perspective prevailed, then the planning and procurement of *all* these "outputs" could be viewed as the responsibility of a single overseeing "consumer advocate" agency within each community. That agency would be in charge of helping consumers procure services from the many different organizations—both public and private—that now produce these varied services. The new "consumer advocate" agency might be called —at least for reference in this article—the "Board of Maturation" or the "Youth Development Board" instead of the "Board of Education." The basic responsibility of this board would be to insure that every young person in the community received assistance in developing adequate skills for assuming a productive adult role in society. Rather than channeling all young people along the same path to maturity (such as formal education), it would seek to create a variety of different possible paths and to counsel each family so that its offspring followed the paths best suited for them individually.

The board would receive all the public funds now directed at these different agencies. It would be responsible for allocating those funds in the manner that procured the best "bundle" of services for each of the consumers it was serving. This might require it to alter present allocations among the several service-production agencies concerned. The board would also have to develop much more explicit relationships between educational institutions and private firms that employ young workers. In this case, it would not control the funding underlying those jobs, since that would be part of the internal economics of the firms concerned. Nevertheless, it might be able to supplement private wages with public training or employment funds in ways that would give private employers strong incentives to cooperate closely with the board.

This reorganization of what is now the Board of Education in most communities would require significant restructuring of the existing public bureaucracy. When transformed into the Board of Maturation, this organization would cease to be responsible for *producing* education. Instead, it would become a consumer-oriented agency responsible for helping consumers plan what youth development services they needed and then helping them procure those services from a variety of sources. Undoubtedly, most of the planning and procurement would at first be done by the board and its staff rather than by consumers themselves. But greater consumer participation could evolve in the future, especially if the board set up a counseling service as one of its major functions.

The separation of this board from the existing public school system would require designating the present administrators of the school system as responsible for its *production* activities. Thus, the Superintendent of Schools would become the head of the school system seen as a service production and delivery system. Since he was formerly the head of the staff for the board, the board would need a new professional staff to advise it and carry out the day-to-day functions of service planning and procurement. Hence, this separation of functions appears to multiply the number of levels in the bureaucracy, making red tape worse instead of better.

But this apparent deterioration would be more than offset by an added element of interbureau competition. Such competition would be created by broadening the board's scope to include the activities of other service-production agencies besides the public school system. Then, as noted above, the board could make—or "threaten" to make—at least marginal shifts of resources among these agencies where their services overlapped in terms of their function for consumers. The increased competition among these agencies in these overlapping areas would force them to become more innovative, flexible, and sensitive to consumer desires than they are now. Hopefully, these effects would produce significant net benefits in spite of the added layer of bureaucracy represented by the board's own staff. In fact, I believe this basic change in structure might produce a whole new public service environment. If it worked, it would introduce powerful consumer advocacy into the heart of the service production processes now almost totally dominated by producers themselves.

This new structure is compatible with several different kinds of funding arrangements. It could be based upon pooling the funds now used by the public agencies concerned, while raising funds the same way they are raised now. Or it could be linked to new funding ideas, such as the "educational trust fund" concept proposed by Edward Clarke and John Fyfe in a recent paper.[2] They suggested that each

---

[2] Edward H. Clarke, "The Education and Training Investment Program," and John Fyfe, "The Effectiveness of Education: Some Guides to Education Finance Reform," in Selma Mushkin, Ed., *State Aids for Human Services in a Federal System* (Washington, D.C.: Public Services Laboratory of Georgetown University, May 1974).

state guarantee all students a basic minimum level of public school funding (a "first tier"). It would also provide a "second tier" in the form of a per-student allowance controlled by the parents, which could be used for conventional schooling, vocational schooling, other job training, or even a wage subsidy. This would provide a strong element of consumer choice in determining how public funds were to be used in providing the optimal maturation path for each child. Still other forms of funding could be adapted to the basic approach suggested in this paper.

Whatever funding mechanism was used, I believe it should provide consumers with a significant element of choice in determining how the public funds assigned to their children should be used to help those children reach maturity. This would require a major new input of consumer counseling services. It might involve development of several alternative "packages" of maturation-aiding programs tailored to different types of young people. Students in public high schools already exercise significant degrees of choice among subjects—and even among schools. Hence, it would not be beyond their capabilities—assisted by their parents and some added counseling—to exercise similar choices among different combinations and sequences of conventional schooling, vocational education, on-the-job training, and part-time or full-time employment.

A BRIEF LOOK AT A SECOND EXAMPLE

The idea of combining (1) separation of service planning and procurement from production and delivery and (2) a broadened scope of services under the purview of a single "consumer advocate" agency could also be applied to many other types of public services. I have not tried to run down the standard list of government services to see how well it fits each of those normally provided, though I believe this should be done. But I can suggest one other potentially fruitful possibility. At present, most local police departments both enforce the law and provide a variety of social services unrelated to law enforcement but derived from their 24-hour availability and immediate responsiveness to calls for help. Why not redesignate the police commissioner as the Commissioner of Law Enforcement and On-Site Social Services? This might shift his perspective significantly, especially if his purview were broadened to incorporate some private security agencies and some social welfare and emergency aid organizations. Rather than attempting to explore all the ramifications of this suggestion, I will provocatively leave them for readers to ponder.

SOME UNRESOLVED DIFFICULTIES

Admittedly, the basic approach proposed in this article involves many potential problems and difficulties that I have not confronted. These include the following:

1. How could a Board of Maturation enlist the close cooperation of business firms needed to more fully integrate work experiences and work opportunities with public education?
2. How could society keep the Board of Maturation—or any comparable agency—from drifting away from a consumer-advocacy posture towards a producer-advocacy posture as most regulatory agencies originally set up to "police" specific industries have done in the past? (Examples are the Interstate Commerce Commission, the Federal Power Commission, and the Federal Communications Commission.)
3. What specific funding arrangements would be used to finance the added activities required by the board's new staff?
4. How would this entire institutional structure be related to property taxation in a manner that would satisfy the new legal challenges to traditional educational funding?

I do not pretend to have answered these questions or even to have raised all the key challenges to this approach that could be made. Nor can I do so within the confines of this article. Nevertheless, I believe the application of this approach to the field of education does offer hope of achieving something many observers have long believed crucial: a broadening of the number of respectable paths to maturity that society makes available and attractive to young people. We need this so the many young people not suited to the presently dominant college-degree path can find alternatives that are equally satisfying psychologically, financially, and in terms of both their self-respect and the respect of society generally. The fact that this general approach at least in theory offers a means of attaining this key goal makes me believe it is well worth analyzing further.

CONCLUSION

The major purpose of this paper has been to stimulate further exploration of this whole approach rather than to urge its immediate application. Our need to improve the way we use human resources in the public sector is already urgent. It will become even more crucial as government employment becomes a larger percentage of our total labor force and government decisions assume greater importance in shaping our entire society. I believe there is enough promise of major improvement in the concept of separating the planning and procurement of public services from their production and delivery to warrant intensive and widespread evaluation of this idea at all levels of government, especially the state and local levels. If we can introduce a powerful consumer advocate into the heart of the service-production process, generate some innovation-stimulating competition among public agencies, and help consumers greatly expand their own choices, we may work a quiet but immensely important revolution in the public sector.

13
Competition and Community Schools

To an economist, many of the criticisms recently made against big-city public school systems have a familiar ring: they are identical with the complaints that consumers have leveled against monopolies for centuries. Since big-city school boards, administrations, and teachers' organizations are all essentially monopoly organizations, this similarity of discontent is no coincidence.

The classic antidote to monopoly is competition. By introducing alternative sources of supply, competition expands the choice available to consumers. Moreover, these alternative sources are likely to use different methods and approaches, or even to develop wholly new products, so greater variety makes expanded choice really meaningful. Since consumers can shift their trade from suppliers who do not please them, suppliers have a strong incentive to provide what the consumers want. This attitude also means competitors regard innovations positively, as potential means of winning more business (if they can protect new ideas from instant duplication by competitors). In contrast, monopolists usually view innovations negatively, as a bother designed to upset established routines for no good reason. Clearly, if greater competition causes these results in general, it might produce some tremendous improvements in big-city school systems.

Community schools could represent a limited form of competitive influence within such systems if these new types of schools were orga-

Reprinted from *Community Control of Schools*, edited by Henry M. Levin (Washington, D.C.: The Brookings Institution, 1970), pp. 219–49. Copyright 1970 by The Brookings Institution.

nized, operated, and related to other schools in certain ways. The shifting of power in education from a single, monolithic administration to many decentralized boards would be quite similar to the breaking up of a monopoly into many competitors—that is, if consumers really had the power to choose among the competitors, and did not merely find themselves faced by many small monopolists rather than one big one. In this chapter, I will examine some of the possibilities, implications, and problems of introducing more competition into big-city public school systems, and show how they can be related to community schools.

REQUIREMENTS FOR EFFECTIVE COMPETITION

In order to provide the major benefits of competition, any system of production must possess certain fundamental characteristics. It is not possible to explore all of these here. Instead, five key characteristics will be described and related to existing conditions in most big-city school systems.

Means for Consumers to Evaluate Outputs

If consumers cannot tell a good product from a bad one, they cannot exercise consumer sovereignty so as to pressure the production system into giving them what they want. In our highly technological society, it is often difficult for consumers to evaluate the quality of products offered them. Is a Ford station wagon better or worse than a Chevrolet station wagon of comparable size and cost? Few people are expert enough to determine the answer. However, since both Fords and Chevrolets are readily available, consumers can directly compare certain measurable traits, such as size, design, and accessories. They can even hire experts to make impartial tests of more complex things, such as acceleration, braking, speed, and stability under loads.

Similar comparisons of more abstract products—such as schooling —require the same basic ingredients. That is, there must be well-defined outputs from different producers; those outputs must be measurable in some way; such measurements must be made; and information about those measurements must be available to consumers. Unfortunately, none of these conditions prevail today in big-city public school systems. There are few agreed-upon definitions of what public school systems are supposed to produce; measuring those products that can be identified is extremely hard; they are rarely measured because doing so is expensive and potentially threatening to many teachers, administrators, and parents; and such rare information as does exist is usually a closely guarded secret.

Nevertheless, some information is available about the quality of education provided in different parts of the nation. It has generated strong discontent among many parents of children in low-income, big-city areas, especially those where ethnic minorities live, because it shows how poor are the results of public schools there as compared to other areas. But effective competition within, or outside, big-city public school systems can never be stimulated without vastly improving the quality and quantity of information evaluating the outputs of different schools and educational methods. How this can be done will be discussed later.

The Existence of Alternative Suppliers

Few "perfect" monopolies exist. Most consumers can usually find some alternative source of supply if they look hard enough, and users of big-city school systems are no exception. Parents living in big cities can send their children to private schools, buy entry into suburban schools without moving (in some cases), or actually move into the jurisdictional area of some other school within the big-city system or into a suburban system. But these alternatives are all far more expensive than using the neighborhood public school. Therefore, low-income households cannot employ such alternatives. And even middle-income nonwhite households are restricted from moving into many all-white areas where superior schools are found. Thus, for thousands of households in big cities, there are no educational choices available except sending their children to that public school which has a district encompassing their residence.

Creating realistic alternative choices for these households will not be easy. Even placing control over local schools in the hands of many decentralized school boards will not expand real choices if each family must still use the nearest public school. Consumers—including the lowest-income consumers—must be able to choose among several, at least two and preferably more, alternatives if competition is to have any real effects. Therefore, individual schools must have attendance areas that overlap to some degree. For example, consider an area containing five elementary schools run by a single board of education. Each of these schools exclusively serves an attendance area surrounding it; that is, all students living in that area must attend that school, whereas no one living outside the area can attend that school. Now assume that control of these schools is shifted from a single centralized board into five decentralized boards. This does not create any expansion of choice for individual families if the same attendance policy is retained. However, such an expansion could be achieved by merging all five attendance areas into a single inclusive area, in which any family could apply to attend any school. Or additional public schools (perhaps run by outside firms or agencies) could be introduced into the area and assigned attendance areas overlapping those of the original five schools. These expansions of choice would have to be accompanied by some scheme providing public payment of the extra transportation costs resulting from parents' sending their children to schools other than the ones closest to their homes. Otherwise, low-income families would be under economic pressure to continue using the nearest school, even if other options were theoretically available to them.

Inescapably, awarding consumers some freedom of choice creates uncertainty among producers concerning what "share of the market" each school will actually "capture." For example, if each of the five schools serves 20 percent of all students initially, allowing consumers free choice might result in 40 percent applying for entry into one school, and only 10 percent into another. Coping with such an outcome raises difficult administrative and capital-planning considerations relevant to the next two requirements for effective competition.

Freedom to Offer Significantly Varying Products

Multiplicity of outlets does not guarantee true competition concerning a given product; it must be accompanied by freedom among several producers to vary the nature of the products they offer. If every car dealer sold only red Ford two-door sedans all with the same accessories and at the same price, vastly increasing the number of dealer outlets would not expand consumer choice. Similarly, providing parents with the ability to choose among several schools for their children would not really increase their freedom of choice if exactly the same subjects, approaches, types of teachers, and materials were used in all the schools. True, individual personality differences among principals and teachers always produce some differences among schools, even when they are all governed by identical regulations. But a meaningful range of variation in educational contents and quality can be offered to parents only if principals of individual schools, or supervisors of relatively small districts, have real freedom to vary the products they offer consumers. Thus, decentralization of control over a significant part of what goes on in individual schools is an essential prerequisite for effective competition in education. Moreover, such decentralization must cover most of the key elements of educational contents. It is a sham to announce that individual principals or district superintendents are free to innovate and then retain centralized and standardized control over hiring and firing of teachers, teachers' salary levels, selection of textbooks, allowable classroom size, a large part of the curriculum, most administrative procedures, and capital expenditures for new buildings and equipment.

This means that competition among several schools for students cannot be the force that generates decentralized control of those schools. Allowing parents to choose among different schools might set up much stronger pressures accentuating those limited product differentiations that could be developed within existing centralized rules and regulations. But those rules and regulations must be greatly relaxed to allow wide variation among individual schools before competition can exert its maximum impact. To create fully effective competition requires overcoming all the frustrating and difficult obstacles that have so far blocked significant decentralization of control in most big-city systems.

Nevertheless, I do not believe it is feasible to wait for complete decentralization before initiating major experiments in greater competition. At least a few competitive units in which the local board, the principal, or individual teacher had significant autonomy could initially be set up outside the existing public school system, or as special, additional units supplementing it in certain areas. Similarly, competition among units within the system could be started even though only marginal decentralization of control existed (though this is inferior to the proposal just mentioned). But to postpone using competition until "perfect" decentralization is achieved is to forgo using it forever—even though it could be an immediate force exerting at least some added pressure to create greater decentralization of control.

Consumer Control Over Significant Resources

In a free enterprise economy, consumers vote with dollars for the products they like and against those they dislike. They can do so because they have the power to allocate those dollars to whatever producers they prefer (except for a few monopolies like the telephone company). Since the income represented by consumers' dollars is vital to producers, consumer-spending choices tremendously influence producer behavior. Similarly, if competition is to have any meaningful impact upon big-city public school systems, the consumers must have control over at least some resources used in their operation.

Some control is already exercised by school consumers. As voters, they decide on bond issues and sometimes indirectly upon other tax increases affecting the total resources available to the system. When a family moves from one place to another to gain access to better schools, it shifts its taxable resources into the new area. This increases the tax base there, and perhaps decreases it in the original area. It also moves its children from one school to another, and children are significant educational resources in several ways. First, they influence the total attendance figures used by each school as part of its formula for obtaining state aid. Second, the quality of education in each school is markedly influenced by the nature of the students attending it. In general, students from middle-income, upper-income, or other homes with strong cultural environments represent an educational asset to any school. But students from culturally deprived homes may represent an educational liability—considered solely from this viewpoint. Thus when parents move a child from one school to another, they affect both the financial and nonfinancial resources available to the two schools concerned. Naturally, they also affect the demands placed upon those schools by their student loads.

But what about parents who cannot afford to move in pursuit of better schools or are prevented from doing so by racial prejudice or some other force? If they are offered true choices among alternative schools, they can at least shift their children from one school to another instead of shifting their homes. However, this might result in a marked disparity between the number of students asking to attend each school and its physical capacity to handle them. If 500 students apply to a school with a capacity for 100 students because it provides unusually desirable educational opportunities, how can the available places be rationed among the applicants?

At present, this problem is solved by setting boundaries so that the situation does not arise. But at the same time this eliminates any true choice among alternatives. Private schools often handle this problem by raising their tuition. But such price rationing discriminates against poor families and hence is inappropriate for public schools. The simple rule of first-come, first-served may be used, but this tends to favor students from the most intelligent and culturally advanced families, since they are more likely to plan ahead. The only remaining methods of allocation I can think of are random selection and use of geographic quotas. The latter can be illustrated by a system which divides the total attendance area into five parts with equal student population; classifies all applicants by location into five groups corresponding with these zones; sets a quota of 20 percent of total enrollment for each zone; and fills that quota from the applicants for each zone through random selection among them. If the boundaries of the five areas are carefully drawn in relation to the socioeconomic and ethnic traits of the population, this system can result in a well-balanced student body providing both ethnic and social-class integration in combinations likely to remain stable (that is, parents of one group will not withdraw their children to avoid the resulting balance).

Nevertheless, as long as any such rationing system still allocates the same proportion of total resources to each school as an exclusive district system, consumer choices are not really affecting the distribution of resources in the system. The worst school would still get 20 percent of all students, state aid, and other resources. Furthermore, parents whose children were assigned to that school would not really be exercising the kind of free choice vital to a truly competitive system. Many would have preferred to send their children to some other school, but it was too crowded. This brings us to the final requirement for a truly competitive system.

Freedom for Consumer Preferences to Influence Resource Allocation

A key long-run advantage of competitive markets is that they cause the production of those goods consumers like to expand, and the production of those they dislike to contract or disappear. This same characteristic is essential to effective competition within big-city public school systems. Consumers must be able to use their power over resources to alter the long-range output of different types of education. At present, this is possible in theory when consumers move from one city to another. If most of the residents of City A were so repelled by its schools that they moved to much-preferred City B nearby, then the schools in City A would be forced to contract their operations— and those in City B would expand.

Unfortunately, the economic ability to shift locations in search of better schools is unevenly distributed in society. Wealthier people can and do move to areas where the schools are reputed to be excellent. Those schools consequently expand. They can do so partly because the arrival of more middle-income or upper-income families within their attendance areas gives them the taxable resources they need for expansion. Furthermore, most students from such homes are positively oriented to education and benefit from relatively cultured home environments. Hence, their very presence in classrooms improves the quality of education. In contrast, poor students whose families cannot afford to move are left in the schools considered relatively undesirable. The departure of middle-income and upper-income students from those classrooms causes a higher concentration of students from relatively deprived homes, thereby lowering the quality of education. Moreover, rising concentration of poor families within the attendance areas of such schools reduces the per-student taxable resources available to support them. Thus, making alternative choices available to the wealthier families in society but not to the poorer, and to middle-income whites more than to middle-income nonwhites, tends to create long-run effects beneficial to the wealthier—especially whites —and detrimental to the poorer—especially nonwhites. What other tactics might help public school consumers gain the long-run advantages of competition without this undesirable result?

We have already described a system for allowing parents to express choices among five elementary schools all serving the same merged attendance area. But if all the parents who wanted to send their children to the best-liked school actually were allowed to do so, it might become extremely overcrowded. At the same time, the worst-liked school would be nearly empty. This would result in an inefficient use of invested capital, and might significantly reduce the quality of education in both schools. Yet adopting any system of student rationing that ultimately allocates 20 percent of all resources to each school does not result in any expansion of the most-preferred school or contraction of the least-preferred one. However, such expansion and contraction could be encouraged by either or both of the following tactics.

The first tactic is the use of a certain amount of flexible classroom and other school capacity that could be moved from one place to another. For example, if a school system consisted of 60 percent permanent buildings and 40 percent mobile classrooms, then the latter could be shifted around each year to accommodate parents' preferences for specific schools. Teachers and other resources would also be shifted correspondingly. This kind of arrangement could be put into effect quickly in cities with rapidly growing populations and school enrollments. A high proportion of the new physical capacity they add each year could consist of portable facilities. In cities that already have fixed plants adequate for present and future enrollments, addition of such mobile capacity would represent a huge added expense and cause underutilization of existing capacity. However, in such cities, if some older facilities must be retired because of obsolescence, they could be replaced with portable units so as to arrive at the desired balance without added expense.

This tactic has two decided disadvantages. First, most parents— and many teachers—regard portable facilities as inferior per se and as stigmatizing to the schools concerned. Second, moving such facilities —and other resources—each year would be expensive and might be administratively disruptive.

The second tactic is that of shifting control over the nature of education in accordance with the expressed votes of parents' attendance choices while still using the same buildings and classrooms. For example, assume there are five equal-sized schools in an attendance area containing 1,000 students. If 500 of these students apply to attend School X because its approach is preferred or well-liked (or for any other reasons), then the methods used in School X would be extended to at least one and perhaps one and a half other schools. This could be done either by expanding the administrative and curriculum jurisdiction of the principal of School X to these other schools or by putting pressure on the principals of the other schools to adopt the methods used in School X. Both of these tactics imply that some central agency exists within the system to perform these reallocations of resources or authority. They also imply that the methods used in School X can be extended almost instantaneously, or at least quite rapidly, to other schools without loss of quality. This is highly unrealistic, but it could be rendered more feasible if a longer period of adjustment were allowed.

Both of these tactics probably seem utterly impractical to the people who actually operate big-city school systems. Yet some version of them must be incorporated into those systems if competition is to have meaningful impact upon public education in large cities. Even now, there is an implicit assumption that each centralized school administration will somehow seek out and discover the most effective methods of education, and introduce them into the classrooms throughout its system. But it is precisely the failure to incorporate the most desired educational methods—and to reduce those least desired—that is one of the chief complaints against existing big-city systems. Moreover, a key response to this failure is continuing migration of middle-class families with children from big cities to their suburbs. Consequently, even if big-city school administrators believe the kinds of responsiveness to consumer preferences indicated by the above tactics are impossible, many consumers clearly believe they are both desirable and possible—and act accordingly.

THE NEED FOR A COMPREHENSIVE EVALUATION SYSTEM

The preceding analysis emphasized the critical need for accurate and easily available information which evaluates both the educational performance of public schools and the methods of education used in them. Without such information, consumers cannot tell whether their children are really getting proper training or to what extent certain parts of that training is fine, and others are terrible. Parents make such judgments now, but they do so only on the basis of personal impressions gained from comparing experiences in different schools with their friends and acquaintances or with the few national test scores that professionals release to them. Many parents in low-income neighborhoods do not even have these elements upon which to base accurate judgments. Therefore, it would be pointless to make the other institutional changes necessary to introduce competition into big-city public school systems without first creating an accurate and comprehensive educational evaluation system, putting it into operation throughout the system, and making the results known to parents.

Such a system might also create pressures on individual schools, principals, local boards, and teachers to adopt those methods that have proved most effective in training various specific kinds of students. Revelation of the success of certain approaches, and the failure of others, would generate both parental and professional pressure to expand the former and contract the latter. Hence, an accurate and widely publicized evaluation system could act as a substitute for the two tactics described in the previous section which seem both so necessary and so impractical.

Furthermore, an evaluation system of this type could greatly improve the efficiency of resource allocation within our enormous national education system. It is astounding that around $100 billion will be spent on education of all types in the United States in 1975; yet there is no systematic way of measuring the effectiveness of this giant expenditure. Few accurate measurements of relationships between costs and effectiveness are made anywhere in the system, and none are regularly applied, even to large parts, to measure comparative performance. As a result, widespread disparities in both effectiveness and efficiency appear and continue without any corrective action. It is widely believed that public schools in the South are generally inferior to those in the North. Many observers also believe that public schools in the East have higher academic standards than those in the West (especially in California). Yet even these conclusions are based mainly on a few national achievement tests in a narrow range of subjects, casual inspection of expenditure-per-pupil data, and personal observations. Admittedly, I am no expert on the nature of educational research, and I may be ill-informed about much pertinent analysis in this area. Moreover, in the past few years, a systematic effort to conduct a National Educational Assessment has been started, using standard achievement tests on nationwide samples of students at various ages. Nevertheless, I believe it is fair to conclude that existing methods of evaluating educational performance are grossly inadequate. They can neither identify nor encourage the adoption of many potentially huge gains in effectiveness from our current national spending on schools.

Accurate evaluation of educational effectiveness will be especially important if community schools become widespread in the United States. The shift of control over curricula to many decentralized school boards will probably lead to a wide variety of educational approaches in different cities, and even within each large city. Each school board will have a vested interest in claiming that its approach is successful. Unless there is some relatively objective way to evaluate these multiple approaches, neither parents, nor national educational policy makers, nor local taxpayers will know which methods are really working and which ones are failing. Admittedly, they do not know now either. Thus, the case for an accurate, comprehensively applied evaluation system will be no stronger under community schools than it is now. But this case is already overwhelmingly persuasive.

PROBLEMS IN PERFORMANCE EVALUATION SYSTEMS

One of the main reasons why so few school systems have developed comprehensive and accurate means of evaluating their performances is the extreme difficulty of doing so. The need for good evaluation is desperate, but the need alone yields no clue as to how it can be met. In this section, I will identify some of the key problems involved, and suggest some potential approaches to solving them or at least coping with them.

Multiple Aspects of Education

It is widely agreed that children who go to school should learn how to read, write, and perform certain basic mathematical skills with at least minimal proficiency. Their ability to do these things can be objectively measured by means of tests and compared with the abilities of other children of the same age and background. But schooling is also designed to have many other impacts on the children it affects. These include creating or bolstering self-confidence; inculcating certain basic democratic values; encouraging positive attitudes toward work; providing minimal skills and disciplinary habits relevant to work; and teaching basic skills of interpersonal relations. Measuring these things —indeed, just defining them—is extraordinarily difficult; in some cases, it may be impossible. Yet few educators believe that these non-academic aspects of schooling are unimportant, and many believe they are more important than basic reading, writing, and arithmetic.

Therefore, no evaluation system should evade trying to measure the capabilities and changes in capabilities of students regarding these nonacademic aspects of education. Attempts should be made to develop clear definitions of the traits concerned, and descriptions of various states of proficiency concerning them. These will differ from place to place, especially if community schools become widespread. Nevertheless, the different participants in the education system—including teachers, students, parents, and counselors—should be asked to evaluate students using these criteria. Admittedly, subjective judgments may be prominent in such measurements, but trying to meet this problem head on will provide many significant insights, even if really precise interpersonal or interschool comparisons prove elusive.

Multiple Distribution Goals

Viewed as a whole, the nation's public school system (or that of any state, district, or city) expends certain resources in order to attain one or more of the following distributions of educational results:

1. The *minimum-citizenship goal*—there should be some basic minimum level of proficiency and capability for all students regarding the various aspects of education discussed above, especially those most relevant to democratic citizenship.
2. The *maximum-system-output goal*—the total capabilities of all students considered as a group (perhaps best measured by their total resulting productivity) should be made as large as possible within the constraints imposed by the total resources available to the system.
3. The *equal-opportunity goal*—all students emerging from the system (say, upon high-school graduation) should have approximately the same capabilities for entering into the post-school portions of their lives.
4. The *maximum-individual-advancement goal*—each student should be given as much development of his individual potential as possible, within the constraints imposed by total available resources.

Undoubtedly, other worthy goals could also be identified. But I believe these four express the major systemwide objectives of education that are most commonly discussed in the United States.

These goals imply widely differing distributions of publicly supplied educational resources among various types of students and various geographic areas. This is true mainly because such resources are only one of the four basic inputs affecting the educational performance of particular students, as will be discussed later. The degree to which individual students possess the other three inputs varies widely in a rather systematic fashion. This variance is related to such factors as their parents' income and socioeconomic status, their geographic location in the nation and within metropolitan areas, and their ethnic nature. Consequently, pursuing each of the goals exclusively, without regard to the others, would result in very different allocations of pub-licly supplied educational inputs. At one extreme, the equal-opportunity goal would require a heavy concentration of resources among the poorest and most culturally deprived students. They would receive much higher per-student inputs than chlidren from higher-income and more advantaged homes. The minimum-citizenship goal would also require concentrating more inputs per student among the most-deprived children. It might not result in quite as unequal a distribution, since the poorest-qualified children would not have to be brought up to the level of attainment with the best-qualified but only up to some minimum standard of basic achievement. In contrast, the maximum-system-output goal would concentrate publicly supplied inputs on the best-qualified students. This would result in the greatest total gain in technical proficiency per dollar invested.[1] The maximum-individual-advancement goal results in an indeterminate allocation pattern, since it really provides no precisely defined objective. If the goal is interpreted as equal advancement (in contrast to equal achievement), then this allocation would also probably favor the lowest-income and most-deprived students. It takes more dollars of publicly-supplied inputs to advance such students a given amount in achievement than it does students from more advantaged homes.

At present, the allocation of such inputs greatly favors children from middle- and upper-income homes, especially whites, and penalizes those from poorer homes, especially nonwhites. This most closely resembles the allocation appropriate for the maximum-system-output goal. It is so unlike the allocation appropriate for the equal-opportunity goal that any major public emphasis upon that goal would call for radical revisions in the existing distribution of educational resources.

The existence of multiple goals and their call for such widely varying resource allocation patterns for publicly supplied inputs poses a difficult problem for anyone trying to design an educational evaluation system. Such a system should tell its users how well existing education methods achieve some set of goals concerning the performance of the educational system as a whole, as well as the performance of each district, school, or classroom. But which of these systemwide objectives should be used in making this assessment? Since any educational system should probably serve several goals simultaneously,

---

[1] Henry Levin argues that the highest marginal payoff would come from applying added resources to students from the most deprived backgrounds. He assumes that there are constantly declining marginal returns to investment in education. Since deprived children have had fewer total resources applied to their education (by their parents as well as public school systems) than less-deprived children, the more-deprived children are not as "far out" on their marginal payoff curves as less-deprived children. However, I believe that the marginal returns from education are not constantly declining. Translating this jargon into English, it seems to me that children from affluent backgrounds who have already received considerable education can absorb a given additional amount of knowledge, or learn an additional amount of a skill, with less input from teachers or other publicly supplied resources than deprived children can. Admittedly, this is a purely subjective judgment on my part. See Henry M. Levin, "The Failure of the Public Schools and the Free Market Remedy," *Urban Review* 2 (June 1968): 32–37 (Brookings Reprint 48).

the question really becomes what relative emphasis should be placed on each goal? Different groups of consumers would undoubtedly provide widely varying answers to this question. Their answers would depend to a great extent upon how each type of emphasis would affect the total share of publicly supplied inputs going to their own children. Therefore, the evaluation system would probably have to be designed so that it could be used to assess the effectiveness of the system in attaining each of these four goals (and perhaps others) independently. This would allow each consumer group to arrive at its own conclusions concerning whether the system was allocating publicly supplied inputs properly.

Multiple Inputs Affecting Educational Achievement

Recent large-scale studies of educational performance in the nation's schools have dramatically shown that activities in those schools are only one of the basic factors influencing educational achievement.[2] In fact, it is useful to view the output of the educational process as resulting from at least four different inputs for each child: (1) genetically determined capabilities inherited from parents; (2) the child's home environment, both present and past (particularly during the first few years of life); (3) the school system and all its component parts (including teachers, buildings, other facilities, methods, systems of mixing students); and (4) the child's nonhome, nonschool environment, including television and other mass media (even though they are often experienced in the home), which will be referred to as the neighborhood environment. These causal factors could be broken down somewhat differently, but this classification is sufficient to illustrate the key points concerned here.

Educational achievement, however defined, is influenced by all four of these factors simultaneously. Thus, attributing it to only one factor is neither just nor accurate. For example, systemwide testing usually indicates that children in schools serving upper-income white neighborhoods score much better on most tests than those in schools serving low-income nonwhite neighborhoods. Yet it might still be false to conclude that the former schools were doing a better job than the latter. The superior achievement of the higher-scoring students might be entirely attributable to the three nonschool factors. The schools serving the lower-scoring students could conceivably be doing a much better job than those serving the higher-scoring students, thereby

---

[2] See James S. Coleman et al., *Equality of Educational Opportunity* (U.S. Office of Education, 1966), referred to as the Coleman Report. See also U.S. Commission on Civil Rights, *Racial Isolation in the Public Schools* (1967).

causing the achievement gap between these two groups to be smaller than it would have been if both schools had performed with equal effectiveness.

Clearly, any useful educational evaluation system must be able to measure the impacts of the school system itself separately from the impacts of these other factors. Moreover, it should be able to measure the specific effects of various parts of the school system (such as training of teachers, quality of facilities, system of mixing students, attitudes of teachers, methods of instruction, and types of curricula). Only if it exhibits such sensitivity can an evaluation system enable those using it to make effective decisions about what publicly supplied inputs to alter and in what ways. But this kind of analytic separation of causal contributions to a single result is extremely difficult to build into any educational evaluation system. The widespread controversy among statisticians over the meaning of the Coleman Report perfectly illustrates this problem. To cope with this problem will require any workable evaluation system to have the following characteristics:

First, it must be used throughout a large part of the entire American school system simultaneously and in the same manner. Only in this way can a sufficiently large and varied sample be obtained so that the impact of a wide variety of individual factors can be isolated through standard statistical techniques. An evaluation system adopted by a single city might be large enough if that city itself was a big one. But if it is used only in one small suburban area, with a relatively homogeneous population in terms of socioeconomic and ethnic traits, then the evaluations it provides may not be measuring the performance of schools at all. This means that entire states would be much better units for the definition and administration of educational evaluation than individual school districts, and the entire nation would probably be the best base. However, it will be extremely difficult to get statewide or nationwide agreement on any specific method of measuring educational achievement—especially concerning those elements not easily subjected to written performance tests (such as success in building student self-confidence or imparting basic democratic values).

Second, a key part of the system should be comparing the performance of each group of children at different points in time. This would provide before and after results that would isolate the impact of the school since—presumably—the other three factors will not have varied significantly between these testing points. In reality, children's capabilities change significantly merely because they get older and acquire better coordination and more general experience. But this could be largely offset by relatively frequent evaluation (at least once a year and perhaps more) and by the next device described.

Third, major emphasis in evaluation should be placed upon comparisons among parts of the school system serving students from similar home and neighborhood environments. Thus, the performance of schools serving low-income neighborhoods should be compared with each other, rather than with the performances of other schools serving upper-income areas. (This should not preclude the latter kinds of comparison, however, since they are necessary to certain systemwide effectiveness evaluations.) This would be analogous to dividing sailboats into specific categories or classes for comparing the performances of their crews. Such categorization should at least intellectually —though perhaps not emotionally—counteract some of the resistance to evaluation from teachers and administrators who fear that unfair comparisons will be made in criticism of their performances. (Unfortunately, many are equally afraid of fair comparisons.)

Fourth, the specific contents and procedures used in evaluation tests must be adapted to the particular experiences of students with tremendously varying backgrounds. Black children reared in low-income urban slums do not have the same mental images, vocabularies, sense experiences, or even world outlooks as children growing up in wealthy all-white suburbs, on isolated Appalachian farms, or in borderline barrios where English is seldom spoken. Therefore, the techniques used to evaluate children's educational skills and the impact of schools upon them must be adapted to the particular experiences of the various types of children concerned. This implies that a wide variety of evaluation techniques and vehicles must be developed. It also seems inconsistent with the first key trait for an effective evaluation system mentioned above: that it be used throughout a large part of the entire school system simultaneously and in the same manner. Admittedly, creating differently adapted evaluative techniques that still permit intergroup comparisons will not be easy. But reaching the moon was not easy either, yet sufficient national resources were applied to accomplish that task. And in my opinion the potential payoff for developing an effective educational evaluation system is vastly greater than the payoff for reaching the moon. Hence, an effort much greater than our present one should be devoted to this task.

Defining System Boundaries

Selecting the area to be included in any evaluation system will have a crucial impact upon the ways in which that system might be used to influence the allocation of publicly supplied educational inputs. At least two of the other three basic educational inputs are unevenly distributed through space. Thus, each school attendance area, or school district, contains a set of consumers quite different from the average composition of students in the nation or state as a whole.

Families with home environments conducive to relatively high-level educational achievement tend to live mainly in areas with other such families. Together, they create neighborhood environments equally conducive to high-level achievement. Conversely, families with home environments that discourage high-level educational achievement also tend to cluster together. This produces neighborhood environments with similarly discouraging effects. Moreover, since most school systems use the neighborhood school principle to establish student mixtures, such spatial clustering means that students of each type tend to encounter similar type students in their classes. But classroom environment is a key ingredient in any school system. Hence the operation of the school system in such a residentially clustered society tends to further aggravate the inequalities of educational achievement resulting from home and neighborhood environments.

Insofar as the equal-opportunity objective is relevant to public education, it calls for an allocation that uses publicly supplied inputs to compensate for the inequalities resulting from the other inputs affecting educational achievement. But the practical implications of this conclusion for any given school vary sharply. They depend on whether that "system" is considered to be the schools in just one small community, an entire metropolitan area, a state, or the whole nation. At present, states supply a significant part of all publicly supplied inputs to local public schools. But most states do not allocate those resources to any well defined and high priority goal (or set of goals). They largely leave the pursuit of such goals to individual school districts. The formula used to pass out state educational funds is based mainly (though not always exclusively) upon equal per-student distribution. Insofar as the sources of such state funds are regressive (as are property taxes and sales taxes), this approach aggravates income inequalities. But this aspect of the issue is too complex to explore here. However, it is clear that the basic duality of state funding for educational operations—collecting funds on a statewide basis but leaving the decision of their effects up to individual districts—has a profound impact upon the net inequalities of educational achievement in each state.

This result could either be reinforced or counteracted by future educational evaluation systems, depending upon what geographic areas they apply to. If a single evaluation system is used throughout an entire state, it will soon reveal profound inequalities in educational achievements. Experts know that these inequalities now exist. But there are few stark statistics that explicitly identify and measure them in the dramatic ways that a statewide evaluation system would. Political or legal pressure for much greater equality of results would be likely to emerge quickly from such a revelation. This might result in some effort to allocate state-supplied resources to compensate for the in-equalities of distribution of the other causal factors described above. On the other hand, if all evaluation systems are strictly local in nature, they would use varying techniques that would obscure such statewide comparisons. The resulting pressures for greater equalization of edu-cational opportunity would probably be much lower, as they are now.

In my opinion, every state should insist upon statewide evaluation of at least some key components of educational achievement. Since the state supplies a significant portion of public school funds to all districts, it has the right—indeed, the obligation—to ask for some accounting of how effectively its funds are being used, not just whether they are being spent without fraud. Many states already require local schools to teach certain subjects or even use certain textbooks. There-fore, it is certainly reasonable for them to ask localities to appraise the effectiveness of their educational efforts by using certain standardized evaluation methods. As an added encouragement, the federal govern-ment should require every state that accepts any federal educational assistance to institute at least some statewide evaluation system on an annual basis, with results made public for each district and school.

Local Resistance

Most people do not like to have their activities scrutinized and eval-uated by "outsiders." This seems especially repugnant if the results are to be made public and compared to similar examination of other people engaged in the same activities. Such "auditing" of behavior may be both within the rights of the community that pays the auditors and highly beneficial to it, but these truths do not usually diminish community resistance. After all, any competent evaluation of an activ-ity carried out on a large scale, like teaching in elementary and sec-ondary schools, is bound to reveal that only a minority of those eval-uated are superior in effectiveness. By definition, most will be rated as either average or below average. Thus, the majority have little to gain in terms of their own status and prestige, and perhaps quite a bit to lose. Even many parents, who stand to benefit most from evaluating the effectiveness of teachers, are often reluctant to subject the achieve-ment levels of their own children to rigorous comparison with those of other children for fear of losing prestige or status.

This nearly universal resistance to evaluation occurs in many forms. The most obvious is opposing any evaluation schemes at all. More subtle is limiting the scope of such schemes. A third is insuring that control over the design and operation of the schemes is main-tained by members of the organizations to be evaluated, so they can exclude the most threatening forms of evaluation. A fourth form of resistance is insisting that the results of any evaluation be kept confidential, or disclosing them to the public in such diluted forms that no individuals or schools can be pinpointed as incompetent or ineffective. The last form is demanding that no remedial actions be based upon the results of evaluation systems—particularly that salaries and other types of compensation be entirely divorced from effectiveness of performance.

In my opinion, the basic motive for all these forms of resistance is the dual fear of being revealed as ineffective, or being pressured to change in ways that might increase individual effort. However, this fear is rarely mentioned by those who support such resistance. Instead, they contend that the particular form of resistance they support is in the public interest. For example, it is commonly argued that "outsiders" should neither design nor control evaluation systems since they are not familiar with local problems, techniques, or educational objectives. Even more frequent is the contention that evaluation schemes cost far more money than already hard-pressed school systems can afford to spend.

It is these forms of defensive resistance, rather than any technical difficulties of designing or operating evaluation systems, that are now and will continue to be the major obstacles to widespread adoption of evaluation systems. Moreover as teachers' unions become more widespread and more powerful, such resistance will greatly increase. Ironically, supporters of community schools are likely to be just as defensive about subjecting themselves to "impartial evaluations" as are the supporters of established school systems who are now accused of ineffective performance—and for the same reasons.

How can such nearly universal—and intense—resistance to evaluation be overcome? I can only offer the following suggestions as possible tactics:

First, state and federal agencies responsible for providing funds to local school districts should insist upon use of evaluation systems with certain basic characteristics as a requirement for receiving such aid. This would provide a strong incentive for adoption.

Second, evaluation systems should be designed and operated by persons outside the district public school administration, but that administration should have some voice in selecting the evaluators. They could perhaps come from local universities or consulting firms in whom the administration has confidence, possibly because of previous experience.

Third, the analogy of public auditing done by outside accountants should be used to persuade congressmen, other officials, citizens, and major public media that evaluation systems not only make sense but are necessary to protect the public's legitimate interest in using its money wisely. The growing understanding and support for planning, programming, and budgeting systems provides further intellectual underpinning for effectiveness evaluation systems.

Fourth, proposed evaluation schemes should not be linked to mechanisms that would translate evaluation results into changes in school behavior. Deciding what to do in response to such results should be left up to the parents, educators, and politicians in each district. Thus emphasizing only the provision of accurate data may reduce the threatening image of evaluation systems in the minds of those who fear any loss of local control over public education.

Finally, evaluation schemes could initially be restricted to community schools. The diversity of approaches likely to appear in these schools makes the need for some means of measuring their performance seem plausible. Also, their experimental character fits in well with the need to innovate in the design of evaluation systems. Even more important, the majority of existing educators will not be involved in running community schools; thus they would not feel threatened by evaluation systems aimed only at those schools. Using evaluation systems only in community schools could even have a vindictive appeal to those educators who believe that community schools cannot work. Even if community schools did fail to improve educational effectiveness directly, they would still be making an important contribution to overall educational effectiveness by thus opening the door to widespread employment of accurate evaluation systems.

Scarcity of Resources

Most big-city public school systems are desperately short of financial resources. Therefore, they regard any diversion of available funds from educational programs to other activities as too wasteful or luxurious to contemplate. The argument that diversion of ½ of 1 percent of all their funds into evaluation might result in a 10 percent or greater improvement in the effectiveness of the remaining 99.5 percent of all funds has so far failed to sway this resistance. However, I believe this is largely because there is so little evidence that effective evaluation systems can actually be designed. Once the possibility of creating and using such systems effectively has been demonstrated, school boards throughout the nation will be far more receptive to installing them. The initial, key task, then, is getting a few well-designed systems under way.

This is a "natural" situation for the use of foundation funding or federal experimental funding. Money for development of a large-scale evaluation system over a five-year period might be tied to money for some other kind of program a big-city system especially desires. This would "sweeten" the package so as to make acceptance of an evaluation system more likely. One such program, which could also be used as a testing ground for the evaluation system, might be the development of prototype community schools on an experimental basis. Once an evaluation system was placed in operation, its success (or failure) at stimulating improvements in the schools concerned would greatly increase (or further reduce) the incentive of other school boards to launch similar programs.

ALTERNATIVE WAYS TO INTRODUCE COMPETITION INTO BIG-CITY PUBLIC SCHOOL SYSTEMS

Assuming that greater competition in big-city public school systems is generally desirable, there are several specific ways to attain it. Some are mutually exclusive, but most could be used in combination.

Widespread and Well-Publicized Use of Evaluation Systems

The simplest way to create greater competition among public schools would be to design, install, and use educational effectiveness evaluation systems along the lines discussed earlier. Although such systems would probably encounter great initial resistance, their use would actually require no significant institutional or administrative changes in existing public school systems. They would generate greater competition solely by revealing to the consumers of education, and to all the professionals concerned, the relative effectiveness of each school, district, educational approach, or other element subject to any kind of measurement. Presumably, the persons in charge of those aspects that appeared to be least effective would receive heavy pressure from those they served, from their own professional pride, and from other educational professionals to adopt elements revealed as more effective.

Competition through better information would be most furthered by evaluation systems that measured: (1) the objective level of achievement of the students in each school (or even each classroom) related to analogous levels for all the other students in the system concerned, in the entire state, and in the whole nation, and particularly to other students in similar homes and neighborhood environments; (2) the contribution to that achievement of the school itself and of specific elements within the school (such as teachers, methods, student mixture); (3) the contribution of the school to the attainment of nonacademic goals of education; and (4) the effectiveness of various specific educational techniques in relation to their costs (not just in relation to their results, as is typical of existing educational evaluations).

As noted earlier, formidable technical and political obstacles inhibit the early use of evaluation systems to stimulate competition in big-city school systems. Therefore, two types of compromises concerning evaluation systems appear necessary. First, any evaluation scheme that is at all sensible should be encouraged and initiated as soon as possible, even if it does not exhibit all or most of the desirable qualities described above. Second, there is no reason to wait until effective evaluation systems are designed before using the other forms of competition, as set forth below. It may be hard for parents to assess the quality of the alternative educational products offered them by competition without a good evaluation system. Nevertheless, any significant increase in competition is likely to produce desirable results and generate healthy pressures on present big-city school monopolies.

Use of Community Schools to Encourage Diversity

Community schools would also encourage a degree of competition within public school systems if they had at least two key attributes. The first is a diversity of educational approaches. This would presumably arise if a wide variety of communities actually had control over significant portions of the curricula in schools serving them. The second is an evaluation system that would measure the effectiveness of these different approaches and promulgate the results throughout the system. Both of these attributes would generate some of the benefits of competition even if students in each part of the city are compelled to attend the school serving their area of the city rather than being given a choice of several schools. Again, knowledge of what worked and what failed should generate at least some pressure on schools that are failing to adopt the successful approaches used in those that are succeeding—or at least doing better.

Use of Overlapping Attendance Areas

There are several ways that overlapping attendance areas, discussed earlier, could be used to create greater competition within an existing public school system.

Expansion of existing attendance areas. If attendance areas for several schools located close to each other were merged, then students anywhere in the enlarged area could attend any school among those serving it. This would cause a concentration of applicants at the schools considered the best, and a shrinkage of applicants at those considered the worst. The approach would generate higher total transportation costs than the pure neighborhood school system. It might also require some form of student-rationing system other than geographic location. However, because simply merging attendance areas would not involve deliberately planned diversity, differences in quality within the system would result mainly from accidents of supervisory abilities. Most parents would probably continue to send their children to the school that was geographically most convenient, rather than encouraging them to go longer distances to find higher quality. Hence, the magnitude of the extra transportation costs involved, and the pressure to use nongeographic rationing, would probably not be great over the whole system; nor would the impact of the resulting competition become very significant.

Expansion of attendance areas plus creation of community schools. This approach is similar to the one above, but would involve more deliberately planned diversity among schools. Hence, the ability of students to choose from among several reasonably proximate schools would represent a more meaningful choice. This might result in a greater convergence of students on certain schools regarded as superior, and more avoidance of those regarded as inferior. Consequently, the whole system would not be so dominated by sheer geographic convenience (though I believe that would probably remain the single most significant factor in parental choice of schools). Transportation costs would rise significantly, and the pressure to adopt some kind of nongeographic student rationing system would also mount. Furthermore, the appearance of much greater diversity of educational approaches would create greater pressure to allow parents in any given area to send their children to schools located elsewhere, even though doing so would be less convenient. This would occur because some parents in each neighborhood would surely disagree with the particular educational approach or emphasis adopted by the community school serving that neighborhood. To insure proper freedom of choice, these parents would have to be allowed to send their children to some alternative schools. These alternatives could be either community schools elsewhere or schools still run by the centralized school administration, or both.

Community schools can be either entirely new structures (or at least structures newly used for schooling) added onto the existing system (in which case, the central authorities might still operate schools in almost every neighborhood), or conversions of existing schools into community-controlled schools (in which case, the central authorities would be running fewer schools). But in either case, use of enlarged attendance areas would be extremely important as a means of introducing and maintaining competition within the system.

Expansion of attendance areas plus creation of experimental schools. This approach is very similar to the one just described, except that the alternative schools would be run by innovation-oriented groups (such as private firms, universities, or local volunteers) rather than community-oriented groups—or perhaps in conjunction with the latter. For example, a community school board might select a basic approach to education, and then contract with a private firm to carry out that approach. This mixture of public control and private administration has already been endorsed by such educational experts as Theodore Sizer and Christopher Jencks.[3] It would provide many private firms interested in educational markets with a chance to show what they could do, thereby generating a new source of competition to existing public schools.

Awarding Parents Vouchers to Buy Schooling

Milton Friedman has suggested that competition could be injected into public education by having educational services financed publicly but produced by a wide variety of private, profit-motivated firms. The parents of every child would receive a publicly financed voucher of a fixed sum per child. They could then use this voucher to buy educational services from any "approved" supplier they wanted to patronize.[4] As Henry Levin pointed out in his excellent analysis of this proposal, it would undoubtedly increase the variety of educational services offered to parents, thereby enabling them to find more easily the kinds of educational services they wanted.[5]

But this scheme would also have two less desirable effects. First, it is vital for society as a whole to insure that all citizens receive a minimum quality education regarding certain skills and knowledge necessary for effective citizenship. Yet experience with other forms of private consumption shows that ignorant, low-income consumers can be exploited by unscrupulous producers who persuade the consumers to pay exorbitant prices for inferior-quality goods. To prevent this outcome from occurring in education, it would be necessary for public authorities to exercise some form of regulation over all private producers of educational services. Such regulation might become nearly as extensive and standardized as existing public production of education.

Second, wealthier parents could add more funds to the voucher

---

[3] See Christopher Jencks, "Is the Public School Obsolete?," *Public Interest* 2 (Winter 1966): 18–27; and Theodore Sizer, "Reform and the Control of Education" (processed; Harvard University, Graduate School of Education, 1967).

[4] Milton Friedman, "The Role of Government in Education," *Capitalism and Freedom* (University of Chicago Press, 1962), pp. 85–107. At least one major experiment employing vouchers is now underway in a California school district.

[5] Levin, op. cit.

to buy better-quality services, but poor parents could not. Wealthier parents would evoke high-quality schools that would attract the best teachers and use the best facilities; poor parents would be compelled to give their children much lower-quality educations. Thus, direct price discrimination based on incomes would accomplish precisely the same result that geographic discrimination based on incomes now achieves. This would aggravate existing inequalities of educational opportunity rather than diminish them.

However, this second disadvantage could be offset by awarding a much larger voucher to low-income families than to higher-income families, as Levin points out. He describes two methods: a sliding scale with payments varying inversely with income, and provision of such aid only to the lowest-income families. He rejects the first as politically unrealistic, but regards the second as politically possible—perhaps because it is essentially a novel version of the aid provided under Title I of the Elementary and Secondary Education Act of 1965.

For purposes of this analysis, I will assume that some form of providing either full vouchers or bonus payments to students from low-income households, and allowing them to choose where to apply such grants, could be used to inject a significant degree of competition into big-city public school systems. Every such voucher or bonus should be at least large enough to pay for the extra inputs needed to offset the disadvantages imposed on the child's education by deficiencies in his nonschool environment. In fact, any voucher or bonus should be made large enough to convert each low-income child from a liability into an asset, as seen from the viewpoints of the suppliers of education and of the parents of other children in the schools involved. Then, the voucher or bonus would create a surplus over and above the marginal cost of educating the low-income child. That surplus could then be applied to improving the quality of the entire school which accepted such a child. This would provide a positive incentive for schools to accept or even seek out such children. However, it is unlikely that society will presently pay the relatively large "amounts" needed to accomplish this outcome.

A voucher or bonus arrangement favoring low-income students could be used in any one of the three basic forms describing the use of overlapping attendance areas. That is, it could be employed in conjunction with an expansion of existing attendance areas into large and overlapping zones, or with a similar expansion plus the development of community schools, or with a similar expansion plus the development of experimental schools (which might be related to community control). In the last case, special schools catering only to students with vouchers or bonus payments might be developed. They would be able to use very high levels of expenditure per student. In the first case, special schools with geographic quotas or bonus-student quotas could be developed. They could provide a socially integrated educational environment that would still take advantage of the added resources made possible by the bonus payments. But in all cases, the parents of low-income children would have to be allowed at least some discretion about where their children would use their bonuses if the benefits of true competition were to be generated.

CONCLUSION

Large bureaucratic organizations almost never make major changes in established behavior patterns unless strongly pressured by outside forces.[6] The most powerful form of such pressure is a direct threat to their continued existence or to their current perquisites of office. This kind of threat can usually be created only by an alliance of all or most of the outside agents who support the bureaucracy. They must get together and demand that the bureaucracy change or else they will remove or drastically reduce their support. But when the bureaucracy produces some vital service, they can reduce their support only by creating a competitive institution to provide that service. Competition has the advantage of generating sustained, almost automatic, pressure upon the organizations involved to keep adapting their production to consumers' wants, without constant vigilance by the consumers themselves.

Big-city public school systems are huge bureaucracies. Therefore, one of the potentially most effective ways of getting them to change their unsatisfactory behavior is to introduce significant elements of competition into their operation. It would be totally unrealistic to assume that most, or even any large fraction, of the existing school systems in large cities could soon be replaced by competitive systems created or run by outsiders. There are simply not enough qualified—or even unqualified—teachers around to create truly parallel systems that could compete with existing public school systems across the board. Moreover, the additional capital investment required to build physical facilities for such an all-out system would be prohibitive.

Nevertheless, even a small dose of competition in certain forms could produce very important—even radical—changes in the nature and quality of education in big-city public schools. The first and most crucial step is developing and using effective ways of evaluating the

---

[6] This definitive generalization is taken from a source in which I have an unusually high degree of confidence. See Anthony Downs, *Inside Bureaucracy* (Little, Brown, 1967), chaps. II and XVI.

educational performance of public schools. Other devices may also be employed to generate the benefits of competition, with varying requirements concerning the amount of basic institutional change involved.

Community schools are currently being advanced almost as a panacea that will create the clearly needed changes in big-city public school systems. But unless community schools are designed and operated so as to increase competitive pressures within those systems, I do not believe they will have the desired effects. The pressure of competition is the crucial ingredient needed to force big-city school systems to adapt their outputs to what consumers want and need. Without such pressure, those school systems will continue succumbing to the natural tendency of all monopolists: providing what is most convenient for them to produce regardless of its suitability to the true needs of those who must consume it.